OECD Reviews on Local Job Creation

HF761396

Preparing for the Future of Work in Canada

OECD
BETTER POLICIES FOR BETTER LIVES

This document, as well as any data and map included herein, are without prejudice to the status of or sovereignty over any territory, to the delimitation of international frontiers and boundaries and to the name of any territory, city or area.

The statistical data for Israel are supplied by and under the responsibility of the relevant Israeli authorities. The use of such data by the OECD is without prejudice to the status of the Golan Heights, East Jerusalem and Israeli settlements in the West Bank under the terms of international law.

Note by Turkey
The information in this document with reference to "Cyprus" relates to the southern part of the Island. There is no single authority representing both Turkish and Greek Cypriot people on the Island. Turkey recognises the Turkish Republic of Northern Cyprus (TRNC). Until a lasting and equitable solution is found within the context of the United Nations, Turkey shall preserve its position concerning the "Cyprus issue".

Note by all the European Union Member States of the OECD and the European Union
The Republic of Cyprus is recognised by all members of the United Nations with the exception of Turkey. The information in this document relates to the area under the effective control of the Government of the Republic of Cyprus.

Please cite this publication as:
OECD (2020), *Preparing for the Future of Work in Canada*, OECD Reviews on Local Job Creation, OECD Publishing, Paris, *https://doi.org/10.1787/05c1b185-en*.

ISBN 978-92-64-94679-8 (print)
ISBN 978-92-64-34697-0 (pdf)

OECD Reviews on Local Job Creation
ISSN 2311-2328 (print)
ISSN 2311-2336 (online)

Photo credits: Cover © GettyImages/Thomas-Soellner.

Corrigenda to publications may be found on line at: *www.oecd.org/about/publishing/corrigenda.htm*.
© OECD 2020

The use of this work, whether digital or print, is governed by the Terms and Conditions to be found at *http://www.oecd.org/termsandconditions*.

Foreword

This OECD report comes at a time when governments around the world are being challenged by the COVID-19 crisis, which is likely to generate a profound reflection on production and consumption habits. A number of provinces and territories across Canada declared a state of emergency in March 2020, and the subsequent shutdown of the economy to protect public health has led to a labour market shock. As measures related to travel and social distancing are gradually easing, the longer-term labour market impacts will become clearer.

The COVID-19 crisis could accelerate automation, as firms look to expand their use of technology to reduce the number of workers that have to physically be at work. Robots may be in even greater demand to help mitigate future disruptions. Productivity could also be negatively impacted, as the costs of doing business go up. Within this context of increasing costs, firms may also change their hiring practices and look to part-time employees or independent contractors to cut costs and be more nimble.

This OECD report sheds light on the threats and opportunities facing local labour markets in Canada in the face of the future of work. It also highlights needed actions to prepare people, places and firms. The report includes a special focus on the Province of Ontario, which represents almost 40% of Canada's Gross Domestic Product. Even before COVID-19, automation, digitalisation and artificial intelligence were re-shaping local labour markets across Canada. These trends offer the opportunity to boost productivity, increase prosperity and raise living standards. They can, however, also create losers, as workers who lose jobs may not always have the skills needed in a changing labour market and might struggle to find a new job.

This report is part of the OECD Review on Local Job Creation Series within the Programme of Work of the OECD Local Economic and Employment Development (LEED) Programme. Created in 1982, the LEED Programme aims to contribute to the creation of more and better jobs in more productive and inclusive economies. It produces guidance to make the implementation of national policies more effective at the local level, while stimulating innovative practices on the ground. The OECD LEED Directing Committee, which gathers governments of OECD member and non-member countries, oversees the work of the LEED Programme. This report was approved by written procedure by the OECD LEED Directing Committee on 24 June 2020 [CFE/LEED(2020)11].

Acknowledgements

This report has been prepared by the OECD Centre for Entrepreneurship, SMEs, Regions and Cities (CFE), led by Lamia Kamal-Chaoui, Director. This work was conducted as part of the OECD's Local Economic and Employment Development (LEED) Programme with financial support from Employment and Social Development Canada (ESDC).

This report was drafted by Alessandro Kandiah, Policy Analyst, Local Employment, Skills and Social Innovation (LESI) Division (OECD/CFE), under the supervision of Jonathan Barr, Head of the Employment and Skills Unit within CFE/LESI, who also drafted sections of the report and co-ordinated the project. Anil Verma, Professor, Rotman School of Management, University of Toronto contributed drafting inputs and the conceptual framework presented in Chapter 4 of this publication. Karen Maguire, Head of the LESI Division, provided overall guidance. Ida Peltonen and Lucas Leblanc, both from the CFE/LESI Division, contributed to this report through data collection and analysis.

ESDC officials played an instrumental role in helping the OECD to co-ordinate this project, while also providing constructive feedback on the development of the report. In particular, the OECD would like to thank Brodie Berrigan, Executive Director, Tania Claes, Senior Advisor, and Rhonda Fernandes, Director. The OECD would also like to express its gratitude to officials from the Ontario Ministry of Labour, Training and Skills Development, with special thanks to Cheryl Donais, Senior Policy Advisor.

The Brookfield Institute for Innovation + Entrepreneurship provided inputs to the report, notably within the section of Chapter 3 on digital skills. The OECD would like to specifically thank Sarah Doyle, Director of Policy + Research, Viet Vu, Economist, Creig Lamb, Senior Policy Analyst, and Rob Willoughby, Data Analyst. Colleagues from the OECD Directorate for Employment, Labour and Social Affairs, including Glenda Quintini, Senior Economist, and Katharine Mullock, Economist, also provided useful comments on the report.

Feedback and inputs from Ontario Workforce Planning Boards representatives were gathered in Hamilton, Kitchener and London. The OECD would like to thank Debra Mountenay, Executive Director, Elgin Middlesex Oxford Workforce Planning and Development Board, Judy Travis, Executive Director, Workforce Planning Hamilton, and Sohrab Rahmaty, Manager of Employer Relations and Research, Workforce Planning Board of Waterloo Wellington Dufferin.

Lastly, the OECD would like to thank all those individuals who participated in roundtables on the local impacts of the future of work in September 2019 in Hamilton, Kitchener and London. These roundtables brought together over 100 local stakeholders across the three cities.

Table of contents

Tables

Figures

Boxes

Follow OECD Publications on:

http://twitter.com/OECD_Pubs

http://www.facebook.com/OECDPublications

http://www.linkedin.com/groups/OECD-Publications-4645871

http://www.youtube.com/oecdilibrary

OECD Alerts *http://www.oecd.org/oecddirect/*

This book has... StatLinks

A service that delivers Excel® files from the printed page!

Look for the *StatLinks* at the bottom of the tables or graphs in this book. To download the matching Excel® spreadsheet, just type the link into your Internet browser, starting with the ***https://doi.org*** prefix, or click on the link from the e-book edition.

Acronyms and Abbreviations

AI	Artificial Intelligence
BII+E	Brookfield Institute for Innovation + Entrepreneurship
COJG	Canada-Ontario Job Grant
CTB	Canada Training Benefit
CTC	Canada Training Credit
EI	Employment Insurance
EMC	Excellence in Manufacturing Consortium
ER	Economic Region
ESDC	Employment and Social Development Canada
ESS	Employer Skills Survey
GDP	Gross Domestic Product
GFC	Global Financial Crisis
G7	Group of Seven
HPWP	High Performance Work Practice
ICT	Information and Communication Technology
ILO	International Labour Organization
LEP	Local Enterprise Partnership
LEPC	Local Employment Planning Council
LMDA	Labour Market Development Agreement
NEET	Neither employed, nor in education or training
NOC	National Occupational Classification
OECD	Organisation for Economic Co-operation and Development
PIAAC	Programme for the International Assessment of Adult Competencies
PISA	Programme for International Student Assessment
PSW	Personal Support Worker
SLM	Self-learning Machine
SME	Small and Medium-Sized Enterprise

UNIDO	United Nations Industrial Development Organisation
VET	Vocational Education and Training
WDA	Workforce Development Agreement
WIB	Workforce Investment Board

Executive Summary

COVID-19 is severely affecting communities across Canada and it is likely to speed up the adoption of automation in the workplace. Employment fell by 15.7%, or 3 million jobs, in Canada between February and April 2020, exceeding by far declines observed in previous labour market downturns. As of May 2020, employment started to rebound with an increase of about 290 000 jobs. However, the unemployment rate has continued to rise, sitting at 13.7% as of May 2020. This is the highest unemployment rate since comparable data became available in 1976. Unemployment rates across Canada range from a low of 11.2% in Manitoba to a high of 16.3% in Newfoundland and Labrador. Some provinces have started gradually easing public health restrictions, including allowing some non-essential businesses to re-open, but there is much uncertainty about the path to recovery.

Looking to the past, automation often accelerates during economic downturns as firms look to deeply re-organise their business models. With health experts warning that social distancing measures may need to remain in place through 2021, firms may seek to expand their use of technology to reduce the number of staff that have to physically be at work. In other words, firms might want to pandemic-proof their operations. The pandemic is also likely to change consumer behaviour as people develop preferences for automated services over face-to-face interactions.

Even before the COVID-19 crisis, automation was changing local labour markets in Canada. Overall, 15% of jobs face a high risk (e.g. high probability) of being automated, while another 30.6% are likely to face significant change. Automation could impact places differently. In Ontario, which represents almost 40% of Canada's Gross Domestic Product, OECD estimates show that jobs at risk of automation amount to almost 45% of total employment – 14.7% of jobs being at high risk (or about 1.1 million jobs) and another 30.2% likely to experience significant change, representing 2.2 million jobs. The share of jobs at risk of automation across economic regions in Ontario ranges from 41.1% in Ottawa to a high of almost 50% in Stratford-Bruce Peninsula.

While automation could create inequalities in the labour market, new jobs are also likely to be created as a result of technological innovations. The good news is that 23 out of 65 economic regions (35%) across Canada have been creating jobs primarily in less risky occupations since 2011. This means that they are creating jobs primarily within occupations with a lower probability of being negatively affected by automation. Within Ontario, 4 out of 11 economic regions created jobs primarily within occupations less likely to be negatively impacted by automation between 2011 and 2018.

There are certain types of places and people within Ontario that are more likely to be impacted by the acceleration of automation. Communities most at risk of automation tend to have a higher share of jobs in the goods producing sector (e.g. manufacturing, mining, construction, and agriculture jobs). In terms of people, men are more likely to be impacted than women as those occupations facing the highest risk tend to have a higher proportion of males in the labour market. Young people, the low-skilled, and some groups already facing labour market disadvantages, could be disproportionately impacted by the introduction of new technologies within the workplace. That is because they tend to work in jobs that primarily involve simple and repetitive tasks, which can be more easily replaced by a machine.

Automation is more likely to change tasks within jobs rather than replace entire jobs, requiring workers to develop new skills. Despite a growing narrative around the importance of learning to code, for most Canadians, foundational digital skills alongside a suite of non-digital skills — in particular, inter-personal skills, such as good communication, team work, and motivation — are critical to be competitive in the labour market.

Here again, the good news is that local labour markets in Canada are primarily shifting from middle to high-skill jobs. In more than 50 out of 65 economic regions, the employment share of high-skill jobs has increased over the last decade. In addition, the demand for high-skill jobs is projected to grow in Canada over the coming decade. Occupations requiring a university education are expected to have the fastest overall employment growth, contributing to the largest share (36%) of job creation among all skill levels in Canada. Within Ontario, 7 out of 11 economic regions primarily shifted from middle to high-skill jobs between 2011 and 2018.

While policy in Canada will concentrate on supporting local employment activity in the short term in light of COVID-19, efforts in the longer term can focus on preparing communities for the upturn. Canada has already taken important steps to future-proof local communities, including by establishing the Future Skills – a federal government initiative that includes a Council and a Centre devoted to identifying labour market changes and new programme innovations. There are also a range of local initiatives aiming to improve how firms and workers use technology, such as Communitech in Kitchener, Ontario, which could be scaled up and implemented in other regions of Canada.

The following recommendations emerge from this report, focusing on future-proofing people, places and firms:

- **Foster demand-led training and labour market information**: Canada could do so by mainstreaming an employer survey, strengthening sector-focused training programmes, and exploring the feasibility of career pathway programmes that better link young people to emerging local labour market opportunities.
- **Promote economic diversification, building on the skills assets of communities**: Local Workforce Planning Boards as well as Local Employment Planning Councils in Ontario could play a stronger role in the development of local skills ecosystems, which aim to connect the broad range of employment, skills, economic development and innovation players. Local policy makers could also look for opportunities to promote economic diversification into activities closely related to the existing skills base of a community.
- **Ensure the employment and skills system targets workers in need**: Local employment services could be tailored to support workers most at risk of being affected by automation, while programmes targeting low-skill adults could be expanded. This includes looking at how these programmes can help workers before they face a lay-off to better anticipate labour market change.
- **Promote a human-centred response to the future of work**: Workers' perspective could be integrated into policy responses, to ensure that policy addresses people's most pressing needs. Action and co-operation with different social partners can help smooth the transition, while also ensuring that technology enhances worker well-being.
- **Improve the effectiveness of training for SMEs**: Policy makers could encourage SMEs to be aware of their training needs, while raising awareness on existing financial incentives for training and promoting the emergence of employer-led networks around skills development.
- **Ensure firms make use of available skills**: Federal and provincial policy makers could look for opportunities to promote the emergence of high-performance work practices within firms to ensure a better use of skills in the workplace. This could include disseminating good practices among firms, while also developing diagnostic tools to help them identify room for improvement, and promoting knowledge transfer across sectors and places.

1 Assessment and recommendations

Managing labour market uncertainty due to COVID-19

This OECD report comes at a time when Canada and the world is facing the COVID-19 pandemic crisis, which represents a source of great economic uncertainty. Due to confinement measures necessary to protect public health, there has been a shock to the Canadian labour market. For example, following a drop of over 1 million in March 2020, employment fell by about 2 million in April 2020. The magnitude of the decline in employment from February to April (-15.7%) far exceeds declines observed in previous labour market downturns. At the same time, Employment Insurance (EI) claims have soared, with 2 million claims over the last two weeks of March alone. COVID-19 restrictions have started to gradually ease as of May 2020 and have been followed by an initial rebound in employment, but it remains to be seen how the economic recovery will unfold. After rising 5.2 percentage points in April to 13.0%, the unemployment rate in Canada has continued to increase in May, hitting an all-time high of 13.7%.

Prior to the COVID-19 outbreak, the Canadian labour market had been performing very well, albeit with unemployment differences across provinces. In 2019, unemployment stood at 5.7%, slightly above the OECD average of 5.2% but one of the lowest rates in the last 40 years. However, this federal picture does not capture differences across provinces – unemployment ranged from a low of 4.7% in British Columbia to a high of 11.9% in Newfoundland and Labrador.

Automation is likely to accelerate in a post-COVID labour market with different spatial impacts across Canada

The long-term impacts of COVID-19 on local labour market outcomes will become clearer with time, but there is a major risk that it could exacerbate economic and social inequalities. It is also likely to accelerate the pace of automation in the labour market. To reduce their exposure to any potential future social distancing and confinement measures, more firms could decide to invest in technology to automate the production of goods and services. The adoption of automation in the workplace tends to accelerate in times of economic crises, as firms replace workers performing routine tasks with a mix of technology and better skilled workers. Firms worldwide are starting to use robots to perform roles workers cannot do at home. For example, retailers in the United States are using robots to clean floors, while robots in South Korea have been used to measure temperatures and distribute hand sanitiser. It has also been argued that the current economic uncertainty is leading firms to reassess business models that rely on global supply chains.

This OECD report looks at economic regions across Canada to better understand how the future of work is going to affect local labour markets. It includes a special focus on the Province of Ontario, given that it represents almost 40% of Canada's Gross Domestic Product.

Even before COVID-19, automation was having a profound impact in Canada as elsewhere. Overall, the OECD estimates that 45.6% of jobs (as a share of total employment) are vulnerable to automation in Canada, of which 15% are at high risk, meaning that these jobs are made-up primarily of tasks, which could be easily replaced by machines. These estimates are based on the Nedelkoska and Quintini (2018) methodology, building on individual level data from the OECD Survey of Adult Skills (PIAAC), which provides insights into the task composition of each person's job as well as their skillset.

Occupations at high risk of automation tend to be concentrated in some sectors, which are not evenly spread across Canada. In the Province of Ontario, around 45% of jobs are at risk of automation – 14.7% of jobs being at high risk and another 30.2% likely to experience significant change, meaning the job will remain but the skills required to succeed could fundamentally change. This is the equivalent of almost 1.1 million jobs at high-risk and another 2.2 million jobs that could significantly change across the Province of Ontario (see Table 1.1). The risk of automation varies from a low of 41.1% in the Ottawa economic region to a high of almost 50% in the Stratford-Bruce Peninsula economic region. Across Ontario, the regions of Ottawa and Toronto face the lowest risk of losing jobs to automation. This can be partly explained by the sectoral composition of these local economies, which rely on finance and science and engineering, as well as services and public administration professionals that typically face a lower risk of automation.

There are a number of regional labour market characteristics that make some places more vulnerable. Economic regions in Ontario facing a higher risk of automation tend to have larger employment shares in goods-producing sectors, a higher prevalence of rural areas and a lower share of working-age population. They also tend to have a higher proportion of people in the labour force with lower levels of skills.

Table 1.1. How could the future of work affect economic regions in Ontario, Canada?

Automation could have substantial impacts on local labour markets across Ontario

Economic region	Total employment (2018)	Jobs at high risk of automation		Jobs vulnerable to significant change	
		Number of jobs	Share of total employment	Number of jobs	Share of total employment
Hamilton-Niagara Peninsula	746 459	117 586	15.8%	231 533	31.0%
Kingston-Pembroke	201 995	31 050	15.4%	61 598	30.5%
Kitchener-Waterloo-Barrie	722 500	112 939	15.6%	221 266	30.6%
London	332 186	55 211	16.6%	105 162	31.7%
Muskoka-Kawarthas	171 266	28 234	16.5%	54 486	31.8%
Northeast	245 777	39 151	15.9%	76 573	31.2%
Northwest	92 295	14 101	15.3%	28 536	30.9%
Ottawa	703 418	88 330	12.6%	200 542	28.5%
Stratford-Bruce Peninsula	151 555	26 391	17.4%	48 418	31.9%
Toronto	3 503 584	493 044	14.1%	1 044 197	29.8%
Windsor-Sarnia	299 670	50 152	16.7%	94 528	31.5%
TOTAL	**7 170 704**	**1 056 188**	**14.7%**	**2 166 839**	**30.2%**

Note: 'High risk of automation' refers to the share of workers featuring a risk of automation of 70% or above. 'Significant change' reflects the share of workers with a risk of automation between 50% and 70%.
Source: OECD calculations on Labour Force Surveys.

While much of the attention often goes to the downside adjustments to automation, the good news is that 23 of 65 economic regions across Canada (35%) created jobs primarily in less risky occupations between 2011 and 2018. Less risky means that the jobs being created are primarily within occupations that tend to have more complex tasks, which are less likely to be replaced by a machine. All together, these 23 economic regions account for about 60% of the overall Canadian labour force. In Ontario, this includes the four economic regions of 1) Hamilton-Niagara Peninsula; 2) Kitchener-Waterloo-Barrie; 3) Toronto; and 4) Windsor-Sarnia.

Table 1.2. Many regions in Ontario have created jobs at lower risk of automation

Change in job creation between 2011 and 2018, economic regions in Ontario

Creating jobs, predominantly in less risky occupations	Creating jobs, predominantly in riskier occupations	Losing jobs, predominantly in riskier occupations	Losing jobs, predominantly less risky occupations
Hamilton-Niagara Peninsula	London	Muskoka-Kawarthas	Kingston-Pembroke
Kitchener-Waterloo-Barrie	Northwest		Northeast
Toronto			Ottawa
Windsor-Sarnia			Stratford-Bruce Peninsula

Source: OECD calculations on Labour Force Survey.

The OECD has developed these four scenarios as a framework to guide place-based actions that respond to particular community needs. For example, in those regions that are able to generate jobs in occupations which are less subject to automation, it would be important to focus on increasing labour market participation, especially from under-represented groups. In regions such as Hamilton-Niagara Peninsula, Kitchener-Waterloo-Barrie, Toronto, and Windsor-Sarnia, more focus can be placed on mentoring programmes, which connect people to work. Training programmes can also focus more on providing adults with new opportunities to re-skill to keep their jobs and advance in their career.

For those regions creating jobs but in risky occupations, more can be done to look at how firms are deploying and using technology. Here, community colleges in Ontario can play an important economic development role by working directly with employers to raise the demand for skills. This includes helping companies move into higher value-added products and service market strategies. Community colleges can work with employers to improve local skills utilisation and productivity through management training, the co-development and dissemination of relevant R&D, product testing and technology transfer.

For regions losing jobs in riskier occupations, there is an opportunity to focus on leveraging the entrepreneurial ecosystem to stimulate new job creation. Local leaders can focus on working directly with SMEs to help them grow and access new markets – both domestic and international. This could include supports for business incubators and supporting knowledge transfer among firms to spread a digital culture.

Finally, for those regions losing jobs, predominantly in less risky occupations, they appear to be in a more difficult structural adjustment situation. In these cases, local leaders need to identify policy complementarities between employment, skills and economic development programmes to leverage new job opportunities, especially in occupations that are less vulnerable to automation. Workforce development programmes should focus on providing "on" and "off" ramps for people to re-skill, while economic development policies should focus on leveraging the existing human capital base to diversify the economy into more productive employment opportunities.

Structural shifts across regional labour markets were already impacting the quality of jobs and employer demand for skills

Canada, as most OECD countries, has also experienced changes in the skills composition of employment over the past two decades, characterised by a shift of employment shares towards high-skill jobs. Labour markets across the OECD have become more polarised, with declining employment shares of middle-skill jobs relative to jobs with higher or lower skill levels. Looking at the 1998-2018 period, Canada experienced an increase in the employment share of high-skill jobs, while both middle-skill and low-skill jobs declined. Polarisation dynamics in Canada partly reflect increases in the supply of skills over the past decades.

All provinces have witnessed a rise in the employment share of high-skill jobs and a decline in the share of middle-skill jobs between 2011 and 2018, but regional differences are pronounced. For example, in Ontario, while Kingston-Pembroke has experienced a clear polarisation pattern over the last decade, in Muskoka-Kawarthas the employment share of middle-skill jobs increased between 2011 and 2018. The higher concentration of middle-skill jobs in some regions might pose challenges in the longer term, as middle-skill occupations often involve routine and repetitive tasks that could be subject to automation.

Alongside automation and job polarisation, labour and skills shortages are affecting some sectors and occupations more than others in Canada. Prior to COVID-19, companies were reporting labour and skills shortages in Canada, and the pandemic crisis is likely to increase demand for some occupations and specific skills. The 2018 ManpowerGroup Talent Shortage Survey reported that labour shortages represented an issue for 41% of employers in Canada. Shortages are affecting some sectors more than others. Surveys undertaken with more than a thousand Canadian entrepreneurs by Business Development Canada show that manufacturing and retail trade are the sectors where the largest share of companies report difficulties in hiring (56% and 54% respectively). Difficulties in hiring typically reflect challenges both on the labour supply (e.g. shortage of applicants, workers lacking the experience and skills needed for the job) and demand (e.g. conditions offered by employers). Automation and new technologies could represent an opportunity to tackle shortages and boost productivity in sectors at high risk of automation facing shortages, such as manufacturing and retail trade.

The increasing sophistication of technology in the workplace is also making some skillsets obsolete while increasing the demand for others. COVID-19 is likely to affect both workforce and skills needs in Canada. For example, it has been suggested that the pandemic crisis could cause labour shortages in essential services and affect infrastructure in Canada. The agriculture sector is also reported to be experiencing labour shortages, as COVID-19 has led to delays in arrivals of temporary foreign workers that the industry relies on. COVID-19 is also making digital skills more important than ever. It has been suggested that it will be crucial for employees to develop higher cognitive, social and emotional skills as well as greater adaptability and resilience in a post-COVID labour market.

Many actions are being taken at the federal and local level to anticipate labour market change

It should be highlighted that Canada has already taken important steps to ensure that local communities are ready for the future of work. For example, in February 2019, Future Skills was launched to encourage collaboration amongst public, private, labour and not-for-profit organisations to generate reliable evidence and drive transformative change in Canada's workforce skills development policies and programmes. Future Skills includes:

- The Future Skills Council: an advisory Council to the Minister of Employment, Workforce Development and Disability Inclusion with members from public, private, labour, education and training providers, not-for-profit and Indigenous organisations. It provides advice on emerging skills and workforce trends, promoting transformative changes within Canada's skills development system through a multi-sectoral approach.

- The Future Skills Centre: an independent applied research and innovation centre that prototypes, tests and evaluates new approaches to skills assessment and development, and disseminates the results widely to encourage broader adoption of proven practices.

Another example includes the Sectoral Initiatives Program, which aims to address current and future skills shortages by supporting the development and distribution of sector-specific labour market intelligence, national occupational standards, and skills certification and accreditation systems.

While the Government of Canada provides funding under the Labour Market Development Agreements and the Workforce Development Agreements, provinces and territories have the flexibility to design and deliver employment programmes and services best suited to the needs of their local labour markets. These agreements with provinces and territories contain devolved funding arrangements that enable place-based responses to workers facing structural adjustment as well as those who are far away from the labour market and need support to re-enter the labour force.

In Ontario, Employment Ontario delivers employment and training services to the public across the province. This employment service is under reform to become more responsive to individual workers and firms. Ontario has also a network of Workforce Planning Boards as well as Local Employment Planning Councils that aim to balance the supply and demand of skills by producing local labour market information, as well as tools and resources to inform their community about future jobs.

In the short term, it is clear that policy will concentrate on supporting employment and economic activity, as communities throughout the country suffer from the ongoing COVID-19 pandemic. Canada is working to address socio-economic challenges linked to the crisis, for example by rolling out a 75% wage subsidy to help employers keep workers on payroll through the crisis. A new temporary salary top-up for essential workers earning less than CAD 2 500 per month has also been introduced, aiming to boost income of front-line hospital workers, those caring for seniors, as well as workers engaged in the supply chain of food and essential goods. Workers who have already lost their income will be able to turn to the new Canada Emergency Response Benefit, which provides CAD 2 000 a month for up to four months. Several measures have been taken in support of young people in Canada. The Canada Emergency Student Benefit provides financial support to post-secondary students and recent post-secondary and high school graduates who are unable to find work due to COVID-19 and do not qualify for the Canada Emergency Response Benefit. The Canada Student Service Grant provides up to CAD 5 000 to support students post-secondary education costs in the fall. Youth are also being supported with the suspension of repayment and interest on their loans until 30 September 2020.

Over the longer term, policy responses could prepare workers for the upturn, while addressing the specific challenges facing people, places and firms in keeping pace with the future of work. This will require targeted action to build the skills in-demand in local labour markets and promote adult learning opportunities, while also fostering economic diversification towards sectors facing a lower risk of automation.

What are the policy opportunities in Canada going forward?

Helping places leverage local assets to make the transition

The increasing sophistication of technology in the workplace is making some skillsets obsolete while increasing the demand for others. Demand-led training systems are better able to ensure that workers build the skills needed in the local labour market. Ad-hoc initiatives in Ontario have been undertaken to measure and collect data on employers skills needs. As an example, the Conference Board of Canada, a Canadian not-for-profit think tank, conducted the Ontario Employer Skills Survey in 2013 to obtain a clear picture of employers' skills needs.

A comprehensive employer survey does not seem to be regularly conducted in Canada. As labour market demands rapidly shift, employment and training providers will need to work more closely with employers to understand and respond to these shifts. Previously, at the federal level, a Workplace and Employee Survey had been in place to examine the way in which employers and their employees respond to the changing competitive and technological environment. Such a survey could be re-visited. The need for collecting information on employers skills needs becomes even more crucial today, as the COVID-19 pandemic crisis is likely to heavily affect employers needs and skills demand going forward.

In Ontario, the employment and training system has recently experimented with innovative initiatives to prepare people for the future of work that could potentially be scaled up. For example, the SkillsAdvance Ontario pilot funds partnerships that connect employers with the employment and training services needed to recruit workers with the right skills. It also supports job seekers to get into jobs by providing them with sector-specific services. Ontario has also tested the feasibility of a career pathways approach, focusing on building the academic and workplace skills that learners need for entry-level positions within demand sectors, while also providing a bridge to more advanced college credentials and employment opportunities. There is a clear opportunity to assess the success of these initiatives and determine the feasibility of scaling them up across the province.

Across the OECD, there is renewed interest in the role of industrial policy to strengthen relevant sectors of the local economy. The tradable sector – which includes all those economic sectors that produce goods or services that can be traded across regions and international borders – is recognised as a driver of productivity growth. Jobs in this sector, however, typically face a higher risk of automation, as they often entail routine and repetitive tasks. This is mostly due to the fact that the tradable sector includes many economic sectors that have an especially high risk of automation, such as agriculture and manufacturing. However, tradable services, which form a small but growing part of the tradable sector, are most likely at much lower risk of automation. Policy makers need to embrace the long-term benefits from shifting towards the tradable sector as productivity growth can lead to better wages and standards of living, while also addressing the risks related to automation that come from this shift. In the context of the future of work, policies can look within the tradable sector and identify how to steer support towards occupations with tasks that are less vulnerable to automation. Given that industrial and skills development policies often pertain to different government departments, policy co-ordination is crucial.

Local skills ecosystems can be instrumental in providing access to relevant specialised knowledge and skills. There may be benefits to be generated by focusing on clusters of expertise as well as regional strengths through a local skills ecosystem approach with the goal of creating a diversified labour market. Local skills ecosystems have a high level of social capital and strong multi-sector linkages between employment services, training organisations, as well as economic development actors, providing local firms with easy access to specialised support to innovate into new activities. Local skills ecosystems can emerge organically and in some cases governments can play a role in providing incentives for their development. The establishment of a local skills ecosystem is often dependent on a strong anchor institution, such as a higher education or vocational education institution as well as a catalyst for change (e.g. evidence suggesting that the region is likely to experience significant adjustment as a result of automation).

Building on local skills ecosystems, policies could promote diversification into activities that are closely related and connected to the existing skills base of the population. As communities respond to structural adjustments resulting from automation, evidence suggests that local networks connecting industries with overlapping skill requirements are predictive of where firms are most likely to diversify economic activities. A successful example of this diversification approach can be found in Akron, Ohio, United States, which was the location of four major tire companies in the 1990s. After experiencing major economic and jobs decline in this activity, the city invested in polymer technology, establishing a National Polymer Innovation Centre, which has since been a new source of job creation in the city. The city has managed to leverage the existing skills base and local knowledge and applied it to new technology and production processes.

"Smart Specialisation" strategies within Europe could also provide useful examples for Canada. They generally aim to focus local development activities in areas where there is a critical mass of knowledge and innovation potential.

Recommendations to help leverage local assets and respond to the future of work

Foster demand-led training and labour market information

- *Mainstream an employer skills survey across Canada* to collect comprehensive data and information on skills challenges that employers report both within their existing workforces and when recruiting, the levels and nature of investment in training and development as well as the relationship between skills challenges, training activity and business strategy. One option could be to build on the coverage and scope of existing surveys, such as the 2018 Business Council Skills Survey.
- *Strengthen programmes with sector-focused training.* There is an opportunity at both the federal and provincial levels in Canada to build on the SkillsAdvance Ontario pilot programme to target skills training to local sector needs, by testing, replicating and scaling sector-focused training.
- *Explore the feasibility of career pathway programmes* that would support post-secondary institutions (i.e. both colleges and universities) in building stronger relationships with employment service providers and employers. This could take the form of providing more flexible funding options that enable post-secondary institutions to offer shorter credential programmes as well as invest in student support services and employer engagement capacity.

Promote economic diversification building on local skills assets

- *Local Workforce Planning Boards as well as Local Employment Planning Councils in Ontario could play a stronger role in the development of local skills ecosystems.* Local skills ecosystems are clusters of firms working horizontally across a value chain, with the education and training system, to foster knowledge exchange and co-ordination. Currently, local boards and councils in Ontario mostly produce labour market information. They could be given more autonomy to manage programmes that aim to better connect both the demand and supply of skills available in a local economy.
- *Promote economic diversification into activities at lower risk of automation related to the existing skills base of the population.* For some workers, developing completely new skills can be challenging, for example if they have been doing the same job throughout their entire work life. The establishment and promotion of local industry networks can help to identify opportunities to build on the existing skill base of the labour market to shift employment towards occupations facing a lower risk of automation. The Future Skills Centre may wish to pilot and evaluate new innovation projects that help transition workers from declining to growing economic sectors. The Labour Market Information Council also has an important role in articulating how skills can be transferred across industries and sectors.

Supporting people to make the digital transition

While fears of "technological unemployment" mount across the OECD, automation is more likely to change tasks within jobs rather than replace entire jobs. This requires workers to access up-skilling opportunities to remain employable. Digital skills are reported by employers among the skills most in need across Ontario and Canada. Canadian employers require a skillset that includes general workforce digital skills and a suite of "soft" skills, needed to make workers more flexible and adaptable to future labour market changes. Despite a growing narrative around the importance of learning to code, for most Canadians, foundational digital skills alongside a suite of non-digital skills — in particular, interpersonal skills — are critical foundations to be competitive in the labour market.

Changes in the world of work will affect everyone, but adults with low skills are most at risk of experiencing a deterioration in their labour market prospects. While more adults participate in training in Canada compared to the OECD (52% and 41% respectively), gaps in access are present across segments of the population. Across OECD countries, low-skilled workers participate much less than higher-skilled workers in training, but this gap is particularly large in Canada (28 percentage points relative to 23 percentage points). Many of these individuals can be stuck in a "low-skills trap" in a lower-level job with limited opportunities for on-the-job training and professional development. As the COVID-19 pandemic crisis poses new and unexpected economic challenges, low-skill workers might suffer more than others.

While a range policies and programmes have been implemented in Canada, there is an opportunity to leverage local action and scale up best practices that support people to transition into digitally intensive jobs. This would be particularly important for Indigenous people, immigrants, persons with disabilities as well as older workers that typically face disadvantage in the labour market. In Kitchener, Ontario, Communitech is an excellent example of a community-based initiative designed to promote and grow digital jobs. This local organisation provides support to all companies (e.g. from start-up to major corporations) to think more critically about how technology can help them improve their business organisation, while also raising awareness about skills training opportunities for all groups of people that are needed to transition workers into tech jobs.

At the local level, worker engagement is an important element to ensure a human-centred policy response to the future of work. Workers that are facing disruption due to technological changes often experience multi-faceted challenges linked to the labour market and are excluded from conversations about the future of work. Many of the workers most at risk of automation often face the greatest burdens of job instability and insecurity.

Recommendations to support people to make the digital transition

Ensure the employment and skills system targets workers in need

- *Tailor employment services to support workers who could be affected by automation.* As the labour market changes, employment services will need to serve not just the long-term unemployed and those facing barriers to the labour market, but workers affected by labour market disruptions and technological change.
- *Expand the scope of programmes targeting low-skill adults.* Targeted training opportunities for low-skill workers and jobseekers exist, but their scope could be expanded. For example, as part of the SkillsAdvance programme of Employment Ontario, a course was developed specifically aiming to provide low-skill unemployed people with relevant training to get them into jobs. However, it only graduates 50 people annually.

Promote a human-centred response to the future of work

- *Surveys and interviews of workers in occupations and sectors facing a high-risk of automation could help provide workers perspective on the future of work.* Such surveys could gather information on workers challenges, needs and perception of the future of their work, while also learning about their daily-life challenges and aspirations.
- *Integrate worker perspectives into local policy response.* This information would play an important role in ensuring the future of work policy agenda places workers at the centre. Policy could build a positive narrative about the opportunities emerging from the future of work, while also tackling the multi-faceted barriers workers face. Future Skills is considering this in its approach but more could be done at both the provincial and federal level. For example, non-profit organisations as well as unions are part of the groups being engaged in discussions with the Council and the Centre. Since unions represent a decreasing percentage of the Canadian workforce, it could be helpful to identify additional ways to consult workers to address their needs.

Ensuring firms have access to skills and training opportunities

Digitalisation and the changing nature of work bring a range of benefits; however, SMEs often struggle more than larger companies in accessing training opportunities. In general, digitalisation has the potential to ease firm access to skills through better job recruitment sites, outsourcing and online task hiring. Digital technology gaps for SMEs are not only related to technical skills, but also the managerial skills to accompany the adoption of digital technologies. The ongoing COVID-19 crisis has placed further focus on the importance of digitalisation for SMEs, as their lower level of technology adoption compared to bigger firms heavily affects their ability to survive.

In Canada, the gap in training participation between SMEs and large firms employees is larger in Canada than on average across the OECD. It amounts to around 15 percentage points. As SMEs account for 60% of employment in Canada, it is crucial to develop targeted strategies to ensure SMEs invest in preparing their workforce for future changes in the labour market. SMEs often face training barriers due to a lack of financial resources and technical expertise to engage in effective workforce development and human resources planning.

Policy has a role to play in providing the right incentives for firms to get the skills needed in the future of work. Having the right incentives to training employees in place is important, especially for SMEs, as they face more challenges than other firms in securing the financial resources to conduct workforce training. The OECD Survey of Adult Skills also shows that the lack of time, due to workload and childcare or family responsibilities, as well as the lack of information, are other challenges typically preventing SMEs from accessing training.

The Government of Canada has introduced the Canada Job Grant Program, providing opportunities for employers, individually or in groups, to invest in their workforce, and undertaken external evaluations to assess and improve its effectiveness. The Canada-Ontario Job Grant (COJG) is funded by the Government of Canada and delivered by the Government of Ontario. The programme foresees flexibility in terms of training co-financing, to ensure that SMEs have a lower burden compared to large firms. Employers with 100 or more employees need to contribute half of training costs, while employers with less than 100 employees need to contribute one-sixth of training costs. A review of the Canada Job Grant Program undertaken in its second year (2016) found that the majority of employers receiving grants were small businesses (i.e. with less than 50 employees). The review found that, while the programme is generally meeting the needs of employers and many participants benefited from the training (e.g., acquired skills, earned a credential/certificate), the achievement of expected outcomes in terms of increasing labour market attachment and improving the employment situation of participants could be improved. Recommendations emerging from the review pointed to the need to ensure increased employer investment in training through the grant and the need for flexibility in the use of funds to meet local labour market needs. In the context of some provinces, an important challenge was that many employers, particularly small businesses, do not have a good understanding of their training needs and therefore might not be optimising the use of the grant. The creation of networks of businesses within the same sector or partnerships between SMEs can play a crucial role in helping SMEs navigate labour market changes and better understand opportunities that can emerge from good training programmes. In February 2020, the Ontario Ministry of Labour, Training and Skills Development has started carrying out a comprehensive evaluation of the Canada-Ontario Job Grant programme to inform re-design and programme improvements.

Finally, to address the changes brought by the future of work, firms will also need to make better use of their existing skill base. For local economies to grow and individuals to succeed in the labour market, skills need to be put to productive use at work. Traditionally, workforce development initiatives have focused on the supply side of labour markets, however, there is increasing recognition of the value of demand-side efforts, including engaging employers in making optimal use of their employees' skills. Promoting the emergence of high-performance work practices could be a means to putting skills into good use across local communities in Canada. Such practices include, for example, employee reward programmes, more flexible working hours, mentoring and leadership development courses, as well as a company culture that promotes training and development.

Recommendations to ensure firms have access to skills and training opportunities

Improve the effectiveness of training for SMEs

- *Encourage SMEs to be aware of their training needs.* For this to happen, it would be important to foster increased take-up of programmes aiming to help SMEs better understand their training needs and offer training accordingly.
- *Raise awareness on existing financial incentives available*, for example through public campaigns and/or online guides. This would help SMEs take informed decisions on how to finance workforce training.
- *Promote the emergence of employer-led training networks*, which could actively define training requirements and deliver programmes.

Ensure firms make use of available skills

- *Support the emergence of high-performance work practices.* Support could be targeted to staff and management training, or to the use of external experts to undertake diagnosis and upgrading of workplace organisation and technology. Funding for action-oriented business research could be another alternative.
- *Build awareness of the benefits from effective skills use*, for example through targeted campaigns or by setting up award mechanisms for employers who implement high-performance work practices.

2 The local impacts of automation in Canada

Despite positive labour market trends over the past decades, the ongoing COVID-19 pandemic crisis poses new and unexpected challenges to labour markets in Canada, with some places likely to be hit harder than others. The pandemic could also accelerate automation in the workplace, as firms seek to replace the production of goods and services with machines. This chapter highlights the potential threats and opportunities posed by automation with a special focus on regions within the Province of Ontario, Canada's largest economy and most populous province. It highlights places that have the highest risk of being impacted by automation as well as which types of jobs are most at risk.

In Brief

Automation could have different impacts across regions in Canada, which will likely be accelerated by the ongoing COVID-19 pandemic

- **The ongoing COVID-19 pandemic crisis is causing widespread disruption in Canadian labour markets, leading to a new spike in unemployment**. Following a drop of over 1 million in March 2020, employment fell by about 2 million in April 2020, bringing the total employment decline since the beginning of the COVID-19 economic shutdown to over 3 million. The magnitude of the decline in employment between February and April (-15.7%) far exceeds declines observed in previous labour market downturns. As some provinces gradually lift restrictions, employment has started to rebound in May 2020, with the creation of 290 000 jobs. The unemployment rate has also declined in some provinces, but continued to increase in Canada overall to 13.7%, the highest rate since comparable data became available in 1976. Before COVID-19, Canada had enjoyed a low unemployment rate. Unemployment sat at 5.7% in 2019 – the lowest point in more than 40 years.
- **The COVID-19 crisis could accelerate automation in the workplace**. There is a wide body of evidence which shows that firms are more likely to invest in automation following economic crisis periods.
- **Automation could re-shape labour markets in Canada**. OECD estimates show that a number of jobs are at high risk of automation in Canada (15.0% of total employment in 2018) but many more are likely to face significant change (30.6%). Canadian provinces face a similar risk of automation, but disparities within provinces are significant. For example, looking at economic regions, there are almost 15 percentage points of difference between the economic regions with the highest and lowest share of jobs at risk of automation within British Columbia, while in Ontario, the difference is 8.3 percentage points.
- **Some factors affect local labour market vulnerability to automation**. In Ontario, the share of jobs at risk of automation varies from a low of 41.1% in Ottawa to a high of 49.4% in Stratford-Bruce Peninsula. Ontario regions facing a higher risk of automation are characterised by a lower share of working age population, a higher prevalence of rural areas, poorer employment and skills levels, and higher employment shares in good-producing sectors.
- **Many places are making the transition**. The good news is that 23 out of 65 economic regions in Canada, accounting for about 60% of the overall Canadian labour force, created jobs predominantly in less risky occupations between 2011 and 2018. New jobs are going to be created, providing new sources of growth if places are ready to seize the opportunity. The future of work can also provide more flexible working opportunities for both people and firms.

Introduction

Megatrends related to digitalisation, automation and artificial intelligence (AI) are having a profound impact on local labour markets across the OECD. Some people and places are more at risk than others. The ongoing COVID-19 pandemic crisis is posing unprecedented challenges to local labour markets across Canada, and risks accelerating automation going forward. This chapter is structured as follows. Section

2.1 provides an overview of regional labour market trends across Canada. Sections 2.2 and 2.3 analyse the impact of automation on local labour markets in Canada with a special focus on the Province of Ontario. Section 2.4 shows trends in the rise of non-standard work, which provides both challenges and opportunities for individuals.

2.1. The ongoing COVID-19 crisis is posing unprecedented challenges to Canadian labour markets, which had performed well before the outbreak

2.1.1. The COVID-19 outbreak is disrupting labour markets in Canada

While necessary for public health reasons, the COVID-19 confinement and social distancing measures have put unprecedented pressure on local labour markets in Canada. As of May 2020, many provinces have gradually eased restrictions and re-opened the economy. However, the longer-term impacts will depend on the length of lockdowns, the scale of indirect impacts such as drops in consumer spending, and the effectiveness of the policy responses. The employment impacts of COVID-19 have exceeded initial estimates, dwarfing those of the 2008 financial crisis and any other recession in recent memory.

As a result of COVID-19, Canada has experienced a historical job loss between February and April 2020. Following a drop of over 1 million in March, employment fell by about 2 million in April, bringing the total employment decline since the beginning of the COVID-19 economic shutdown to over 3 million. The magnitude of the decline in employment between February and April (-15.7%) far exceeds declines observed in previous labour market downturns. Compared with February, employment in April declined by more than 10% in all provinces, led by Quebec (-18.7% or -821 000). The unemployment rate rose 5.2 percentage points in April to 13.0%, and it increased in all provinces. This followed an increase of 2.2 percentage points in March. Total unemployment grew by 1 285 000 (+113.3%) from February to April 2020. By comparison, during the 1981-1982 recession unemployment rose by 763 000 (+88.6%) over the course of 16 months. In April, almost all (97.0%) of the newly-unemployed were on temporary layoff (not seasonally adjusted), indicating that they expected to return to their former employer as the shutdown is relaxed (Statistics Canada, 2020[1]) (Statistics Canada, 2020[2]).

Employment has started to rebound in May 2020, but there is uncertainty on how the economic recovery will unfold. In May, employment rose by 290 000 (+1.8%), while the number of people who worked less than half their usual hours dropped by 292 000 (-8.6%). Combined, these changes in the labour market represented a recovery of 10.6% of the COVID-19-related employment losses and absences recorded in the previous two months. The unemployment rate started to decline in some provinces, but increased in Canada overall, standing at 13.7% in May 2020, the highest recorded since comparable data became available in 1976. The gradual easing of COVID-19 restrictions and the re-opening of the economy presents both opportunities and challenges for employers and workers. For employers, this includes adapting workplaces while adjusting to disruptions in global supply chains and uncertainties in consumer demand. For workers, the challenges vary, from returning to a previous employer, to looking for a new job, adapting to new ways of working, or making child care arrangements (Statistics Canada, 2020[3]).

Figure 2.1. Unemployment has increased across all provinces in Canada due to COVID-19

Unemployment rates by province, February, April and May 2020

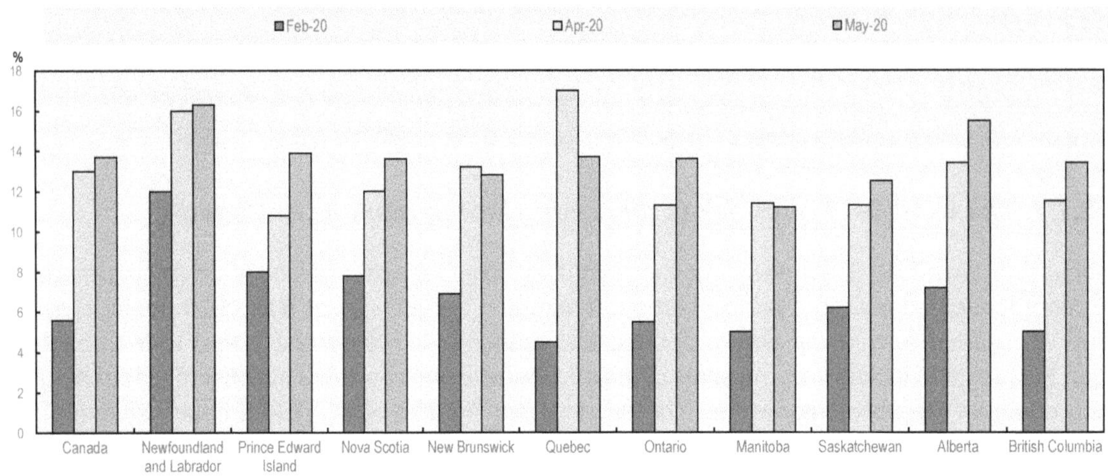

Source: Statistics Canada. Table 14-10-0287-01 Labour force characteristics, monthly, seasonally adjusted and trend-cycle, last 5 months. DOI: https://doi.org/10.25318/1410028701-eng.

StatLink https://doi.org/10.1787/888934149987

2.1.2. The impacts of the pandemic outbreak could be geographically concentrated

The economic consequences of COVID-19 are likely to affect local economies throughout Canada differently, with tourist destinations and large cities suffering the most in the short-term. Regions have different sectoral specialisations, exposure to global value chains, focus on tradable vs. non-tradable sectors, and shares of non-standard employment. Recent OECD work shows that sectors most at risk during the confinement period include manufacturing of transport equipment; construction; wholesale and retail trade; air transport, accommodation and food services; real estate services; professional service activities; and arts, entertainment and recreation (OECD, 2020[4]).

Some sectors have experienced larger employment losses than others. In March, almost all employment losses were observed in the services-producing sector. In April, by contrast, employment losses were proportionally larger in goods (-15.8%; -621 000) than in services (-9.6%; -1.4 million). Losses in the goods-producing sector were led by construction (-314 000; -21.1%) and manufacturing (-267 000; -15.7%). Within the services sector, employment losses continued in several industries, led by wholesale and retail trade (-375 000; -14.0%) and accommodation and food services (-321 000; -34.3%). Industries which continued to be relatively less affected by the COVID-19 economic shutdown included utilities; public administration; and finance, insurance and real estate (Statistics Canada, 2020[2]). In May, employment rebounded more strongly in the goods-producing sector (+5.0% or +165 000) than in the services-producing sector (+1.0% or +125 000) (Statistics Canada, 2020[3]).

2.1.3. Before COVID-19, the unemployment rate stood at a record low in Canada, but this masked regional labour market variations

Before the COVID-19 outbreak, Canada's labour market had performed well, with economic growth underpinning strong employment growth over recent years. The unemployment rate has been decreasing over the last decades, hitting a 40-year low of 5.7% in 2019, which was slightly above the OECD average of 5.2%.

Despite historical low unemployment rates at the federal level, labour markets in Canada witnessed strong provincial variation. Unemployment rates ranged from 11.9% in Newfoundland and Labrador to 4.7% in British Columbia in 2019, with Ontario and Quebec standing around the OECD average (see Figure 2.2). The relatively weaker performance of Newfoundland and Labrador is linked to the province's ageing population and emigration of high-skilled workers, as well as to spikes in employment linked to large construction projects (Moore, 2018[5]). In addition, the province enjoys a rich endowment of natural resources, with offshore oil and mining accounting for nearly a quarter of GDP. This level of concentration in natural resource sectors means that the local economy is highly exposed to fluctuations in global commodity prices (McKinsey & Company, 2019[6]).

To better understand the duration of labour market shocks, it is useful to analyse unemployment performance between 2008 (just before the financial crisis) and 2019. This can provide some indication about the time needed for recovery after a labour market shock. In 2019, the unemployment rate was still higher compared to 2008 in Alberta (+3.3 percentage points), Saskatchewan (+1.4), Manitoba (+1.1) and British Columbia (+0.1), showing that some provinces indeed did not fully recover in terms of unemployment from the 2008 financial crisis.

Regional employment disparities are also present when looking at economic regions across Canada (see Box 2.1 for more information on the definition of an economic region). Within four provinces in Canada (British Columbia, Nova Scotia, New Brunswick and Ontario), trends in regional employment have gone in opposite directions over the last decade, with some regions having recovered to their 2008 level while others still struggle with higher unemployment (see Figure 2.3). All economic regions in Newfoundland and Labrador and Quebec had lower unemployment rates in 2019 than in 2008. Looking at Ontario, the unemployment rate in 2019 was slightly higher than in 2008 only in Muskoka-Kawarthas and Northeast, while in all other economic regions it had decreased (see Figure 2.4). On the other hand, in Manitoba, Saskatchewan and Alberta, unemployment rates were higher in 2019 across all economic regions compared to 2008, largely reflecting difficulties in the oil sector and consequent negative impacts across the economy.

Figure 2.2. Unemployment varied substantially across provinces in Canada

Unemployment rate, Canadian provinces, Canada and OECD average, 2019

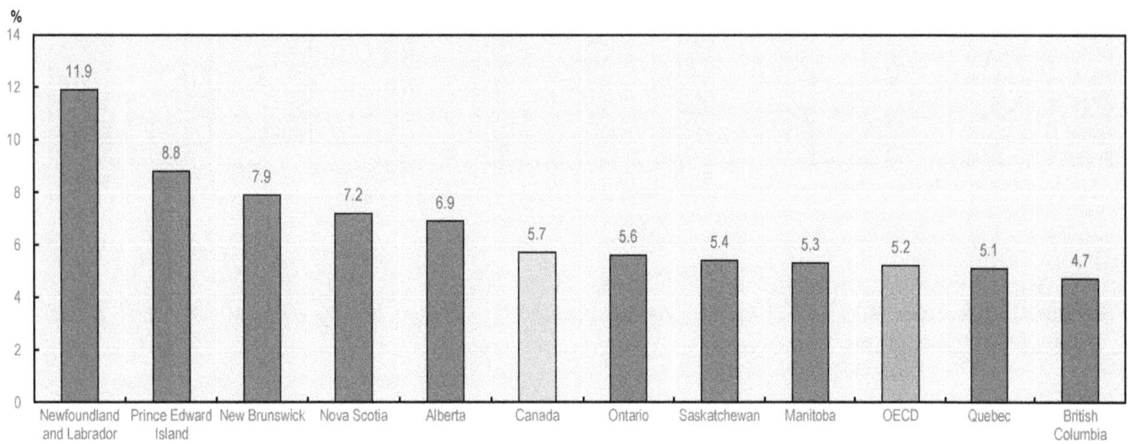

Note: The unemployment rate is the number of unemployed persons expressed as a percentage of the labour force. Estimates are percentages, rounded to the nearest tenth. The figure excludes the territories.

Source: Statistics Canada. Table 14-10-0090-01 Labour force characteristics by province, territory and economic region, annual, https://doi.org/10.25318/1410009001-eng.

Figure 2.3. Almost half of Canadian regions had not recovered to 2008 unemployment levels before the COVID-19 outbreak

Share of economic regions by province having lower or higher unemployment rates in 2019 compared to 2008

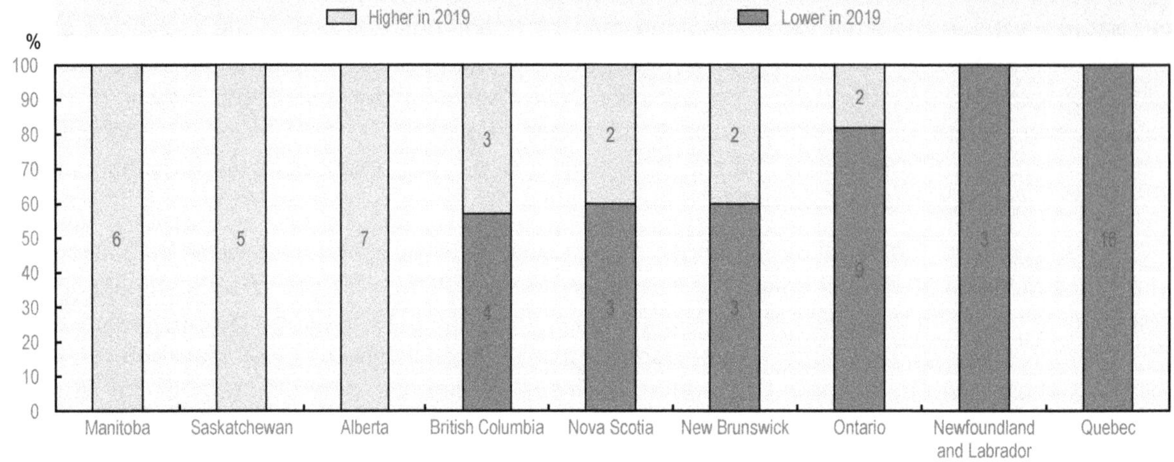

Note: The number in each column denotes the number of economic regions facing lower/higher unemployment rates in 2019 compared to 2008 within each province.
Source: OECD calculations on Statistics Canada.

Figure 2.4. Unemployment in Ontario had decreased in most regions between 2008 and 2019

Unemployment rate, Ontario economic regions, 2008 and 2019

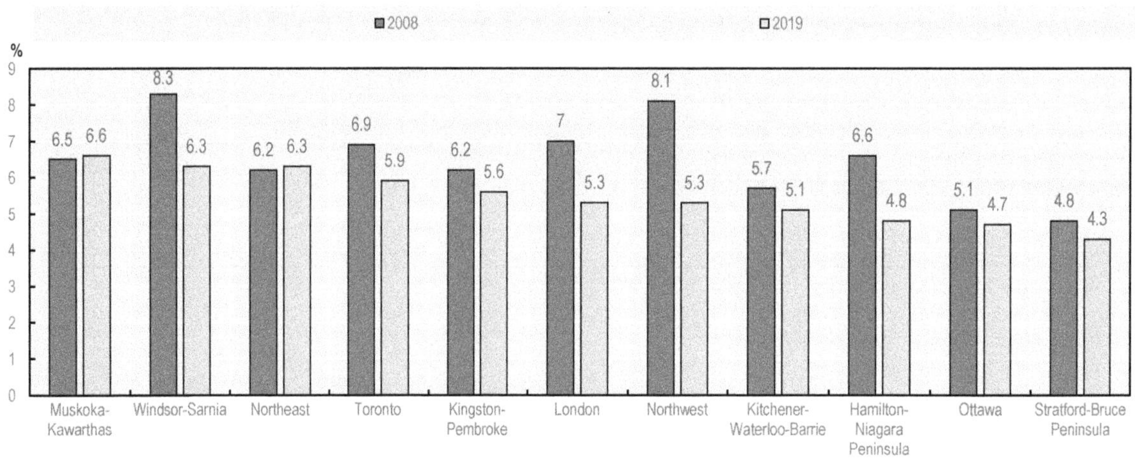

Note: Economic regions are ranked in descending order of 2019 unemployment rates.
Source: Statistics Canada. Table 14-10-0090-01 Labour force characteristics by province, territory and economic region, annual. DOI: https://doi.org/10.25318/1410009001-eng.

Box 2.1. What do we mean by "economic region"?

An economic region (ER) is a grouping of complete census divisions (with one exception in Ontario) created as a standard geographic unit for analysis of regional economic activity. According to the 2016 Canadian Census data, there are a total of 76 economic regions across Canada. However, some areas are too small to enable production of independent estimates and are grouped with a neighbouring region with similar economic characteristics, to obtain a total of 65 economic regions. Within the province of Quebec, economic regions (*régions administratives*) are designated by law. In all other provinces and territories, economic regions are created by agreement between Statistics Canada and the province/territory concerned. In Ontario, there is one exception where the economic region boundary does not respect census division boundaries: the census division of Halton is split between the ER of Hamilton--Niagara Peninsula and the ER of Toronto. Figure 2.5 presents a map of Ontario's 11 economic regions.

Figure 2.5. Ontario economic regions

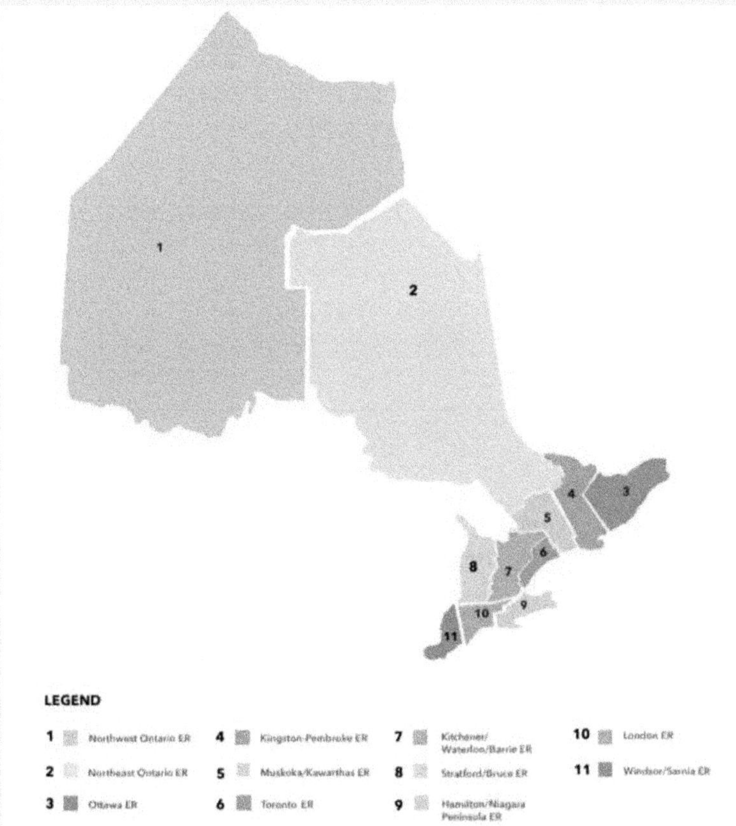

Source: Statistics Canada (2019[7]), Table 1.1 Geographic areas by province and territory, 2016 Census, https://www12.statcan.gc.ca/census-recensement/2016/ref/dict/tab/t1_1-eng.cfm (accessed on 7 May 2020); Ontario Chamber of Commerce (2019[8]), The Great Mosaic: Reviving Ontario's Regional Economies, https://occ.ca/wp-content/uploads/The-Great-Mosaic-Reviving-Ontarios-Regional-Economies.pdf (accessed on 10 March 2020); Statistics Canada (2018[9]), Economic region (ER), https://www150.statcan.gc.ca/n1/pub/92-195-x/2011001/geo/er-re/er-re-eng.htm (accessed on 10 July 2019); Statistics Canada (2016[10]), Economic Regions -Variant of SGC 2016 -Introduction -Definitions, http://www23.statcan.gc.ca/imdb/p3VD.pl?Function=getCET_Page&VD=318020&Item=318531 (accessed on 10 July 2019).

2.1.4. Job creation has been concentrated in some regions and within the services sector between 2008 and 2019

Disparities in local labour market outcomes are reflected in job creation trends across Canada. At the federal level, Ontario, Quebec, British Columbia and Alberta, which are Canada's most populous provinces, have led job creation over the past decade, adding 842 300, 457 200, 317 100 and 289 100 jobs to the economy respectively between 2008 and 2019. Most Canadian provinces, including less populated ones, have experienced employment growth over the past decade, with the only exception of New Brunswick. Provincial employment growth has lagged behind population growth in most provinces (see Figure 2.6).

Job creation has been particularly uneven within provinces, with a concentration in urban regions. For example, in Ontario, employment has grown by 20.8% in the economic region of Toronto over the 2008-19 period, followed by Kitchener-Waterloo-Barrie at 15.2% (see Figure 2.7). Toronto recently led all of North America (including Canada, the United States, and Mexico) in tech job creation and is now home to 240 000 tech workers (InvestinOntario, 2019[11]). On the other hand, negative growth occurred in the Northeast, Muskoka-Kawarthas, Windsor-Sarnia and Kingston-Pembroke regions. A similar picture emerges when looking at other provinces. For example, in British Columbia, Lower Mainland-Southwest experienced strong job growth between 2008-19, amounting to 21.8%, while some economic regions, such as North Coast and Nechako and Cariboo have lost jobs (-4.5% and -3.2% respectively). In Quebec, most regions have created jobs over the last decade but some have experienced decline, including Bas-Saint-Laurent (-2.6%) and Gaspésie-Îles-de-la-Madeleine (-6.4%).

Figure 2.6. Most provinces have created jobs over the last decade, although population has grown faster in most of them

Total employment and population change, percentage, Canada and Canadian provinces, 2008 to 2019

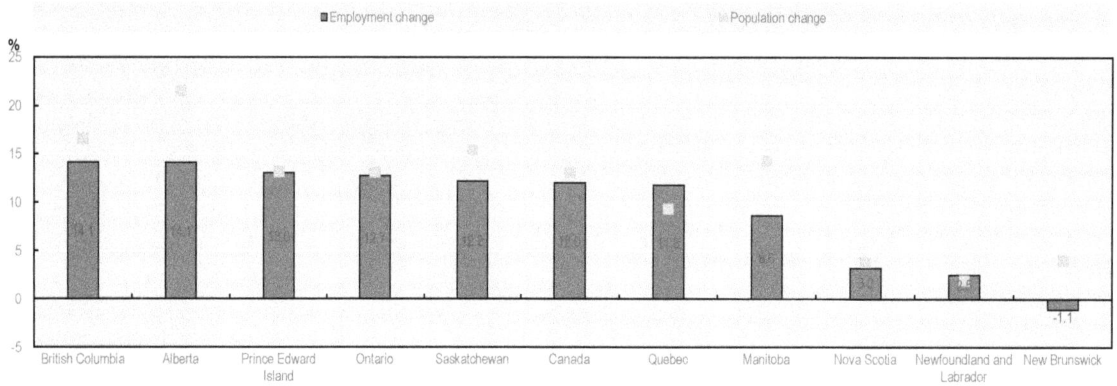

Note: Data does not include the territories.

Source: Statistics Canada. Table 14-10-0312-01 Employment by economic regions and occupation, annual (x 1,000). DOI: https://doi.org/10.25318/1410031201-eng; and Statistics Canada. Table 17-10-0005-01 Population estimates on July 1st, by age and sex. DOI: https://doi.org/10.25318/1710000501-eng.

Figure 2.7. Toronto has been an engine of job growth in Ontario

Total employment change, percentage, economic region in Ontario, 2008 to 2019

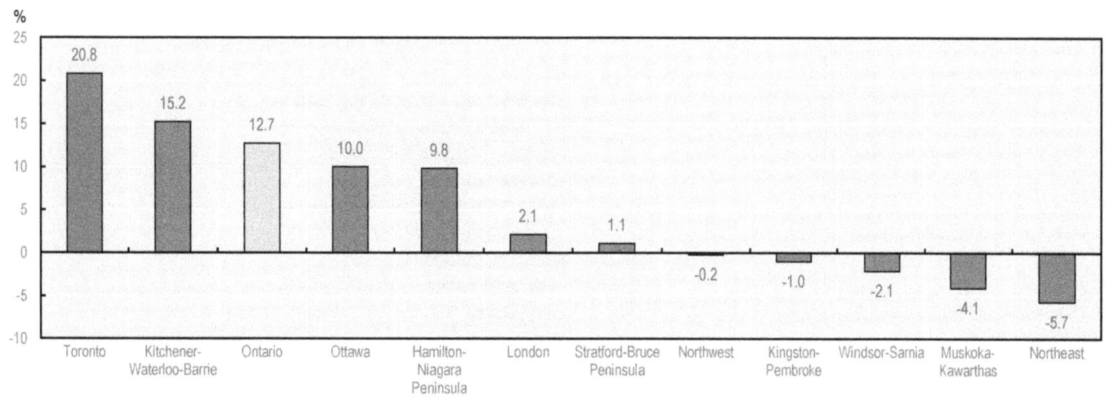

Source: Statistics Canada. Table 14-10-0312-01 Employment by economic regions and occupation, annual (x 1 000). DOI: https://doi.org/10.25318/1410031201-eng.

Trends in job creation have gone hand in hand with changing patterns in sectoral employment in Canada, which mirror OECD trends. Jobs in the services sector have expanded, while goods-producing jobs, such as manufacturing and agriculture, have shrunk both in Canada and across the OECD over the past decades. The services sector accounts for 79.2% of Canadian employment in 2019, compared to 20.8% for goods-producing sectors, which includes manufacturing, construction, agriculture, forestry, fishing and mining, and utilities. Manufacturing alone accounted for 9.1% of total employment in 2019. In addition, over the last decade, the Canadian labour market has experienced a considerable shift away from manufacturing towards services such as professional, scientific and technical services and health care and social assistance (see Figure 2.8). The drop in manufacturing employment has been widespread across regions in Canada, with about 80% of regions having experienced a drop in manufacturing employment. Similarly, agriculture employment has declined, with almost 70% of economic regions across Canada witnessing decreased shares of agriculture employment over the last decade.

The sectoral composition of employment remains diverse across Canada. Looking at Ontario, employment has grown in recent years in the health care and social assistance sectors, driven by the ageing of Ontario's population, and in technology, the fastest growing industrial sector in Canada in 2018 (Fields, Bourbeau and Patterson, 2018[12]) (Patterson, Hazel and Saunders, 2019[13]). Although services are the main source of employment across all Ontario regions, manufacturing remains a relevant employer, especially in Windsor-Sarnia, where it accounts for 18.4% of total employment, followed by London (15.5%) and Kitchener-Waterloo-Barrie (14.5%) in 2019 (see Figure 2.9).

Figure 2.8. Services employment has grown in Canada over the last decade, while agriculture and manufacturing have shrunk

Changes in employment by sector, Canada, 2008 to 2019

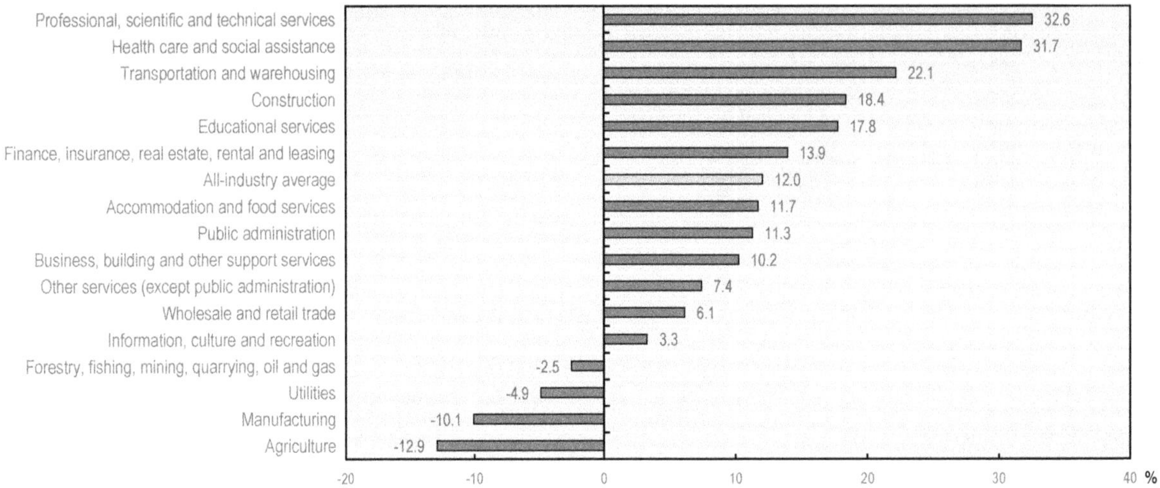

Note: Data does not include the territories.
Source: Statistics Canada. Table 14-10-0023-01 Labour force characteristics by industry, annual (x 1,000). DOI: https://doi.org/10.25318/1410002301-eng.

Figure 2.9. Manufacturing remains an important source of employment across Ontario regions

Manufacturing employment as a share of total regional employment, Canada, Ontario and Ontario economic regions, 2019

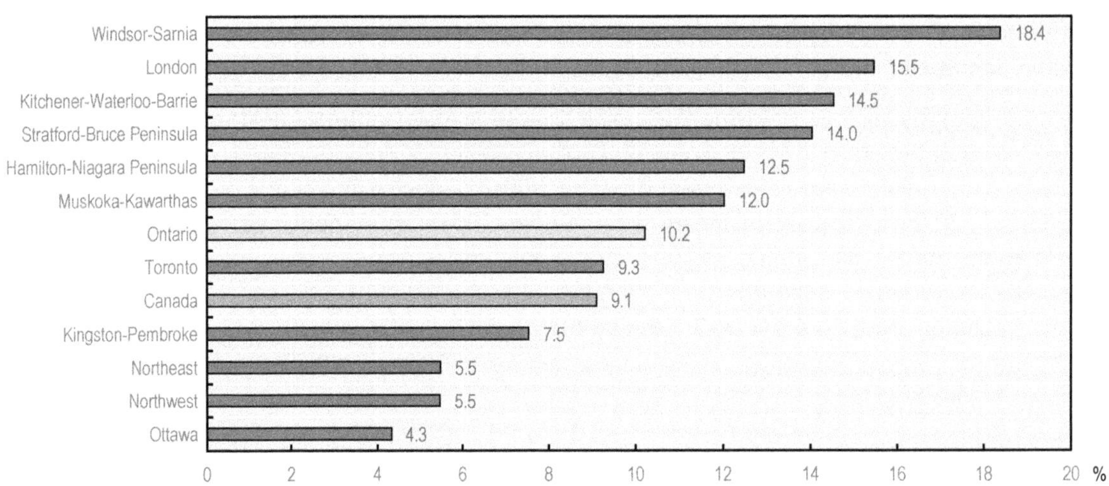

Source: Statistics Canada. Table 14-10-0092-01 Employment by industry, annual, provinces and economic regions (x 1 000). DOI: https://doi.org/10.25318/1410009201-eng.

2.2. Automation could re-shape labour markets across Canada

2.2.1. Fewer jobs are at risk of automation in Canada than on average across the OECD, but many jobs risk disappearing or changing significantly

Automation offers the opportunity to boost productivity, increasing prosperity and raising living standards. Automation can however also create losers, as workers who lose jobs to automation may not always have the skills needed in a changing labour market and might struggle to find new jobs. Automation can also put downward pressure on wages and lead to a polarisation of the skills required in the labour market, potentially exacerbating inequalities (OECD, 2018[14]). The labour share, defined as the share of total federal income that is paid in wages, has been decreasing over recent decades. While there are different potential explanations, the decline in the labour share was at least partially due to greater automation. In addition, the expanding use of robots is also associated with a reduction in wages and in the employment rate (Acemoglu and Restrepo, 2016[15]).

The spread of robots particularly affects sectors with a high concentration of occupations entailing routine tasks, which are easier to automate (Dao et al., 2017[16]) (Autor and Salomons, 2018[17]). These include middle-skill/middle-wage jobs, such as manufacturing and clerical jobs, that typically entail routine and repetitive tasks. While at the beginning of the century 100 000 industrial robots were delivered each year across the world, by 2016 the number of new industrial robots reached 300 000 annually (OECD, 2018[18]). In Canada, robot sales surged by 72% to 4 003 units in 2017, the highest level ever reached. The number of industrial robots per 10 000 employees in the manufacturing industry amounted to 161 in 2017, above both the world (85) and American average (91). Canada's robot density increased to 1 354 units per 10 000 employees in the automotive industry, attaining the highest level in the world for this sector (International Federation of Robotics, 2018[19]).

While only one in seven jobs may be lost to automation, many more could experience significant change in Canada. The OECD has developed a methodology to calculate the probability of losing jobs to automation, building on the model elaborated by Frey and Osborne (Frey and Osborne, 2013[20]) (see Box 2.2). Previous OECD research suggested that 14% of total jobs across the OECD faced a high risk of automation in 2013, while 32% may experience significant change to how they are carried out, with Canada experiencing lower automation risk than the OECD average (see Figure 2.10). Estimates developed for this report, looking at total employment data in 2018, show that 15.0% of jobs are at high risk of automation in Canada, while 30.6% are at significant risk.

The ongoing COVID-19 pandemic crisis is likely to accelerate the speed of automation in the workplace. Automation has historically taken place in bursts, concentrated especially in bad times such as in the wake of economic shocks, when human labour become relatively more expensive as firms' revenues rapidly decline. In these periods, employers are more likely to shed less-skilled workers and replace them with technology and higher-skilled workers, increasing labour productivity in the face of recessions (Muro, Maxim and Whiton, 2020[21]). Acceleration in the adoption of automation poses a dual challenge for Canada. On the one hand, it will be important for Canadian companies to adopt technology during and after the pandemic. This will help companies to solve some immediate challenges, and enjoy the productivity benefits of technology investments during and after the pandemic. On the other hand, accelerated automation can mean that certain workers may see longer-term dislocation from the labour market (Lamb, 2020[22]).

Figure 2.10. Jobs at risk of automation across OECD countries

Percentage of jobs at significant and high risk of automation by country, 2013

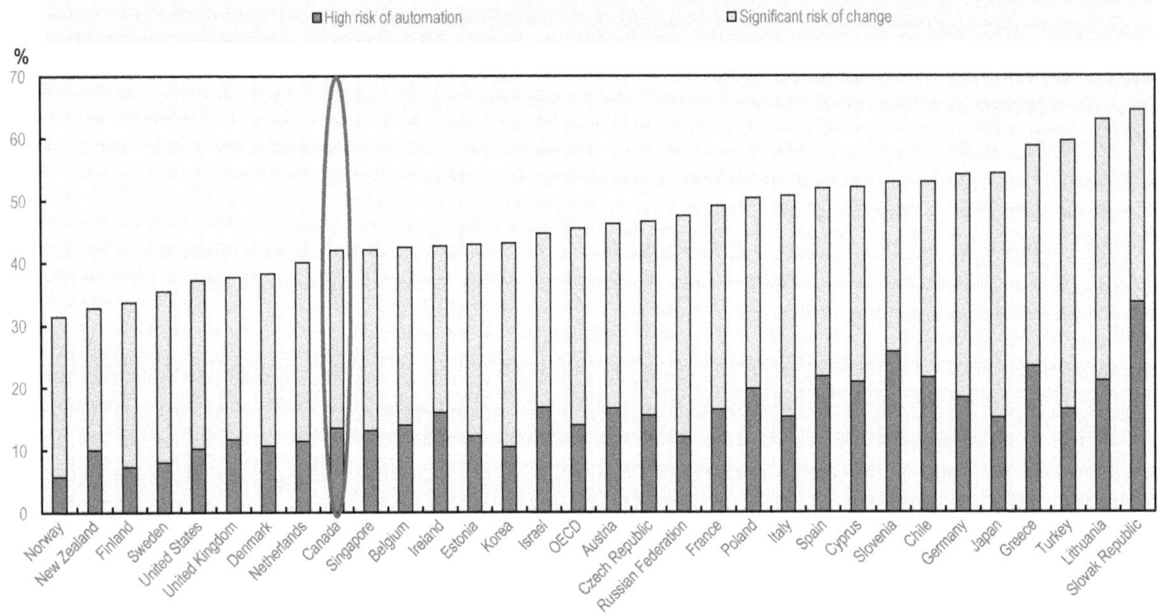

Note: 'High risk of automation' refers to the share of workers featuring a risk of automation of 70% or above. 'Significant risk' reflects the share of workers with a risk of automation between 50% and 70%.

Source: Nedelkoska, L. and G. Quintini (2018[23]), "Automation, skills use and training", OECD Social, Employment and Migration Working Papers, No. 202, OECD Publishing, Paris, https://dx.doi.org/10.1787/2e2f4eea-en.

StatLink https://doi.org/10.1787/888934150006

Box 2.2. Estimating the risk of automation across OECD countries

Frey and Osborne (FO) estimated the number of occupations at high risk of automation in the United States using a two-step methodology. They conducted a workshop with a group of experts in machine learning, whom they provided with a list of 70 occupations and their corresponding O*NET[1] task descriptions. Experts were asked "Can the tasks of this job be sufficiently specified, conditional on the availability of big data, to be performed by state of the art computer-controlled equipment?". This allowed for the coding of each occupation as automatable or non-automatable. FO then used a machine learning algorithm to find out more about the links between the coding to automate and the list of O*NET variables. They were able to identify those variables (and their associated bottlenecks) with higher prediction power. High scores on these bottlenecks are likely to mean that an occupation is safe from automation. They could then compute a "probability of computerisation" for each occupation in the US, leading to the aggregate estimate that 47% of US jobs have a probability of automation of more than 70%.

Table 2.1. Automation bottlenecks

Computerisation bottleneck	O*NET variable
Perception and Manipulation	Finger dexterity Manual dexterity Cramped workspace; awkward positions
Creative intelligence	Originality Fine arts
Social intelligence	Social perceptiveness Negotiation Persuasion Assisting and caring for others

Note: Please refer to (Frey and Osborne, 2013[20]) for further details on the definition of automation bottlenecks.
Source: Frey, C. and M. Osborne (2013[20]), The Future of Employment: How Susceptible are Jobs to Computerisation?, University of Oxford, https://www.oxfordmartin.ox.ac.uk/downloads/academic/The_Future_of_Employment.pdf (accessed on 10 July 2019).

Building on this approach, (Nedelkoska and Quintini, 2018[23]) (NQ) calculated the risk of automation across 32 OECD countries. The approach is based on individual-level data from the OECD Survey of Adult Skills (PIAAC), providing information on the skills composition of each person's job and their skillset. While drawing on FO, this methodology presents four main differences: (i) training data in the NQ model is taken from Canada to exploit the country's large sample in PIAAC; (ii) O*NET occupational data for FO's 70 original occupations were manually recoded into the International Standard Classification of Occupations (ISCO); (iii) NQ uses a logistic regression compared to FO's Gaussian process classifier; (iv) NQ found equivalents in PIAAC to match FO's bottlenecks. PIAAC includes variables addressing the bottlenecks identified by FO, but no perfect match exists for each variable. No question in PIAAC could be identified to account for job elements related to "assisting and caring for others", related to occupations in health and social services. This implies that risks of automation based on NQ could be slightly overestimated.

Table 2.2. Automation bottleneck correspondence

FO computerisation bottleneck	PIAAC variable
Perception and manipulation	Finger dexterity
Creative intelligence	Problem solving (simple) Problem solving (complex)
Social intelligence	Teaching Advising Planning for others Communication Negotiation Influence Sales

Note: Please refer to (Nedelkoska and Quintini, 2018[23]) for further details on the definition of the PIAAC variables.
Source: OECD (2018[18]), Job Creation and Local Economic Development 2018: Preparing for the Future of Work, OECD Publishing, Paris, https://dx.doi.org/10.1787/9789264305342-en; Nedelkoska, L. and G. Quintini (2018[23]), "Automation, skills use and training", OECD Social, Employment and Migration Working Papers, No. 202, OECD Publishing, Paris, https://dx.doi.org/10.1787/2e2f4eea-en.

Recent studies have pointed out the difficulty in predicting the risk of automation, as different models and variables come into play. Frey and Osborne's original examination of the impact of automation on jobs was focused on machine learning and mobile robotics, but these are not the only key technological developments likely to impact the future of skills. Others have identified the rise of various forms of telepresence and virtual/augmented/mixed forms of reality, as well as the expansion of digital platforms as trends that will have important impacts on the future. The inherent unpredictability of technological progress means that within the growing literature, estimates of the jobs at risk of automation can vary widely, and the timeframes within which these impacts are predicted to occur are similarly broad, ranging from 10 to 50 years. Both the shape disruption will take, and its extent, are uncertain. What is certain is that workers will need to learn new skills and develop new competencies to adapt to changes are on their way (Crawford Urban and Johal, 2020[24]).

2.2.2. Regional differences in the risk of automation exist within Canadian provinces

Automatable tasks are more prevalent in certain occupations and sectors, and neither occupations nor sectors are evenly distributed within Canada. Across Canada, provinces face a similar risk of losing jobs to automation (see Figure 2.11), compared to other OECD countries where the gap between the region at highest and lowest risks can be substantial (e.g. 12 percentage points in Spain). Similar automation risks across Canadian provinces reflect similar job creation trends and sectoral employment structures across provinces (OECD, 2018[18]). In the 2011-16 period, the share of jobs at high risk of automation in nine out of ten Canadian provinces fell, due to the creation of jobs in less risky occupations and loss of jobs in riskier occupations. Since 2011, Quebec, Ontario, Manitoba, Saskatchewan, Alberta and British Columbia have created jobs mostly in occupations presenting a lesser risk of automation, although this may entail greater job market polarisation. In Alberta, employment grew in the health sector, education, and business administration, which are at lower risks of automation. Meanwhile, in Prince Edward Island, Nova Scotia and New Brunswick, jobs have disappeared in occupations at higher risk of automation such as food processing, woodworking and garment workers. Standing out among provinces, Newfound and Labrador's economy has created jobs mostly in occupations at a higher risk of automation (OECD, 2018[18]).

However, the provincial picture does not capture substantial differences that exist within provinces (see Figure 2.12). For example, there are almost 15 percentage points of difference between regions facing the highest risk and lowest risk within British Columbia (Northeast with 59%, and Vancouver Island and Coast with 45.2% of jobs at risk of automation respectively). Northeast is a vast area of mountains, forests and lakes. The region's economy is based on natural resources, particularly mining and oil and gas activities. Other important industries in the region include forestry, agriculture and utilities (Government of British Columbia, n.d.[25]). Disparities in terms of risk of automation are also pronounced in Ontario, Quebec and Alberta. This could be partly explained by the coexistence of regions around large metropolitan areas in all provinces, typically drivers of high-skill jobs, and regions where manufacturing and agriculture are a large source of employment. Annex 2.A provides estimates of the risk of automation for economic regions within all Canadian provinces.

Figure 2.11. Canadian provinces face a similar risk of losing jobs to automation

Jobs at risk of automation as a share of provincial employment, 2018

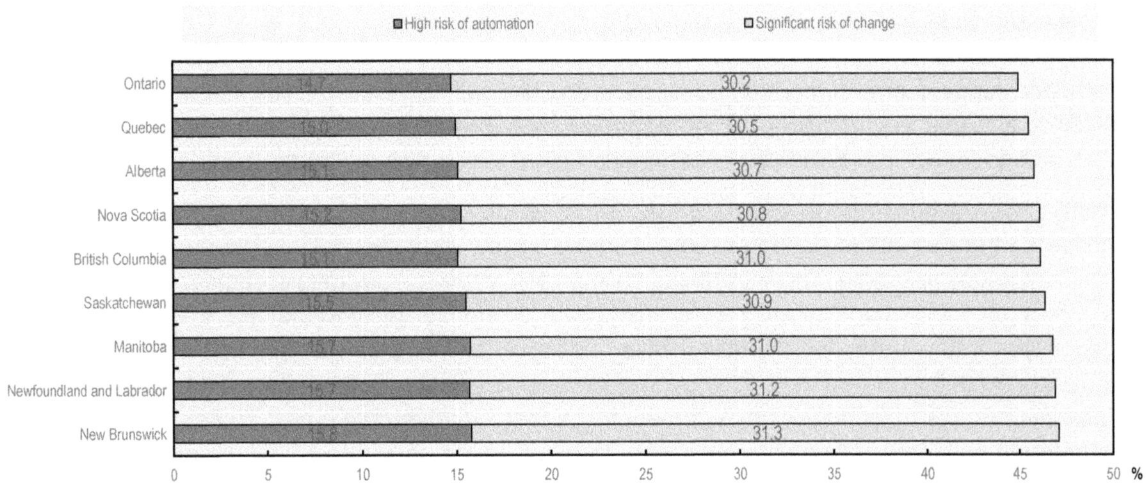

Source: OECD calculations on Labour Force Surveys.

Figure 2.12. Some provinces have wide regional disparities in terms of risk of automation

Jobs at risk of automation, region at highest and lowest risk within each province, 2018

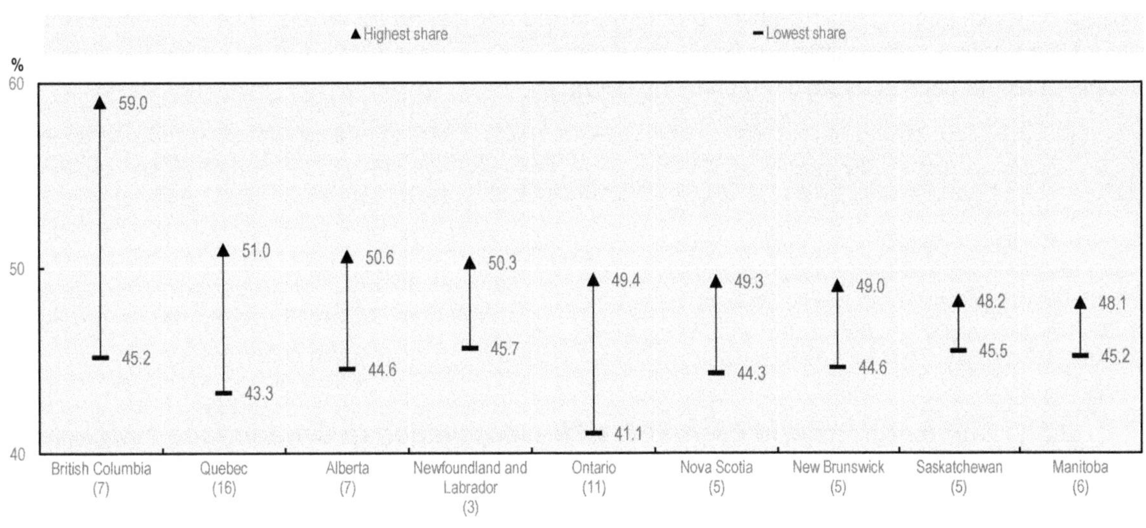

Note: The number of economic regions in each province is included in parenthesis.
Source: OECD calculations on Labour Force Surveys.

Box 2.3. How are the provincial and regional risks of automation calculated?

In order to produce provincial and regional estimates on the risk of automation, the results of Nedelkoska and Quintini (2018[23]) are applied at the provincial and regional scale in Canada. For each province and economic region, the share of jobs at risk of automation is calculated using data on provincial and regional employment by occupation and the estimated probabilities of automation from (Nedelkoska and Quintini, 2018[23]). As an approximation, the method assumes that jobs within the same job category have the same risk of automation across all provinces and regions of Canada.

Importantly, the methodology to estimate the risk of automation in an occupation can account for differences in the risk across countries but it cannot show how the risk of automation within an occupation changes over time. This introduces an important caveat. Countries or regions might respond to the threat of automation not only by shifting into economic sectors that have a lower risk of automation, but also by adapting the task profile of occupations so that they become less susceptible to automation. With the current methodology, it is impossible to capture the latter effect. Estimates that show how the number of jobs at risk of automation changes over time are based on how the number of jobs in different occupations changes over time. In other words, they show how regions gain or lose jobs in risky and less risky occupations.

Annex Table 2.A.1 presents details on the mean, high and significant risk of automation by occupation in Canada and the number of workers affected. These probabilities are defined for each occupation based on the Nedelkoska and Quintini (2018) methodology using PIAAC. Occupations with the highest mean risk of automation typically do not require specific skills or training, and include food preparation assistants, assemblers, labourers, refuse workers, cleaners and helpers. At the other end of the spectrum are occupations that require high level of education and training and which involve high degree of social interaction, creativity, problem-solving and caring for others. The high and significant risk of automation probabilities for each occupation in Canada are used to calculate the number of people at risk in each economic region in the country.

Source: OECD (2018[18]), Job Creation and Local Economic Development 2018: Preparing for the Future of Work, OECD Publishing, Paris, https://dx.doi.org/10.1787/9789264305342-en; Nedelkoska, L. and G. Quintini (2018[23]), "Automation, skills use and training", OECD Social, Employment and Migration Working Papers, No. 202, OECD Publishing, Paris, https://dx.doi.org/10.1787/2e2f4eea-en.

2.3. What could the local impacts of automation look like in Ontario?

2.3.1. Some regions and segments of the population in Ontario face a higher risk of automation

The Province of Ontario is the largest economy in Canada and the most populous province. Ontario's GDP accounts for about 40% of Canada's GDP. With a population of almost 15 million people, Ontario is also home to almost 40% of the Canadian population. The province is made of eleven economic regions, of which the largest by economy and population is Toronto.

Within Ontario, the share of total jobs at risk of automation ranges from 41.1% in Ottawa to 49.4% in Stratford-Bruce Peninsula (see Figure 2.13). The two regions face the lowest and highest shares of jobs at high risk of automation and jobs at risk of significant change. The share of jobs at high risk of automation ranges from 12.6% in Ottawa to 17.4% in Stratford-Bruce Peninsula. On the other hand, many more jobs are at risk of significant change across Ontario, ranging from 28.5% in Ottawa to 31.9% in Stratford-Bruce Peninsula. Stakeholder interviews conducted for this study show that the Ontario workforce perceives that automation is already affecting them and that it will do even more so in the near future, disrupting many sectors. In addition, the prevailing view among Ontario employers is that jobs will be simply lost to automation. Businesses and workers in Ontario have a general sense that automation is here, that its scope is increasing, and that it will disrupt many sectors and change how Ontario works (Birnbaum and Farrow, 2018[26]). Box 2.4 presents estimates of the risk of automation across Census Metropolitan Areas (CMAs) in Ontario.

Differences in the occupational profile of regional labour markets are the drivers behind differences in the risk of automation within Ontario. Occupational differences largely reflect differences in the industrial structure of regions. Industries such as agriculture, manufacturing, food and beverage services, transport and forestry have a higher probability of losing jobs to automation (Nedelkoska and Quintini, 2018[23]). Regions facing a higher risk of automation in Ontario tend to also present relatively high employment shares in goods-producing sectors, including agriculture, utilities, forestry, construction and manufacturing (see Figure 2.14). Stratford-Bruce Peninsula has the highest share of employment in construction and agriculture among Ontario region, amounting to 11.6% and 8% respectively in 2018, while manufacturing employment is highest in Windsor-Sarnia across regions in Ontario.

At the same time, the risk of automation is present in some services sectors, where occupations entailing routine tasks, such as sales workers, administration and personal services, represent a notable share of employment across Ontario regions. For example, London and Muskoka-Kawarthas face a high risk of automation, despite relatively lower employment shares in the goods-producing sector. The risk is driven by services occupations, including for example personal services and sales workers. On the other hand, regions facing lower risks have higher employment shares in services that typically face lower risk of automation as jobs in these sectors involve fewer routine tasks. Toronto is the region in Ontario with the largest share of jobs in professional, scientific and technical services, and finance, insurance, real estate, rental and leasing (11.3% and 10.9% respectively). In Ottawa, public administration remains the largest employer at 17.4%, while employment shares in agriculture, construction and manufacturing are the lowest across all Ontario regions.

Figure 2.13. The share of jobs at risk of automation varies across regions in Ontario

Jobs at risk of automation, Ontario economic regions and Ontario value, 2018

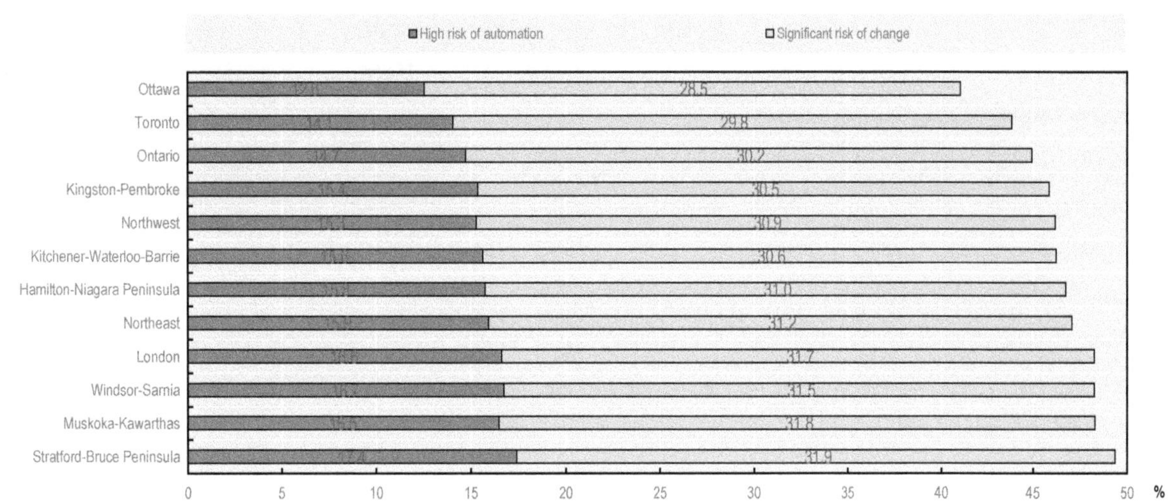

Source: OECD calculations on Labour Force Surveys.

Box 2.4. How could the future of work affect cities in Ontario?

Digging deeper to look at Census Metropolitan Areas (CMAs) in Ontario, OECD estimates show that the variation in the share of jobs at risk of automation is even more pronounced. About 52.1% of jobs are at risk of automation in Brantford, amounting to about 30 000 jobs, the highest share across all Ontario CMAs. On the other hand, the share of jobs at risk of automation is lowest in Ontario's part of Ottawa-Gatineau (39.5%). However, this represents a large number of jobs, given the CMA's total employment, with almost 220 000 jobs at risk.

Table 2.3. Jobs at risk of automation across Ontario CMAs

		Jobs at high risk of automation		Jobs vulnerable to significant change	
CMA	Total employment (2018)	Number of jobs	Share of total employment	Number of jobs	Share of total employment
Barrie	106 750	17 150	16.1%	33 460	31.3%
Brantford	55 500	10 402	18.7%	18 550	33.4%
Greater Sudbury	68 289	10 449	15.3%	21 448	31.4%
Guelph	75 695	11 596	15.3%	23 078	30.5%
Hamilton	409 971	60 307	14.7%	123 319	30.1%
Kingston	77 470	10 539	13.6%	22 701	29.3%
Kitchener-Cambridge-Waterloo	287 332	44 721	15.6%	87 691	30.5%
London	245 879	39 093	15.9%	76 550	31.1%
Oshawa	215 875	32 376	15.0%	66 001	30.6%
Ottawa-Gatineau, Ontario part, Ontario/Quebec	551 893	64 444	11.7%	153 335	27.8%
Ottawa-Gatineau, Ontario/Quebec	733 355	89 634	12.2%	207 593	28.3%
Peterborough	50 871	8 278	16.3%	16 567	32.6%
St. Catharines-Niagara	196 620	32 195	16.4%	62 961	32.0%
Thunder Bay	49 280	7 533	15.3%	15 618	31.7%
Toronto	3 336 159	467 656	14.0%	992 912	29.8%
Windsor	159 836	26 817	16.8%	49 977	31.3%

Source: OECD calculations on Labour Force Surveys.

Figure 2.14. Ontario regions most at risk present higher employment shares in goods-producing sectors

Share of employment in goods-producing sectors and risk of automation, Ontario economic regions and Ontario value, 2018

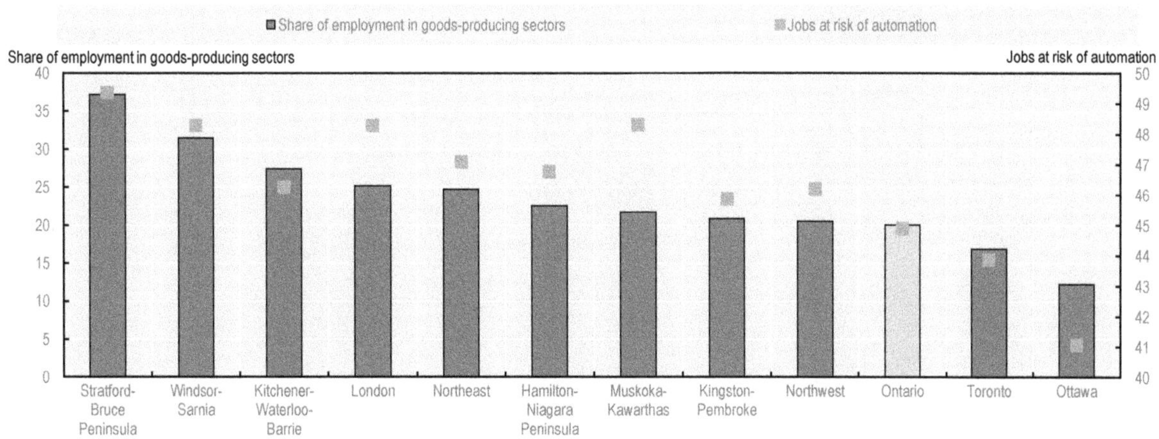

Note: Goods-producing sector includes agriculture; forestry, fishing, mining, quarrying, oil and gas; utilities; construction and manufacturing.
Source: OECD elaboration on Labour Force Surveys and Statistics Canada Table 14-10-0092-01 Employment by industry, annual, provinces and economic regions (x 1,000). DOI: https://doi.org/10.25318/1410009201-eng.

In addition, some segments of the population are more likely to be employed in high-risk occupations than others. Male-dominated occupations face a higher risk of automation, which typically results in men, rather than women, being mostly affected by equipment modernisation in Ontario (see Figure 2.15). This is typically related to higher male employment shares in occupations that entail repetitive and routine tasks. Around 150 000 men working as drivers and mobile plant operators face a risk of automation, compared to less than 30 000 women in Ontario. Similarly, more than 100 000 men working in metal, machinery and related trades face a risk of automation, compared to less than 15 000 women. There are however more women than men working as business and administration associate professionals and sales workers, who face a risk of automation. In addition, OECD work shows that across regions in the OECD, the low-skilled and young people are often in jobs at a higher risk of automation than the rest of the population. Low-skilled jobs are often those at higher risk as they entail elementary tasks easily automatable (OECD, 2019[27]). Young people also tend to be more employed in elementary occupations across the OECD (OECD, 2018[18]).

Figure 2.15. Men typically face a higher risk of automation than women in Ontario

Jobs at risk of automation by gender, 2018

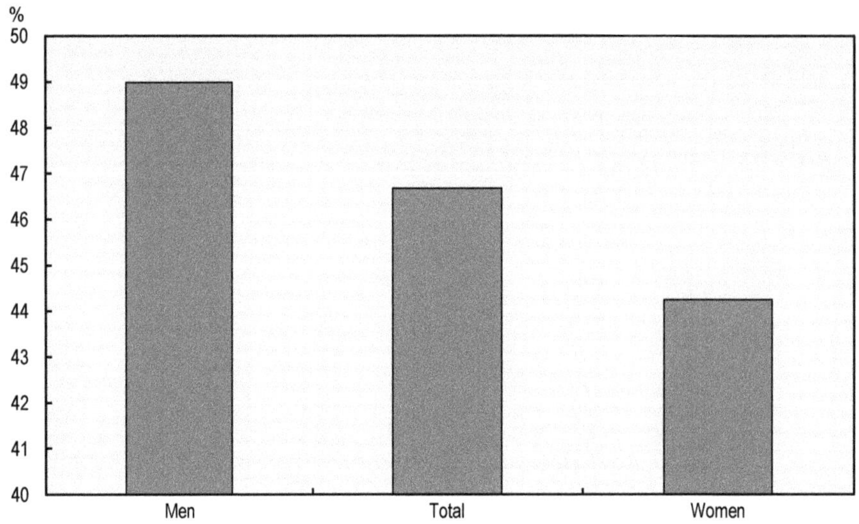

Note: Automation estimates by gender are done using the same methodology as used for other automation calculations, but calculating the estimates for men and women separately instead of for the total number of people employed. The shares of high and significant risk are the same for both genders, the differences come from the allocation of men and women into different occupations.
Source: OECD calculations on Labour Force Survey.

2.3.2. Ontario regions facing a higher risk are characterised by a lower share of working age population and more rural communities

Several studies support the notion that shrinking prime-age working populations pushes firms to source for alternative injections of productivity beyond local labour, such as automation. Using data on robot adoption from the International Federation of Robotics and data on ageing from the United Nations, Acemoglu and Restrepo (2019[28]) have shown that between 40% and 65% of cross-country variation in the adoption of industrial robots can be explained by ageing alone. The analyses focuses on the manufacturing sector and industrial automation. An ageing workforce leads to automation, particularly through robotics, as employers react to a scarcity of middle-aged workers. The relative scarcity of middle-aged workers with the skills to perform manual production tasks increases the value of technologies that can substitute for them. In industries most amenable to automation, ageing can trigger the adoption of robots and as a result lead to greater productivity (Acemoglu and Restrepo, 2019[28]). The increase in the adoption of robots is greater in countries and regions where ageing has occurred more rapidly (Mercer and Oliver Wyman, 2018[29]).

Ontario regions facing a higher risk of automation tend to have a lower share of working age population (i.e. population aged 15-64). On the other hand, regions with lower risk tend to have higher shares of working age population, driven by net migration inflows over the past decades. Toronto, Ottawa and Kitchener-Waterloo-Barrie have the highest shares of working age population, amounting to 68.8%, 66.7% and 66.7% respectively. On the other hand, only 61.4% of the population is in working age in Stratford-Bruce Peninsula and 61.7% in Muskoka-Kawarthas. Toronto is also the region with the lowest share of population aged 65 and more, amounting to 14.5% of the total regional population. On the other hand, almost one in four is older than 65 in Muskoka-Kawarthas. Northeast, Kingston-Pembroke and Stratford-Bruce Peninsula also have more than 20% of the local population in the over 65 year group. Acknowledging the difficult labour market prospects of older workers, the Government of Canada has measures in place to help them transition into new jobs. These include for example specific funding transferred from the federal government to provincial and territorial governments in support of older workers through the Workforce Development Agreements (WDAs).

A prevalence of rural areas[2] is also a feature of regions facing a higher risk of automation in Ontario. Muskoka-Kawarthas and Stratford-Bruce Peninsula are the two economic regions with the largest share of rural population, with one in two inhabitants living in rural areas. On average, 14% of the population is rural in Ontario, compared to 19% for the Canadian average. Regions, which have a low share of the population living in urban areas, have a higher share of jobs at risk of automation. OECD work shows that rural economies tend to have a lower share of service sector jobs that are better protected from automation. Smaller towns and rural areas are also more likely to be highly reliant on a handful of employers or on a single industry. While this does not necessarily increase the risk of automation in and of itself, it makes it more difficult to absorb displaced workers if one of the employers automates on a large scale (OECD, 2018[18]). Developing innovative solutions to provide education and apprenticeship training in rural areas is an important tool to support job transitions, as young people living in rural areas face a number of uniquely rural barriers, particularly concerning access to transport, careers advice, employment and training support, and youth services (OECD/ILO, 2017[30]).

2.3.3. Regions at higher risk also present lower levels of skills and poorer employment outcomes

The risk of automation tends to be higher in regions attaining lower levels of education in Ontario. Jobs facing a lower risk of automation typically require high education levels. Looking across the OECD, high-skill workers are geographically concentrated, often in more urban areas, and this concentration has increased over time. In Ottawa and Toronto, the two regions where the risk of automation is lowest, more than 30% of the population had a university certificate in 2016. On the other hand, less than 15% did so in Stratford-Bruce Peninsula and Northeast. OECD work shows that there is a negative relationship between the risk of automation and the share of workers with tertiary education. Regions that have the highest share of jobs at risk of automation also have the lowest share of workers with tertiary education (OECD, 2018[18]).

Poorer labour market outcomes are also a characteristic of regions showing a higher risk of automation. Looking at job creation trends over the last decade, regions that have experienced lower job creation (or job loss) tend to experience a higher risk. On the other hand, regions facing lower risks, such as Toronto and Ottawa, are those that have driven the creation of jobs. The combination of low jobs growth over the last decade and high risk of automation risks posing challenges for regional policy makers.

Regions with lower productivity have more potential for further automation and hence a higher risk of future job loss. OECD work highlights that automatable jobs are more likely to be concentrated in regions where productivity is low (OECD, 2018[18]). At least partially, this is because regions with low productivity make less use of advanced machines. Since automation tends to increase labour productivity, regions with low levels of productivity also tend to have low levels of automation.

Figure 2.16. Regions facing a higher risk in Ontario tend to have a less educated workforce

Share of population attaining university certificate or above and risk of automation, Ontario economic regions and Ontario

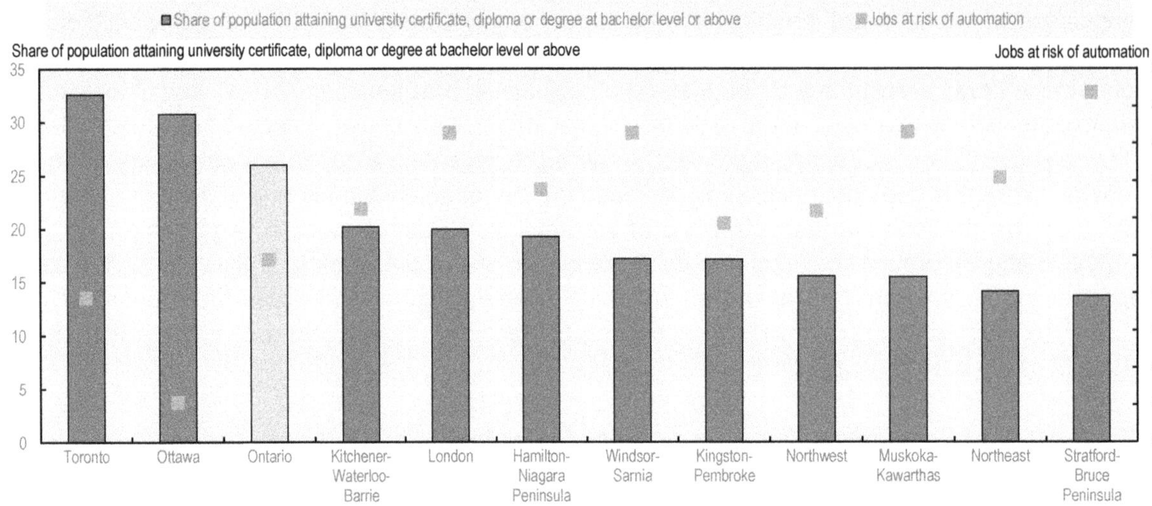

Note: Data on university attainment is from the 2016 Population Census.
Source: OECD elaboration on Labour Force Survey and 2016 Census.

2.3.4. The good news is that many regions in Ontario have created jobs in occupations at lower risk over the past decade

The creation of jobs in occupations at lower risk of automation has been sustained in Ontario over the 2011-2018 period (see Figure 2.17). The occupation that has grown the most is Business and Administration Associate Professionals, having added around 140 000 jobs. This is followed by other high-skill and professional occupations, such as Business and Administration Professionals and Science and Engineering Professionals, which have added around 70 000 and 60 000 new jobs respectively between 2011 and 2018. The number of Health Professionals and Teaching Professionals has also increased, by about 55 000 and 40 000. Some middle-skill occupations that typically face a rather high risk of automation, such as General and Keyboard Clerks, Customer Service Clerks and Numerical and Material Recording Clerks, have shed jobs. However, jobs have been created also in occupations facing a higher risk of automation over the 2011-2018 period, although not as many as in low-risk occupations. Two examples are Sales Workers and Drivers and Mobile Plant Operators, that have created around 30 000 jobs respectively. Other Canadian provinces have also created jobs predominantly in occupations at lower risk of automation between 2011 and 2018, including Alberta, Manitoba, Quebec and Saskatchewan. On the other hand, Newfoundland and Labrador and Prince Edward Island have lost jobs predominantly in riskier occupations, while New Brunswick and Nova Scotia have lost jobs predominantly in less risky occupations.

The Ontario economic regions of Hamilton-Niagara Peninsula, Kitchener-Waterloo-Barrie, Toronto and Windsor-Sarnia, have created jobs between 2011-2018 predominantly in occupations at a lower risk of automation (see Table 2.4). Box 2.6 and Box 2.7 present a spotlight on the economic regions of Hamilton-Niagara Peninsula and Kitchener-Waterloo-Barrie. In both regions, manufacturing, construction and transportation typically represent relevant sources of employment. However, recent years have seen the expansion of sectors such as professional and technical services, and information, culture and recreation. The risk of automation has also decreased in Muskoka-Kawarthas, but due to job loss in occupations at a higher risk of automation. Jobs at risk of automation have increased in other Ontario regions. London and Northwest have created jobs in riskier occupations. Job creation in occupations at risk of automation represents a critical trade-off for local policy makers. It can help improve labour market outcomes in the short term, but it also risks creating further risks for the future. Kingston-Pembroke, Ottawa, Northeast and Stratford-Bruce Peninsula have lost jobs predominantly in less risky occupations.

In the majority of regions across Canada, the risk of automation has decreased over the past decade (see Figure 2.18). Between 2011 and 2018, 35% of regions have created jobs predominantly in less risky occupations, while 20% have lost jobs predominantly in riskier occupations. However, the risk of automation has increased in the remaining regions, with 11% creating jobs predominantly in riskier occupations and 34% losing jobs predominantly in less risky occupations.

Figure 2.17. Ontario has mainly created jobs at lower risk of automation in the past decade

Job creation and automation risk by occupation, 2011 to 2018 where blue is high-skill, orange is middle-skill and green is low-skill jobs

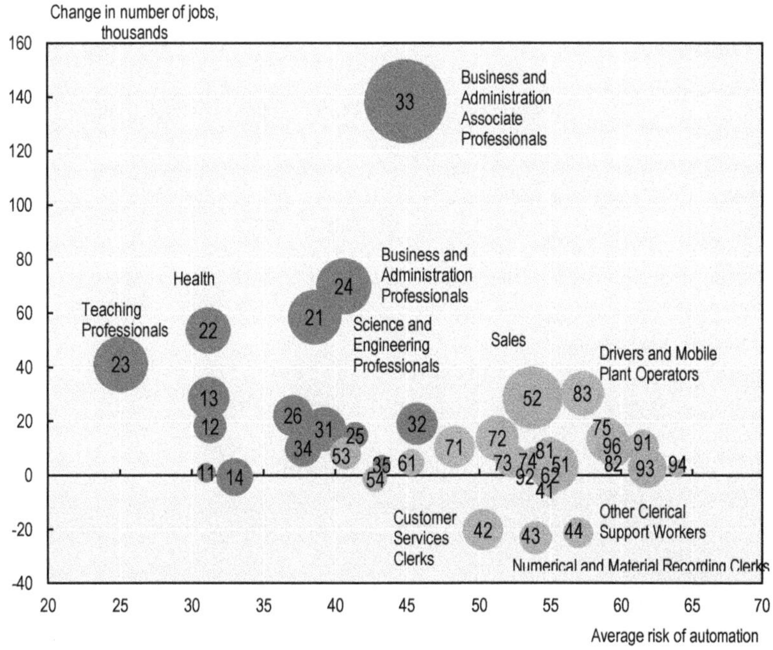

Note: Change in the number of jobs in thousands is a change between 2011 and 2018.
Source: OECD calculations on Labour Force Survey.

StatLink https://doi.org/10.1787/888934150025

Table 2.4. Many regions have created jobs at lower risk in Ontario

Change between 2011 and 2018, economic regions in Ontario

A. Creating jobs, predominantly in less risky occupations	B. Creating jobs, predominantly in riskier occupations	C. Losing jobs, predominantly in riskier occupations	D. Losing jobs, predominantly in less risky occupations
Hamilton-Niagara Peninsula	London	Muskoka-Kawarthas	Kingston-Pembroke
Kitchener-Waterloo-Barrie	Northwest		Northeast
Toronto			Ottawa
Windsor-Sarnia			Stratford-Bruce Peninsula

Note: Data is the change between 2011 and 2018. Type A and Type C regions experienced an increase in the share of jobs at low risk of automation with respect to occupations at high risk of automation. Type B and Type D regions experienced an increase in the share of jobs at high risk of automation. In both Type A and Type B regions aggregate employment grew, while in the Type C and Type D regions employment declined.
Source: OECD calculations on Labour Force Survey.

Box 2.5. A regional typology for employment creation in the face of digitalisation and automation

Regions can be classified into four categories depending on whether they gain or lose jobs and whether the gains or losses occur in sectors with high or low risk of automation. Ontario regions are classified according to whether they created jobs in the period 2011-2018, and further divided according to the type of occupation in which they created or shed employment. This classification provides insights into the short-term and long-term employment situation of a region (OECD, 2018[18]).

Table 2.5. The typology

Creating jobs		Losing jobs	
Predominantly in less risky occupations	Predominantly in riskier occupations	Predominantly in riskier occupations	Predominantly in less risky occupations
These regions improve their job situation in the short term and also reduce their long-term risk of unemployment from automation	These regions improve their short-term job situation, but do so at the expense of moving towards a riskier job profile in the future	These regions have the typical profile of regions in the process of undergoing a structural change caused by automation. While jobs are being lost to automation today, the risk of further job losses due to automation decreases	These regions face the greatest challenge. They suffer current job losses combined with an increasing risk of further job losses in the future due to automation

Figure 2.18. Most Canadian regions have created jobs in less risky occupations

Change between 2011 and 2018, all economic regions in Canada

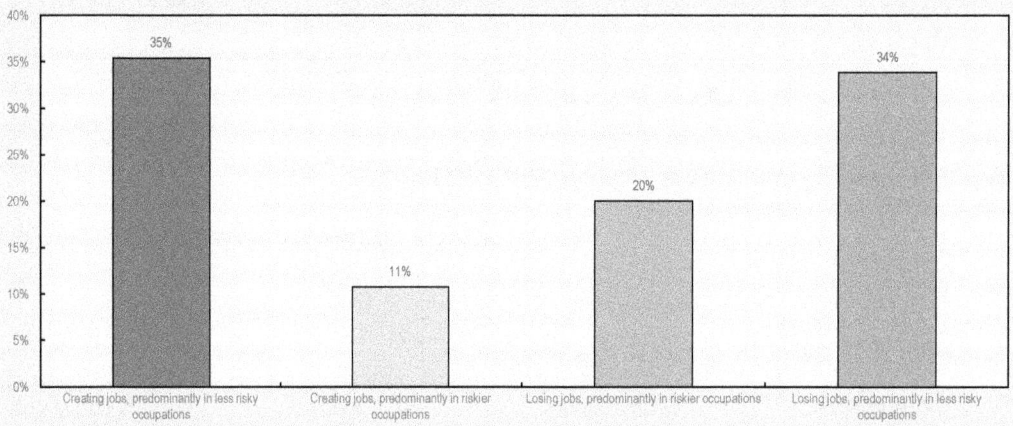

Source: OECD calculations on Labour Force Survey; OECD (2018[18]), Job Creation and Local Economic Development 2018: Preparing for the Future of Work, OECD Publishing, Paris, https://dx.doi.org/10.1787/9789264305342-en.

StatLink https://doi.org/10.1787/888934150044

Box 2.6. Spotlight on Hamilton-Niagara Peninsula

The Hamilton-Niagara Peninsula region has experienced improving employment outcomes over the past decade. After peaking at 9.2% in 2009, in the aftermath of the global financial crisis, the unemployment rate has been steadily declining, but it has fluctuated since 2016. The rate stood at 5.4% in 2018, among the lowest in the province. However, labour force participation and employment rates remain relatively low in comparison with the rest of the province. Labour force participation has declined from 66.3% to 63.9% from 2008 to 2018, while the employment rate has decreased from 62% to 60.9% over the same period.

In Hamilton-Niagara Peninsula, 46.8% of jobs are at risk of automation, representing around 370 000 jobs. The risk of automation is slightly higher in Hamilton-Niagara Peninsula than across Ontario on average. About 15.8% of jobs (almost 120 000 jobs) are at high risk in Hamilton-Niagara Peninsula, while 31% (around 250 000 jobs) are at significant risk of change. Hamilton-Niagara Peninsula has been among the four regions in Ontario that have created jobs predominantly in occupations at lower risk of automation over the 2011-2018 period.

Professional, scientific and technical services and information, culture and recreation are the sectors that have experienced the largest increase in employment (33% and 26.4% respectively, adding a total of 11 700 and 7 300 new jobs to the economy). On the other hand, agriculture has experienced the largest drop (-18.8%, or -2 600 jobs), followed by utilities (-13.2%, or -700 jobs) and transportation and warehousing (-5.9% or -2 100 jobs). Manufacturing has traditionally represented an important source of employment in the region. More than 100 000 people were employed in manufacturing in Hamilton-Niagara Peninsula in 2008. Over the past decade manufacturing employment has experienced substantial decline. About 93 200 people were employed in manufacturing in 2018, accounting for 12.4% of regional employment. The manufacturing industry accounted for 14% of the Hamilton-Niagara Region's total GDP in 2016. Only finance and insurance (17%) holds a larger share of GDP in the region. While manufacturing remains an important part of the region's economy, its share of GDP has declined by more than 5% between 2006 and 2016 (Canadian Skills Training and Employment Coalition, 2016[31]).

Figure 2.19. What sectors have expanded and contracted the most in Hamilton?

Change in employment, top 5 and bottom 5 sectors witnessing the largest change, 2011 to 2018

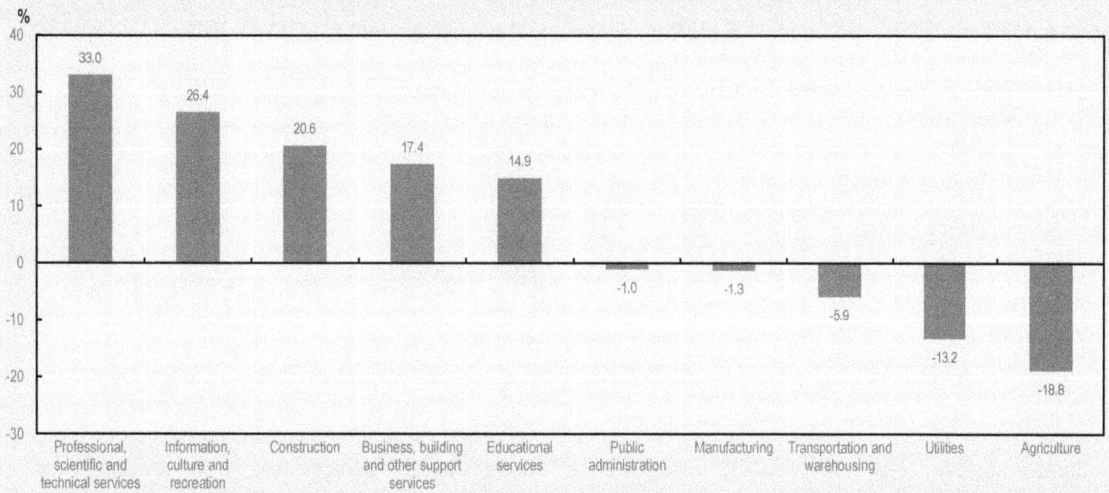

Source: Statistics Canada. Table 14-10-0092-01 Employment by industry, annual, provinces and economic regions (x 1 000). DOI: https://doi.org/10.25318/1410009201-eng; Canadian Skills Training and Employment Coalition (2016[31]), Regional Manufacturing Profile: Hamilton-Niagara Region, http://cstec.ca/sites/cstec/files/reports/MANUFACTURING-PROFILE-%20Hamilton-Niagara.pdf (accessed on 28 February 2020).

Box 2.7. Spotlight on Kitchener-Waterloo-Barrie

The region of Kitchener-Waterloo-Barrie includes the census metropolitan areas (CMA) of Kitchener-Waterloo-Cambridge, Barrie, and Guelph, as well as Dufferin and Simcoe regions. The region had a total population of 1 299 265 in 2016. Important economic drivers in the region include a large high-tech sector, manufacturing and agriculture among other industries.

Businesses from the Kitchener-Waterloo-Barrie region were among the least confident in their organisation's economic outlook, according to a 2014 survey from the Greater Barrie Chamber of Commerce, the Ontario Chamber of Commerce and Leger Marketing. A more recent survey undertaken by the ManpowerGroup however showed that the region was among the top 5 regions for hiring federally, as 35% of employers surveyed in 2018 expected to hire in the first quarter of 2019, while only 2% were expected to make job cuts. Among employers surveyed in 2019, 20% planned to hire in the first quarter of 2020, while 3% expected to make job cuts. The unemployment rate stood at 4.7% in 2018, lower than pre-crisis levels. The rate had substantially increased in 2009, when it totalled 9.1%, up from 5.7% in 2008. Although declining, labour force participation and employment rates are higher than on average across Ontario (67.3% versus 64.5% and 64.1% versus 60.9%).

Kitchener-Waterloo-Barrie faces a higher risk of automation than on average across Ontario, with 46.3% of jobs at risk of automation in 2018, corresponding to more than 450 000 jobs. About 15.6% of jobs (around 140 000 jobs) are at high-risk in Kitchener-Waterloo-Barrie, while 30.6% (around 310 000 jobs) are at significant risk of change. However, between 2011 and 2018 employment has grown predominantly in occupations facing a lower risk of automation. Looking at sectoral development, utilities (+ 29.3% or 1 200 new jobs), health care and social assistance (+17.6% or 12 400 new jobs), professional, scientific and technical services (16.3% or 7 100 new jobs), and information, culture and recreation (15% or 4 200 new jobs) are the sectors where employment has experienced higher growth rates. However, construction and transport sector employment has also grown (14.9% and 12%, adding 7 800 and 3 300 new jobs respectively). Manufacturing is the largest industry in the region by employment, accounting for 16.7% of total employment, or 121 300 jobs in 2018. In addition, manufacturing employment has continued to grow between 2011 and 2018 (+3.3%, or 3 900 new jobs). This poses potential labour market challenges for the future, as manufacturing and construction jobs are among those typically facing a higher risk of automation.

Figure 2.20. What sectors have expanded and contracted the most in Kitchener?

Change in employment, top 5 and bottom 5 sectors witnessing the largest change, 2011 to 2018

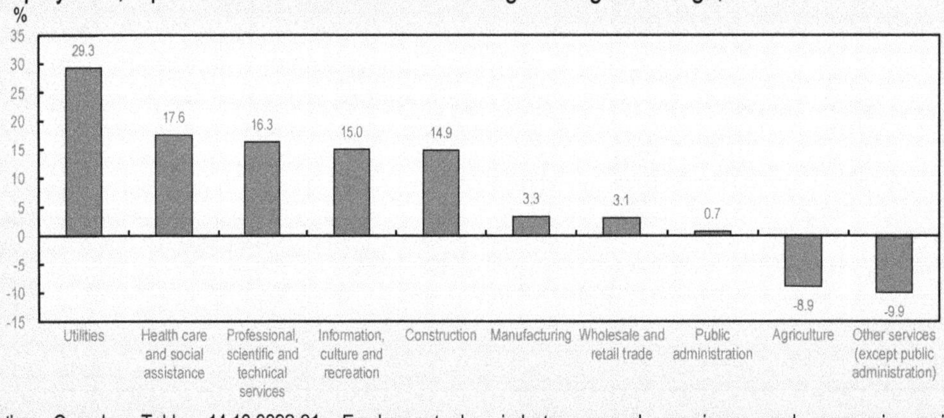

Source: Statistics Canada. Table 14-10-0092-01 Employment by industry, annual, provinces and economic regions (x 1 000), https://doi.org/10.25318/1410009201-eng; Nielsen, K. (2019[32]), Kitchener-Cambridge job market to cool in 2020: ManpowerGroup, https://globalnews.ca/news/6278877/kitchener-waterloo-region-jobs-market-2020-manpower-survey/ (accessed on 19 Feb 2020); Nielsen, K. (2018[33]), Kitchener, Cambridge job market looking solid for 2019: survey, https://globalnews.ca/news/4754727/kitchener-cambridge-job-market/ (accessed on 19 Feb 2020); Barrie Chamber of Commerce (2014[34]), Business confidence in Kitchener-Waterloo-Barrie region lower than provincial average*, http://barriechamber.wsiefusion.net/member-blog/business-confidence-in-kitchener-waterloo-barrie-region-lower-than-provincial-average (accessed on 19 Feb 2020); Greater Barrie Chamber of Commerce (2014[35]), Regional Economic Outlook: Kitchener-Waterloo-Barrie, http://barriechamber.com/2014/REO2014_GBCC_r1.pdf (accessed on 19 Feb 2020).

2.3.5. High-skill occupations are projected to drive job creation in Ontario

The demand for high-skill jobs is projected to grow in Canada over the coming decade. To take advantage of future developments in the labour market, re-skilling and up-skilling will be essential. While technological developments are likely to lead to the automation of tasks within different occupations, high-skill jobs, such as managerial jobs, are typically less vulnerable to automation, as they require fewer routine and repetitive tasks to be performed.

Employment and Social Development Canada (ESDC) has undertaken estimates of job growth in Canada for the period 2019-28 based on the 2016 National Occupational Classification (NOC). Occupations that usually require a university education are expected to have the fastest overall employment growth contributing also to the largest share (36%) of job creation among all skill levels. This is mostly the result of strong growth expectations in occupations related to professional services in health, as well as in the natural and applied sciences fields, including occupations in the information and technology sector. Occupations that usually require a college education or apprenticeship training are projected to have the second largest contribution to employment growth (33%). In comparison, occupations requiring high school education or on-the-job training are expected to account for a much lower share of total job creation (16% and 9% respectively). Sectors can be divided in three categories, based on their projected employment growth:

- Sectors projected to experience above average employment growth (i.e. above or around 0.9% annually). These include professional and scientific services (such as computer system design), health care and social assistance, arts, entertainment and recreation services, food services, some transportation services, metal fabrication and machinery, and elementary and secondary schools;
- Sectors projected to undergo average or moderate employment growth (i.e. between 0.4% and 0.9% annually). This is the case of some manufacturing and commercial services industries, as well as the construction, oil and gas, and mining industries;
- Sectors projected to experience weak employment growth or declines in employment. These are mainly manufacturing and primary industries that have already experienced weak growth or decline over the past years, including wood products, textiles, clothing, furniture, paper, printing, agriculture, forestry and fishing.

Figure 2.21. High-skill occupations are projected to create thousands of jobs in Canada in the coming years

Distribution of Expansion Demand by Skill Level, 2019-28

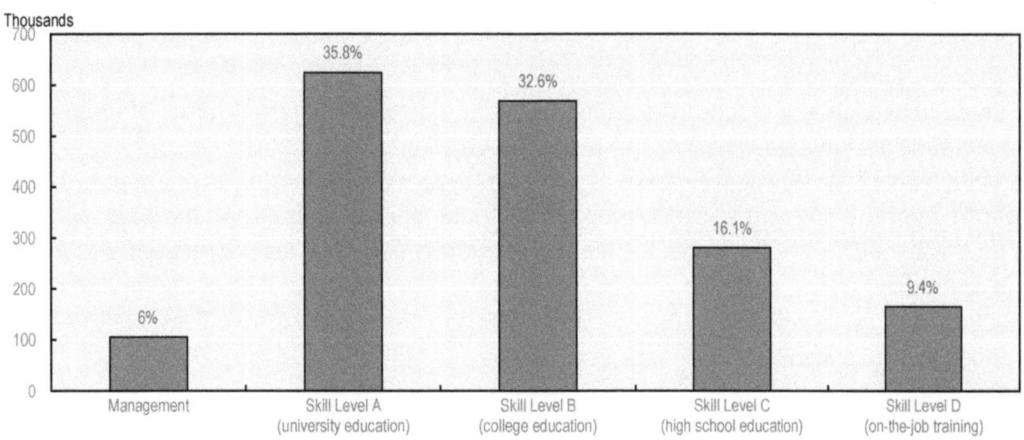

Source: Statistics Canada (historical) and ESDC 2019 COPS Projections.

2.4. What other challenges and opportunities could impact local labour markets in in Canada?

2.4.1. Non-standard forms of work can offer flexible work arrangements

A relevant labour market development witnessed across OECD countries over the last three decades is the gradual transition from the traditional open-ended contracts to non-standard forms of work (see Box 2.8 for information on the definition of non-standard work). Technological developments are an important mechanism behind the rise of non-standard forms of work. Consumers' preferences on one hand have increasingly favoured customised services and just-in-time delivery. Technological developments within firms have also allowed to increase job flexibility and task outsourcing, including freelance contractors, temporary help agencies or others.

Non-standard work represents an opportunity for some workers. For example, it can help people ensure a better matching between work time with family care, allowing many people – mostly women – to get a job at all. It can also help young people transition into the labour market and gain experience, which can lead to other job opportunities in the future (OECD, 2018[18]).

However, non-standard work can also be associated with a deterioration of working conditions. It reduces employment stability, increasing income volatility and potentially hampering career progression. Non-standard workers also traditionally have less access to training. Wages in fixed term contracts tend to be lower than in permanent ones, while work-related strain and job insecurity are higher. Flexible and more precarious forms of work may represent a way for firms to reduce labour costs, and, to the extent that they do not foster labour participation or career progression, these forms of work would reduce workers' welfare. In particular, non-standard workers are usually worse off in terms of job security and social protection, and tend to receive less training and face barriers to accessing employment programmes (OECD, 2018[18]).

Box 2.8. Defining non-standard work

Non-standard work (NSW) arrangements are defined by what they are not: full-time dependent employment with a contract of indefinite duration – or what is generally considered the "standard" work arrangement. NSW therefore includes:

- Temporary workers - workers in fixed-term contracts, including casual employees (duration is not fixed, but hours can vary), and seasonal workers in the Canadian context;
- Part-time workers;
- The self-employed.

While this definition may be considered problematic – as it lumps together precarious and non-precarious forms of work – the convention is followed by a large part of academic research as well as by international organisations. For this reason, this chapter adopts this definition.

An additional challenge lies in the fact that the distinction between different forms of employment has become increasingly intricate. In particular, there is a growing grey area between self-employment and wage employment. The growing numbers of self-employed working for just one company represent a group on the border between two categories. While these blurred lines are at the heart of the current debate on the benefits and downsides of the gig economy, data that allows researchers to settle the debate is scarce

Source: OECD (2018[18]), Job Creation and Local Economic Development 2018: Preparing for the Future of Work, OECD Publishing, Paris, https://dx.doi.org/10.1787/9789264305342-en; OECD (2015[36]), "Non-standard work, job polarisation and inequality", in *In It Together: Why Less Inequality Benefits All*, OECD Publishing, Paris, https://dx.doi.org/10.1787/9789264235120-7-en.

2.4.2. Temporary work has increased in Canada and across the OECD

Temporary work has been on the rise in Canada with some gender differences depending on its form. Around 12.8% of dependent workers were in temporary work in Canada in 2019. The latest share for the OECD average is 11.7% in 2018. Temporary jobs slightly increased from 12.3% in 2008. Although temporary employees represent a smaller share of total employment as compared to permanent workers, growth in temporary employment in Canada has outpaced permanent employment since 2000. Over the past two decades, the large share of growth in temporary employment in Canada can be attributed to increases in the number of people with a term or contract job. Women are as likely to be in temporary jobs as men in Canada (14% and 13% respectively in 2018). Among temporary employees, women are however more likely than men to have a casual, term or contract job (85% and 73%), but less likely to have a seasonal job (14% and 27% respectively). About 10% of women employed in temporary contracts had multiple jobs in 2018, compared to 6% of men (Statistics Canada, 2019[37]).

Temporary work is associated with lower earnings. In 2018, temporary workers earned on average CAD 21.80 per hour, compared to CAD 27.71 for permanent employees, and worked fewer hours on average per week (27.8 hours compared with 33.3), causing lower weekly earnings for temporary employees. Temporary workers also have lower median hourly wages than permanent employees (CAD 18.75 and 25 respectively). At the same time, about four out of ten temporary employees worked part-time, compared with 14% of permanent employees. Differences in the hourly wage also exist between unionised and non-unionised temporary workers across Canada, amounting to CAD 27.37 and CAD 19.56 per hour respectively (Statistics Canada, 2019[37]).

The pervasiveness of temporary contracts varies almost two-fold across provinces in Canada (see Figure 2.23). Seasonal employment is prevalent as a form of temporary work in Atlantic provinces, as it is highly dependent on fluctuations in commodity prices. The share of temporary employment was highest in Newfoundland and Labrador (23.6%) and Prince Edward Island (20.7%) across Canadian provinces in 2019. On the other hand, Manitoba, Alberta and Ontario had the lowest proportions of temporary employment in 2019 (11.7%, 12.1% and 12.2% respectively). Temporary employment has experienced limited fluctuations across provinces in Canada over the past decade. Alberta has experienced the largest increase in temporary employment between 2008 and 2019, amounting to 2.1 percentage points. On the other hand, temporary employment has decreased by 1.9 percentage points in Prince Edward Island and New Brunswick.

Figure 2.22. Non-standard employment has been on the rise in most OECD countries

Share of temporary work, 2000 and 2016

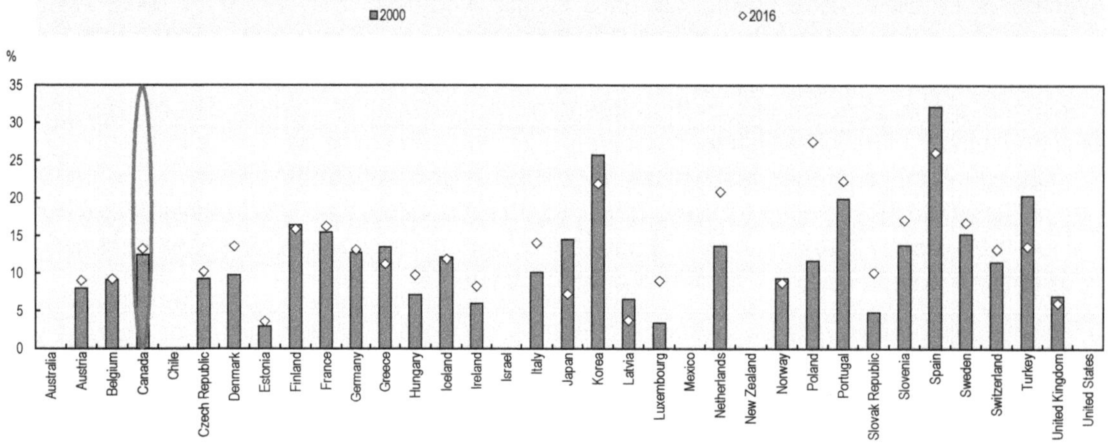

Source: OECD (2018[18]), Job Creation and Local Economic Development 2018: Preparing for the Future of Work, OECD Publishing, Paris, https://dx.doi.org/10.1787/9789264305342-en; OECD (2018), "Labour Market Statistics: Employment by permanency of the job & Full-time part-time employment - common definition: incidence", OECD Employment and Labour Market Statistics (database), http://dx.doi.org/10.1787/lfs-data-en.

Figure 2.23. Temporary employment in some provinces is almost double the rate of others

Percentage of permanent and temporary employees over total employees, Canada and Canadian Provinces, 2019

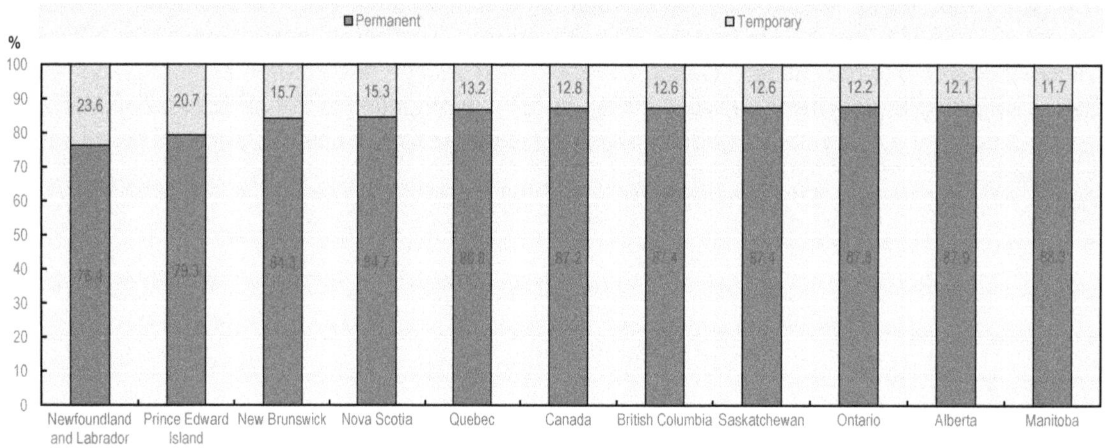

Source: Statistics Canada. Table 14-10-0072-01 Job permanency (permanent and temporary) by industry, annual (x 1 000), DOI: https://doi.org/10.25318/1410007201-eng.

2.4.3. Part-time work has slightly increased in Canada

The share of part-time work, including those workers who usually work less than 30 hours per week at their main or only job, has increased in most OECD countries over the past decades, including a slight increase in Canada (see Figure 2.24). The share of part-time workers amounted to 18.9% in 2019 in Canada. The share was highest in British Columbia, where it amounted to 21.9% in 2019, followed by Manitoba at 19.6%. The share of part-time work is lowest in Prince Edward Island and New Brunswick, where 15.1% of employees work part-time. In Ontario, part-time work stood at 18.6% in 2019.

Part-time employment is more pronounced in some Ontario regions than others. A slight increase in part time employment was recorded in Ontario in the aftermath of the global financial crisis, with part-time employment up to 19.6% of total employment in 2009 and 2010. The incidence of part-time work over total employment was highest in Kingston-Pembroke than the rest of Ontario economic regions in 2019 (see Figure 2.25). Toronto has the lowest share of part-time work, amounting to 17.4% in 2019. Going to school and personal preference are the main reason for working part-time in Ontario, as in all other Canadian provinces (see Figure 2.26). However, compared to the Canadian average, a larger share of people in Ontario works part-time due to business conditions, whether they did or did not look for full-time employment over the past month (11.1% and 9.4% of part-time workers in Ontario and Canada respectively). There are also gender differences in the reasons for working part-time within Ontario. Caring for children is the reason why about 11.9% of women work part-time in the Province, compared to only 1.8% of men. On the other hand, men are more likely to be going to school compared to women, with about 34.8% of men who work part-time selecting this as the reason, compared to 26.3% of women.

Figure 2.24. Part-time work has increased in most OECD countries

Share of part-time work, 2000 and 2016

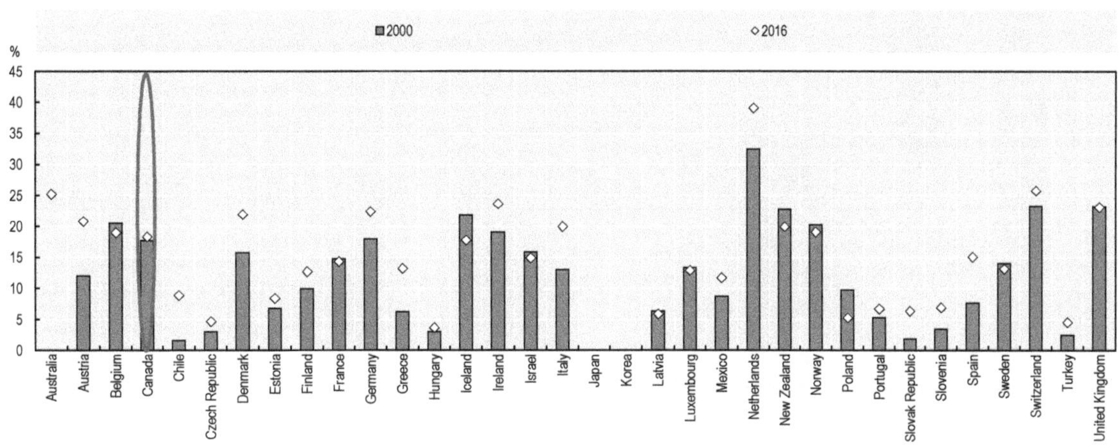

Source: OECD (2018[18]), Job Creation and Local Economic Development 2018: Preparing for the Future of Work, OECD Publishing, Paris, https://dx.doi.org/10.1787/9789264305342-en; OECD (2018), "Labour Market Statistics: Employment by permanency of the job & Full-time part-time employment - common definition: incidence", OECD Employment and Labour Market Statistics (database), http://dx.doi.org/10.1787/lfs-data-en.

Figure 2.25. Part-time work is highest in Kingston-Pembroke across Ontario regions

Share of part-time workers over total employment, Ontario and Ontario economic regions, 2019

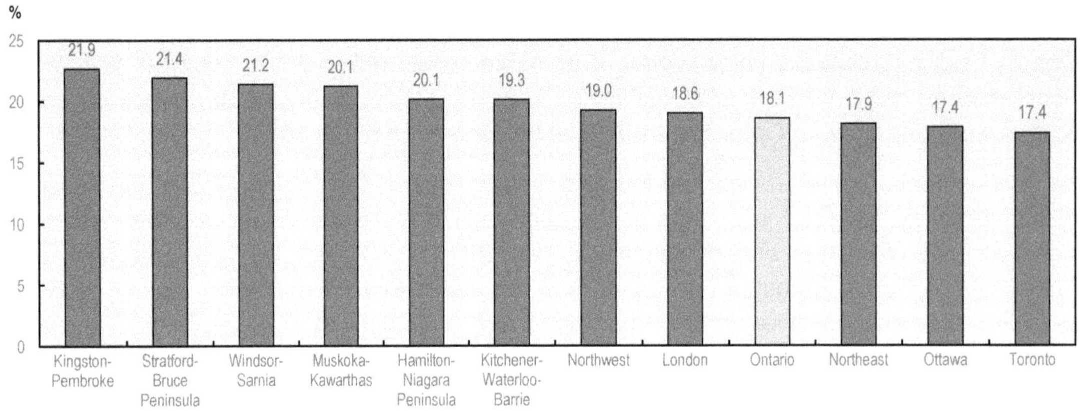

Source: Statistics Canada. Table 14-10-0293-02 Labour force characteristics by economic region, three-month moving average, unadjusted for seasonality (x 1,000). DOI: https://doi.org/10.25318/1410029301-eng.

Figure 2.26. The main reasons for working part-time in Ontario are going to school and personal preference

Reasons for working part-time in Ontario, 2019

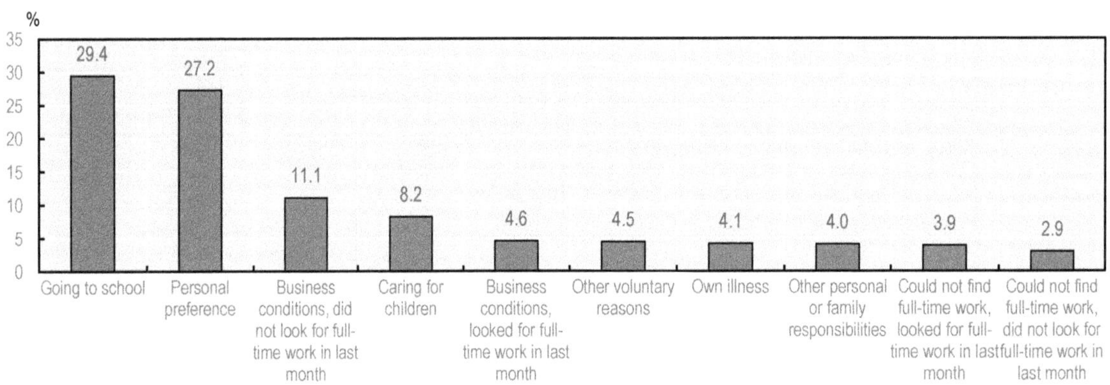

Source: Statistics Canada. Table 14-10-0029-01 Part-time employment by reason, annual (x 1,000), https://doi.org/10.25318/1410002901-eng.

2.4.4. The number of self-employed workers has increased in Ontario

The proportion of self-employed workers across the OECD has remained constant at 15% over the last decade. The OECD defines the self-employed as those who own and work in their own business, including unincorporated business and own-account workers. Self-employed derive some economic benefit from their work, including for example wages, profits, in-kind benefits or family gains, which set them apart from those who undertake voluntary work. The nature of self-employment has substantially changed over the past decades. First, there has been a rise in the share of self-employed workers without employees, partly due to the increase in part-time self-employment—as is the case in the majority of OECD countries. Secondly, the emergence of the digital economy over recent years has created new markets, sectors and occupations, with some self-employed workers exploiting these new opportunities and creating high-value added work for themselves (e.g. freelancers, independent professionals). On the other hand, the digital economy has also generated new forms of precarious self-employment, with a growing number of self-employed workers who work for only one client and have a working arrangement which reflects that of an employee, but are registered as self-employed (OECD, 2018[18]).

In Canada there were 2.9 million self-employed in 2018, accounting for 15% of total employment, on an upward trend over the last decades. British Columbia emerges as the province with the highest share of self-employed workers (17.9%), followed by Saskatchewan (17.4%), Alberta (17.2%) and Ontario (15.5%) (see Figure 2.27). The largest majority of self-employed workers are men (62%), but the share of women being self-employed has increased over the past decade, mirroring an increase in women labour force participation. A growing share of self-employed workers are employed in professional, scientific and technical services, such as occupations in legal services, accounting, architecture, engineering and related services, computer system designs, management, scientific and technical consulting and scientific research and development, which require a high level of education. However, agriculture remains the sector with the highest prevalence of self-employment, with self-employed workers accounting for 57% of agriculture workers in 2018, although this has decreased over the past decades, mainly due to industrialisation and farm aggregation (Yssaad and Ferrao, 2019[38]).

The number of self-employed workers in Ontario has been on the rise over the last fifteen years. This has been led by increases in the number of self-employed unincorporated without paid help (e.g. working owners of businesses and farms, persons who do not have business such as baby-sitters and newspapers carriers), and incorporated self-employed without and with paid help. On the other hand, the number of unpaid family workers has decreased, partly reflecting the decrease in agricultural employment. Data from the 2016 Census shows that across Ontario, Stratford-Bruce Peninsula is the region with the largest share of self-employed workers, accounting for 17.5% of all workers, followed by Muskoka-Kawarthas at 14.5% (see Figure 2.28). The prevalence of self-employment in Stratford-Bruce Peninsula compared to other regions is partly linked to the higher shares of agriculture employment, which accounts for 8% of regional employment, compared to 1% on average across Ontario. On the other hand, less than 8% of workers are self-employed in Northwest.

Figure 2.27. Self-employment is highest in British Columbia

Self-employment by province in Canada, 2018

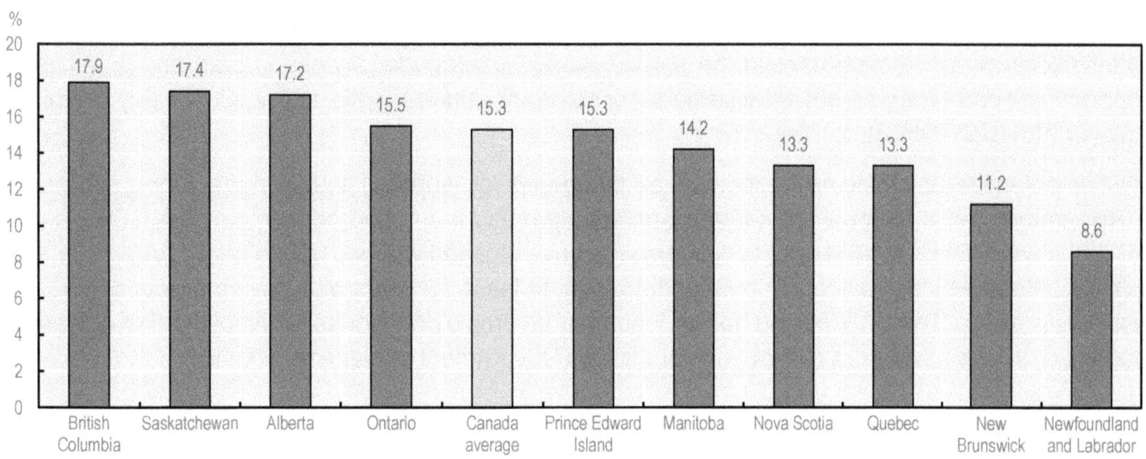

Source: Yssaad and Ferrao (2019[38]), Self-employed Canadians: Who and Why?, https://www150.statcan.gc.ca/n1/pub/71-222-x/71-222-x2019002-eng.htm (accessed on 1 October 2019).

Figure 2.28. Stratford-Bruce Peninsula has the highest share of self-employment in Ontario, driven by agriculture

Share of self-employment over total employment across regions in Ontario, 2016

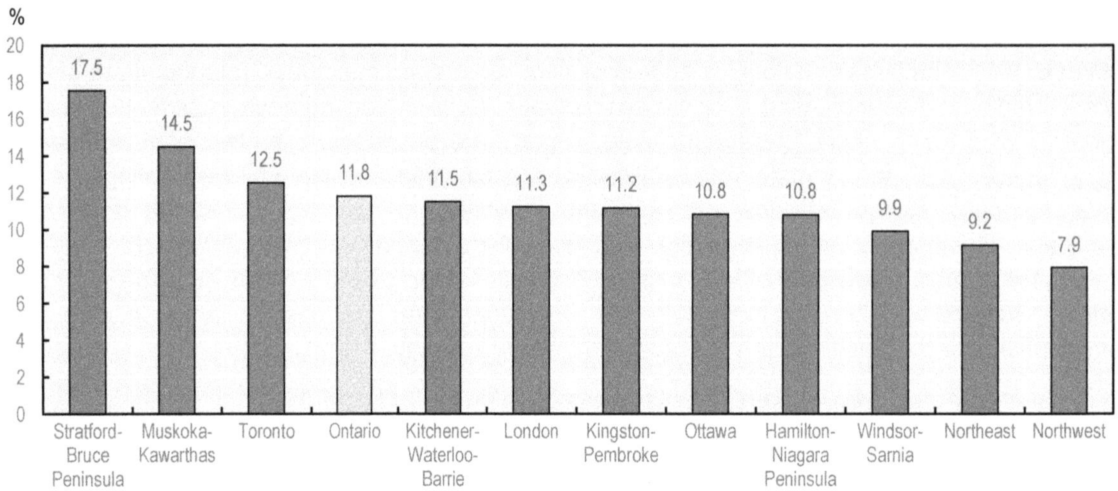

Source: OECD calculations on 2016 Census.

2.4.5. While it provides employment opportunities during the COVID-19 crisis, non-standard work risks posing further challenges to job quality

Non-standard workers are often required to continue working despite the health challenges linked to the COVID-19 outbreak. As an example, in the midst of the COVID-19 pandemic, food delivery drivers continue working, while they can lack sufficient protection against health risks by the platform providers. In the meantime, workers in e-commerce are under increasing work strain and pressure.

In addition, access to paid sick leave can be limited for non-standard workers. Heavy reliance on voluntary employer provisions can mean lower coverage in part-time jobs and for employees on short-time contracts. These gaps are a concern particularly when health risks are elevated for these groups, e.g., because of greater exposure to infection risks in the service sector. In Canada, access to paid and sick leave for temporary and part-time workers is the same as for standard workers, while self-employed rely on voluntary employer provision (OECD, 2020[39]).

With the objective of providing support to all categories of workers, the Canada Emergency Benefit (CERB), introduced in March 2020, targets both standard and non-standard workers. The CERB provides CAD 500 a week for up to 16 weeks to workers who have stopped working due to the COVID-19 outbreak. Eligibility criteria include residence in Canada; being at least 15 years old; having stopped working for reasons related to COVID-19; having had an income from employment or self-employment of at least CAD 5 000 in 2019; and having not quit the job voluntarily (Government of Canada, 2020[40]).

2.4.6. Building an inclusive labour market will be fundamental to sustain employment

Youth, women and vulnerable workers are being hit harder than others by the ongoing COVID-19 pandemic crisis. Among youth aged 15 to 24, employment decreased by 392 500 (-15.4%) in March 2020, the fastest rate of decline across the three main age groups. The decrease was almost entirely in part-time work, and brought the employment rate for youth to 49.1%, the lowest on record using comparable data beginning in 1976. Among people in the core working ages of 25 to 54, the monthly decline in employment for women (-298 500 or -5.0%) was more than twice that of men (-127 600 or -2.0%). Nearly half of the decrease among women was from part-time employment (-144,100 or -14.0%). In general, workers in less secure, lower-quality jobs, were more likely to see employment losses in March. The number of employees in temporary jobs decreased by 14.5% (-274 900) compared with a decline of 5.3% (-749 500) among employees with permanent jobs. Decreases were observed across all types of temporary work, led by those in casual employment (-23.5% or -136 000). There were 5.0% fewer temporary workers with a term or contract position (Statistics Canada, 2020[1]).

Youth had been facing challenging labour market conditions also before the COVID-19 outbreak. The youth (15-24) unemployment rate stood at 11.0% in 2019, almost double the rate for the overall population, mirroring trends across the OECD. Both the overall unemployment and youth unemployment rates went back to 2008 levels only in 2018 – a 10 year period of recovery. Canada's youth unemployment has never fallen below 10% since 1976, even when the economy was doing particularly well and overall employment was high (Janzen, 2018[41]). The share of youth not in employment, education or training (NEET) was slightly lower in Canada than on average across the OECD in 2018, amounting to 11.9% and 13% respectively for the 15-29 year old population.

In addition, some segments of the population, including Indigenous People, older workers, immigrants, people with disabilities and the low-skilled, have typically participated less in the labour force in Canada (OECD, 2020[42]). In 2016, the unemployment rate for Indigenous People was 15.3%, compared to 7.4% for non-Indigenous people. Within Indigenous groups, unemployment was higher for Inuit (22.4%) and First Nations (18%) relative to Métis (11.2%). Indigenous People also have lower levels of education and skills outcomes, which represent a challenge for Indigenous People to access quality jobs (OECD, 2018[43]). The foreign-born population experiences lower labour force participation, and higher unemployment than the native-born population in Canada (OECD, 2019[44]). Labour force participation and unemployment rates stood at 64.5% and 5.9% in 2019 for landed migrants, compared to 66.2% and 5.5% for those born in Canada. Among landed migrants, unemployment is highest for those landed five years of less earlier, while participation is lowest for those landed more than ten years earlier (Statistics Canada, 2020[45]). Recent research shows that labour market challenges in Canada have been most acute for working age men without post-secondary qualifications, whose labour market outcomes outside of the oil-producing provinces have been poor. This cohort seems to be facing a series of secular challenges that threaten their inclusion in broader labour market gains (Speer, 2019[46]).

2.4.7. Ageing and sluggish productivity growth are other concerns for the long term

Challenges linked to an ageing population and weak productivity growth are other crucial concerns for labour market performance in Canada. Due to declining fertility rates and increased life expectancy, Canada, as most OECD economies, is experiencing population ageing. Ageing has reduced the contribution of labour utilisation to growth and the effects of population ageing on potential growth are predicted to intensify over the next decades (OECD, 2018[47]). The share of the population of working age in Canada (aged 15 to 64) has declined in recent years, standing at 66.9% in 2018, down from 69.5% in 2008. This is slightly above the OECD average of 65.1%. The median age was 39.4 years in 2008, while it rose to 40.8 in 2018. The median age in Canada is higher than for other OECD countries such as Australia and the United States (37.3 and 38.2 years in 2018 respectively). In addition, the median age varies across provinces, from 36.9 years in Alberta to 46.5 in Newfoundland and Labrador. Territories are characterised by substantially lower median age, only 34.8 years in Northwest Territories and 26.1 in Nunavut in 2018. The most populous Canadian provinces have witnessed a common trend characterised by a marked increase in the median age over the last decade. On the other hand, the median age slightly decreased in Manitoba and Saskatchewan.

Figure 2.29. Canada has aged more than Australia and the United States, with substantial differences across provinces

Median age across provinces in Canada, 2008 and 2018

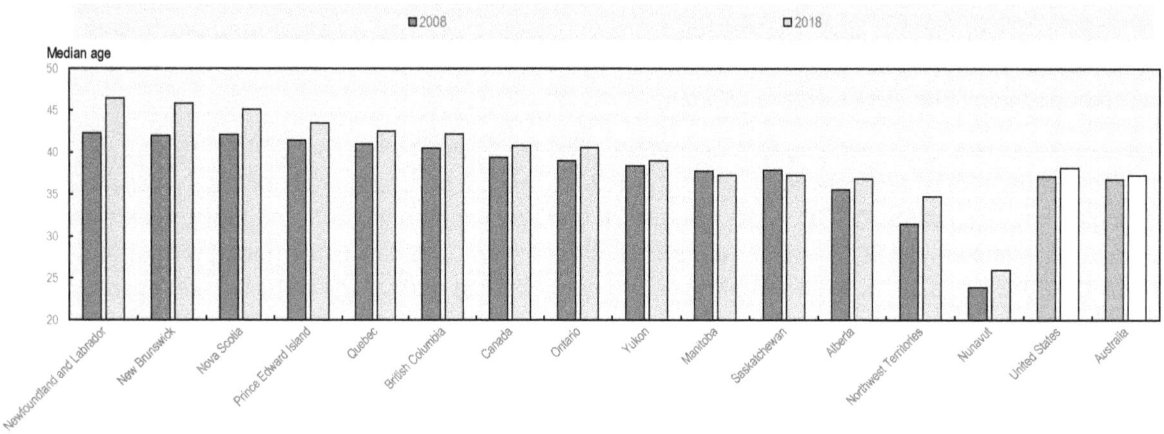

Source: Statistics Canada. Table 17-10-0005-01 Population estimates on July 1st, by age and sex DOI: https://doi.org/10.25318/1710000501-eng; Worldometer (n.d.[48]), Australia Population (live), https://www.worldometers.info/world-population/australia-population/ (accessed on 13 February 2020); Statista, (2019[49]), Median age of the U.S. population 1960-2018 | Statista, https://www.statista.com/statistics/241494/median-age-of-the-us-population/ (accessed on 13 February 2020).

Labour productivity growth in Canada has been subdued, lagging behind many Group of Seven (G7) economies (see Figure 2.30). Labour productivity as measured by hourly GDP (in constant prices 2010 and Purchasing Power Parity) amounts to USD 52.2 in Canada, compared to USD 62.4 across the G7 in 2018 (OECD, 2020[48]). Productivity growth in the Canadian economy has been considerably slower in the post-2000 period than in the pre-2000 period, but it has lagged behind the United States and other G7 since the 1980s (Sharpe and Tsang, 2018[49]) (Rao, Tang and Wang, 2008[50]). Business innovation is identified as an important lever that could help lift Canada's overall productivity performance (The Conference Board of Canada, 2017[51]). It has been argued that the higher number of small firms in Canada relative to the United States may have lowered Canadian aggregate productivity levels. In addition, the gap between the productivity of small firms and that of large firms is estimated to be larger in Canada than in the United States (Statistics Canada, 2015[52]). Other factors that might have driven divergence in productivity between Canada and the United States include: the lower capital intensity of economic activity in Canada; an innovation gap relative to the United States; Canada's relatively less developed high-tech sector; less developed human capital in Canada in terms of proportionately fewer university graduates and scientists and engineers in research and development; and more limited economies of scale and scope in Canada (Sharpe, 2003[53]).

Trends in labour productivity growth have differed by provincial economy in Canada. Manitoba and British Columbia lead labour productivity growth, averaging 1.5% and 1.4% per year between 2008 and 2018. British Columbia's performance is partly linked to the province operating at or above its full capacity during much of the period when the local economy was booming due to activities tied to mortgage debt and real estate (Business Council of British Columbia, 2019[54]). Newfoundland and Labrador is the only province having experienced negative productivity growth over the same period (see Figure 2.31). However, Newfoundland and Labrador remains one of the provinces in Canada attaining the highest levels of labour productivity, amounting to CAD 76 per hour, preceded only by Saskatchewan and Alberta (79.6 and 78.8 respectively).

Dynamics in labour productivity across provinces in Canada depend on the sectoral composition of local economies. The tradable sector, which includes manufacturing, agriculture and extractive industries, as well as some services (parts of finance, advertising and publishing for example), has higher productivity growth rates than the non-tradable sector, which includes locally-rendered services, including health, education, retail and construction (OECD, 2018[55]). Saskatchewan, Alberta and Newfoundland and Labrador top the list when it comes to labour productivity as they have relatively large oil and gas extraction sectors. The large amount of capital investment involved in oil and gas extraction results in a higher overall output per worker. While mining, oil and gas are the sectors with by far the highest labour productivity in Canada, productivity growth has been particularly strong in agriculture, forestry, fishing and hunting, averaging an annual 5.1% between 2008 and 2018. This is partly due to the sector starting from low productivity levels in 2008. On the other hand, productivity growth has stalled or been negative in educational services, health care and social services, construction and administrative and support services.

Ontario has experienced labour productivity growth across sectors over the past decade, with the exception of manufacturing. Productivity growth has been driven by utilities and resource extraction, followed by agriculture, non-tradable and tradable services. The non-tradable services sector includes construction, distributive trade and transport, professional, scientific and technical activities as well as public administration and education. The tradable services sector includes information and communication, financial and insurance activities and other services. Productivity growth in utilities and resource extraction has gone hand in hand with employment losses in the sector. On the other hand, employment growth has been strong in non-tradable sectors, that have added around 730 000 jobs between 2008 and 2018. Also tradable services and agriculture have created jobs in Ontario, adding about 60 000 and 3 000 jobs respectively. Manufacturing has experienced both negative labour productivity growth and employment losses in Ontario over the same period.

Figure 2.30. Labour productivity growth in Canada has been lower than many G7 countries over the last two decades

GDP per hour worked, percentage rate at annual rate

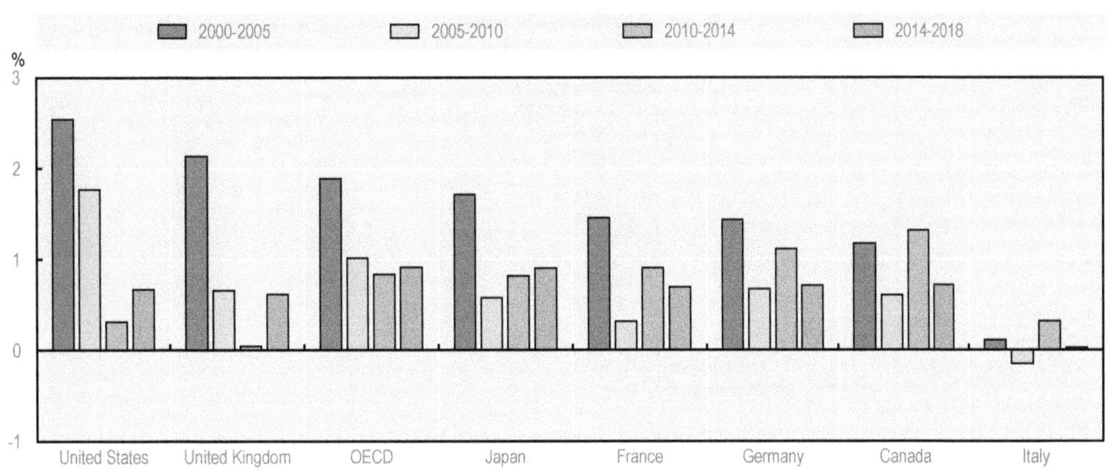

Source: OECD (2019[56]), OECD Compendium of Productivity Indicators 2019, https://dx.doi.org/10.1787/b2774f97-en.

Figure 2.31. Newfoundland and Labrador is the only province having averaged negative productivity growth over the past decade

Average provincial labour productivity annual growth, Canada and Canadian Provinces, 2012 Chained Dollars, 2008 to 2018

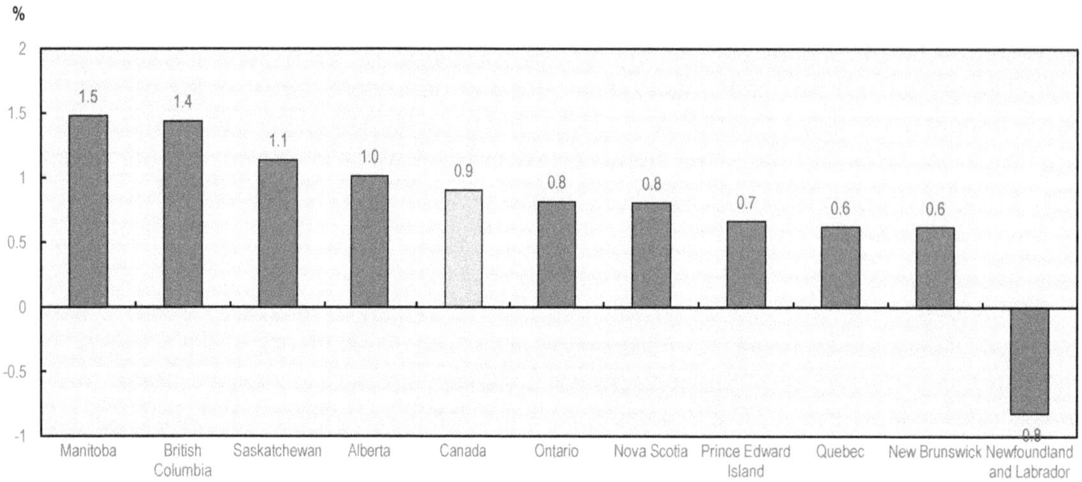

Note: Labour productivity is the ratio between real value added and hours worked. Data does not include the territories.
Source: Statistics Canada. Table 36-10-0480-01 Labour productivity and related measures by business sector industry and by non-commercial activity consistent with the industry accounts. DOI: https://doi.org/10.25318/3610048001-eng.

Figure 2.32. Agriculture has experienced the highest productivity growth in Canada

Average sector labour productivity annual growth, 2012 Chained Dollars, 2008 to 2018

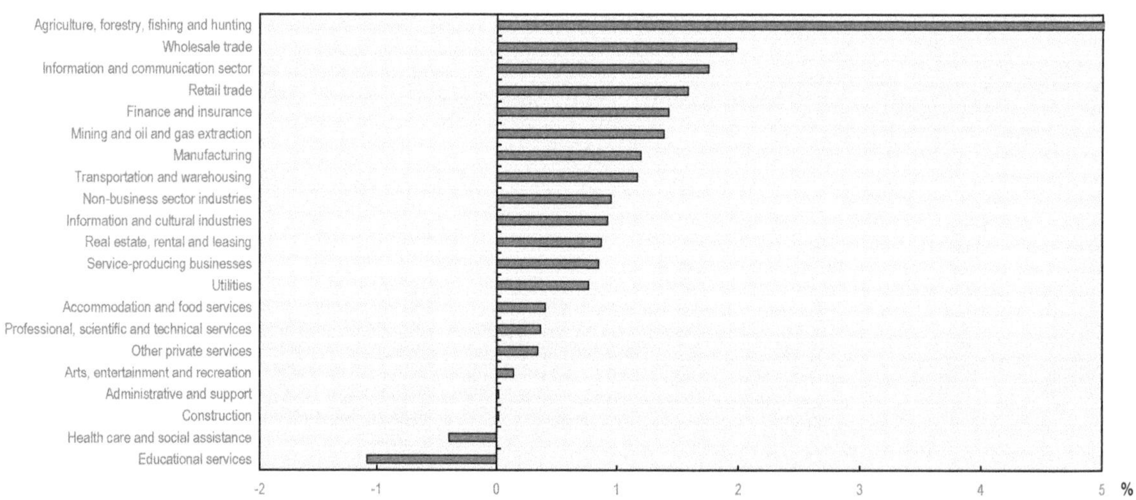

Note: Administrative and support services also includes waste management and remediation services.
Source: Statistics Canada. Table 36-10-0480-01 Labour productivity and related measures by business sector industry and by non-commercial activity consistent with the industry accounts. DOI: https://doi.org/10.25318/3610048001-eng.

Figure 2.33. Agriculture, tradable and non-tradable services have experienced productivity and employment growth in Ontario

Employment and labour productivity growth in Ontario by sector, 2008 to 2018

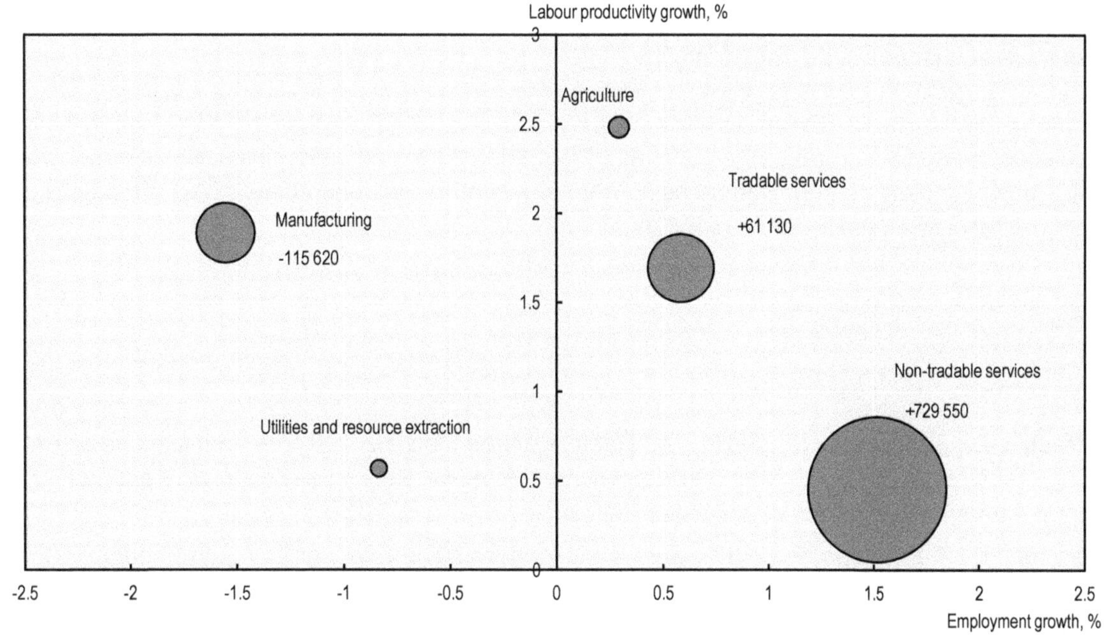

Note: Labour productivity is calculated using real gross value added in USD in constant 2015 prices and PPPs, regional employment and deflators. Employment change is the total change in employment over the period, bubble size indicates the size of the sector in terms of employment in 2008. Tradable services are taken as information and communication (J), financial and insurance activities (K), and other services (RSTU). Non-tradable services are composed of construction, distributive trade, repairs, transport, accommodation, food services activities (GHI), real estate activities (L), business services (MN), and public administration (OPQ). Real estate activities are excluded in this chart.
Source: Calculations on OECD Regional Statistics [Database].

StatLink https://doi.org/10.1787/888934150063

Conclusion

The future of work is having a profound impact on labour markets across Canada. Ontario faces a risk of being impacted by automation which is similar to other Canadian provinces. However, there are substantial differences within provinces. The geographical concentration of occupations at risk of automation has the consequence that different regions face different risks. The ongoing COVID-19 pandemic is posing new and unexpected challenges, and it is likely to accelerate the speed of automation adoption in the workplace. The future of work is however also presenting new opportunities for people to get into jobs. Most regions in Ontario have created jobs in occupations at lower risk of automation and high-skill occupations are projected to drive employment growth in the coming years. In addition, some non-standard forms of work can provide the opportunity to adopt flexible working arrangements. However, they can also create challenges related to job quality. While automation is shaping local labour markets, skills needs are changing. More employers than ever report skills shortages and skills mismatches, which have a negative impact on productivity. This is the focus of the next chapter.

Notes

[1] O*NET provides a set of 277 quantitative variables that serve as descriptions of the skill requirements for each of the 702 occupations in the US classification of occupations. O*NET was originally made up of labour market analysts, although it now also uses continuous surveys of workers and experts in order to keep track of changes in the nature of jobs.

[2] Rural areas (RAs) include all territory lying outside population centres (POPCTRs). Taken together, population centres and rural areas cover all of Canada. Rural population includes all population living in rural areas of census metropolitan areas (CMAs) and census agglomerations (CAs), as well as population living in rural areas outside CMAs and CAs.

References

Acemoglu, D., & Restrepo, P. (2016). *The Race Between Machine and Man: Implications of Technology for Growth, Factor Shares and Employment.* National Bureau of Economic Research, Cambridge, MA. doi:10.3386/w22252

Acemoglu, D., & Restrepo, P. (2017). *Secular Stagnation? The Effect of Aging on Economic Growth in the Age of Automation.* Retrieved 02 19, 2020, from https://www.nber.org/papers/w23077.pdf

Acemoglu, D., & Restrepo, P. (2019). *Demographics and Automation.* Retrieved 05 07, 2020, from https://economics.mit.edu/files/16788

Autor, D., & Salomons, A. (2018). *Is automation labor-displacing? Productivity growth, employment, and the labor share.* Retrieved 02 17, 2020, from https://www.brookings.edu/wp-content/uploads/2018/03/1_autorsalomons.pdf

Barrie Chamber of Commerce. (2014). *Business confidence in Kitchener-Waterloo-Barrie region lower than provincial average*.* Retrieved 02 19, 2020, from http://barriechamber.wsiefusion.net/member-blog/business-confidence-in-kitchener-waterloo-barrie-region-lower-than-provincial-average

Birnbaum, L., & Farrow, J. (2018). *The Impact of Technological Change on Ontario's Workforce.* Retrieved 07 15, 2019, from http://brookfieldinstitute.ca/wp-content/uploads/RPT-RobotTalks-Summary.pdf

Business Council of British Columbia. (2019). *B.C. has mostly caught up with Canada on productivity levels.* Retrieved 02 13, 2020, from https://bcbc.com/insights-and-opinions/b-c-has-mostly-caught-up-with-canada-on-productivity-levels

Canadian Skills Training and Employment Coalition. (2016). *Regional Manufacturing Profile: Hamilton-Niagara Region.* Retrieved 02 28, 2020, from http://cstec.ca/sites/cstec/files/reports/MANUFACTURING-PROFILE-%20Hamilton-Niagara.pdf

Crawford Urban, M., & Johal, S. (2020). *Understanding the Future of Skills: Trends and Global Policy Responses.* Retrieved 05 14, 2020, from https://fsc-ccf.ca/wp-content/uploads/2020/01/UnderstandingTheFutureOfSkills-PPF-JAN2020-EN.pdf

Dao, M., Das, M., Koczan, Z., & Lian, W. (2017). *Why Is Labor Receiving a Smaller Share of Global Income? Theory and Empirical Evidence.* International Monetary Fund, Washington, D. C. Retrieved 02 17, 2020, from https://www.imf.org/en/Publications/WP/Issues/2017/07/24/Why-Is-Labor-Receiving-a-Smaller-Share-of-Global-Income-Theory-and-Empirical-Evidence-45102

Fields, A., Bourbeau, E., & Patterson, M. (2018). *Annual review of the labour market, 2017.* Retrieved 10

09, 2019, from https://www150.statcan.gc.ca/n1/pub/75-004-m/75-004-m2018001-eng.htm

Frey, C., & Osborne, M. (2013). *The Future of Employment: How Susceptible are Jobs to Computerisation?* University of Oxford. Retrieved 07 10, 2019, from https://www.oxfordmartin.ox.ac.uk/downloads/academic/The_Future_of_Employment.pdf

Government of British Columbia. (n.d.). *Northeast - Province of British Columbia.* Retrieved 02 18, 2020, from https://www2.gov.bc.ca/gov/content/environment/natural-resource-stewardship/cumulative-effects-framework/regional-assessments/northeast

Government of Canada. (2017). *Canadian Occupational Projection System (COPS) - Job Openings (2017-2026).* Retrieved 08 01, 2019, from http://occupations.esdc.gc.ca/sppc-cops/l.3bd.2t.1ilshtml@-eng.jsp?lid=17&fid=1&lang=en

Government of Canada. (2020). *Questions and Answers on the Canada Emergency Response Benefit.* Retrieved 04 27, 2020, from https://www.canada.ca/en/services/benefits/ei/cerb-application/questions.html

Greater Barrie Chamber of Commerce. (2014). *Regional Economic Outlook: Kitchener-Waterloo-Barrie.* Retrieved 02 19, 2020, from http://barriechamber.com/2014/REO2014_GBCC_r1.pdf

International Federation of Robotics. (2018). *Executive Summary World Robotics 2018 Industrial Robots.* International Federation of Robotics. Retrieved 07 04, 2019, from https://ifr.org/downloads/press2018/Executive_Summary_WR_2018_Industrial_Robots.pdf

InvestinOntario. (2019). *Toronto adds more tech jobs than Seattle, the Bay Area and Washington D.C. combined.* Retrieved 03 11, 2020, from https://www.investinontario.com/spotlights/toronto-adds-more-tech-jobs-seattle-bay-area-and-washington-dc-combined

Janzen, N. (2018). *What's the problem with Canada's youth labour market?* Retrieved from http://www.rbc.com/economics/economic-reports/pdf/other-reports/Canadianyouthlabour_Jul2018.pdf

Lamb, C. (2020). *Automation, Accelerated: Will technology adoption amidst the pandemic leave Canada further behind?* . Retrieved 05 15, 2020, from https://brookfieldinstitute.ca/commentary/automation-accelerated-will-technology-adoption-amidst-the-pandemic-leave-canada-further-behind-2/

Martel, L. (2019). *The labour force in Canada and its regions: Projections to 2036.* Retrieved 03 10, 2020, from https://www150.statcan.gc.ca/n1/pub/75-006-x/2019001/article/00004-eng.htm

McKinsey & Company. (2019). *Economic Growth Strategy for Newfoundland and Labrador.* Retrieved 05 07, 2020, from https://www.gov.nl.ca/fin/files/publications-pdf-mck-final-report.pdf

Mercer and Oliver Wyman. (2018). *The Twin Threats of Aging and Automation.* Retrieved 02 19, 2020, from https://info.mercer.com/rs/521-DEV-513/images/Workforce-For-the-Future-The-Twin-Threats-of-Aging-and-automation-POV.pdf?mkt_tok=eyJpIjoiTm1NeU9EWTNNbU5pWXpobSIsInQiOiJieXNJVzBpVDdzYjkrRk4yN2tKT0FOaGxwVlpnQUtacWxDSFNzOTRCVHprV0NhYmlzdDZvV2RTdmNqVFBQcTZGVzRZRWQ1UUczc3ZRYTdLeXVMRXFZdlpDVEN2Y0xIUUFLNFZ2UnJmN3pcL0FaVmpad1JTd1wvd2d2YVdpSHJRM0VEMmdBZmczaEh6cDV0SW00V1psdnlXZz09In0%3D

Moore, M. (2018). *Unemployment still on the rise in N.L.: Stats Can.* Retrieved 02 19, 2020, from https://www.cbc.ca/news/canada/newfoundland-labrador/unemployment-rising-newfoundland-labrador-1.4753099

Muro, M., Maxim, R., & Whiton, J. (2020). *The robots are ready as the COVID-19 recession spreads.* The Brookings Institution. Retrieved 04 22, 2020, from https://www.brookings.edu/blog/the-avenue/2020/03/24/the-robots-are-ready-as-the-covid-19-recession-spreads/

Nedelkoska, L., & Quintini, G. (2018). Automation, skills use and training. In *OECD Social, Employment and Migration Working Papers.* OECD Publishing, Paris, https://dx.doi.org/10.1787/2e2f4eea-en

Nielsen, K. (2018). *Kitchener, Cambridge job market looking solid for 2019: survey.* Retrieved 02 19, 2020, from https://globalnews.ca/news/4754727/kitchener-cambridge-job-market/

Nielsen, K. (2019). *Kitchener-Cambridge job market to cool in 2020: ManpowerGroup.* Retrieved 02 19, 2020, from https://globalnews.ca/news/6278877/kitchener-waterloo-region-jobs-market-2020-manpower-survey/

OECD. (2015). Non-standard work, job polarisation and inequality. In *In It Together: Why Less Inequality Benefits All.* OECD Publishing, Paris. doi:https://dx.doi.org/10.1787/9789264235120-7-en

OECD. (2018). Indigenous Employment and Skills Strategies in Canada. In *OECD Reviews on Local Job Creation.* OECD Publishing, Paris. doi:https://dx.doi.org/10.1787/9789264300477-en

OECD. (2018). Job Creation and Local Economic Development 2018: Preparing for the Future of Work. doi:https://dx.doi.org/10.1787/9789264305342-en

OECD. (2018). OECD Economic Surveys: Canada 2018. *2018/11.* doi:https://dx.doi.org/10.1787/eco_surveys-can-2018-en

OECD. (2018). OECD Employment Outlook 2018. doi:https://dx.doi.org/10.1787/empl_outlook-2018-en

OECD. (2018). *Productivity and Jobs in a Globalised World: (How) Can All Regions Benefit?* OECD Publishing, Paris. doi:https://dx.doi.org/10.1787/9789264293137-en

OECD. (2019). *Getting Skills Right: Engaging low-skilled adults in learning.* Retrieved 02 25, 2020, from http://www.oecd.org/employment/emp/engaging-low-skilled-adults-2019.pdf

OECD. (2019). International Migration Outlook 2019. doi:https://dx.doi.org/10.1787/c3e35eec-en

OECD. (2019). OECD Compendium of Productivity Indicators 2019. doi:https://dx.doi.org/10.1787/b2774f97-en

OECD. (2020). *From pandemic to recovery: Local employment and economic development* . Retrieved 05 12, 2020, from https://read.oecd-ilibrary.org/view/?ref=130_130810-m60ml0s4wf&title=From-pandemic-to-recovery-Local-employment-and-economic-development

OECD. (2020). GDP per hour worked. doi:https://dx.doi.org/10.1787/1439e590-en

OECD. (2020). *Supporting people and companies to deal with the COVID-19 virus: Options for an immediate employment and social-policy response.* Retrieved 04 27, 2020, from https://oecd.dam-broadcast.com/pm_7379_119_119686-962r78x4do.pdf

OECD. (2020). Workforce Innovation to Foster Positive Learning Environments in Canada. In *Getting Skills Right.* OECD Publishing, Paris. doi:https://dx.doi.org/10.1787/a92cf94d-en

OECD/ILO. (2017). *Engaging Employers in Apprenticeship Opportunities: Making It Happen Locally.* OECD Publishing, Paris. doi:https://dx.doi.org/10.1787/9789264266681-en

Ontario Chamber of Commerce. (2019). *The Great Mosaic: Reviving Ontario's Regional Economies.* Retrieved 03 10, 2020, from https://occ.ca/wp-content/uploads/The-Great-Mosaic-Reviving-Ontarios-Regional-Economies.pdf

Patterson, M., Hazel, M., & Saunders, D. (2019). *Annual review of the labour market, 2018.* Retrieved 10 09, 2019, from https://www150.statcan.gc.ca/n1/pub/75-004-m/75-004-m2019002-eng.htm

Rao, S., Tang, J., & Wang, W. (2008). What Explains the Canada-US Labour Productivity Gap? *Canadian Public PolicyAnalyse de Politiques, 34*(2), 163-192. Retrieved 02 13, 2020, from https://www.jstor.org/stable/25463606?seq=3#metadata_info_tab_contents

Saunders, D., & Hazel, M. (2018). *Students in the labour market: After the recession.* Statistics Canada. Retrieved 05 07, 2020, from https://www150.statcan.gc.ca/n1/pub/75-004-m/75-004-m2018002-eng.htm

Sharpe, A. (2003). *Why Are Americans More Productive Than Canadians?* Retrieved 03 11, 2020, from http://www.csls.ca/reports/10-03-03_can-us.pdf

Sharpe, A., & Tsang, J. (2018). *The Stylized Facts about Slower Productivity Growth in Canada.*

Retrieved 02 13, 2020, from http://www.csls.ca/ipm/35/IPM-35-Sharpe-Tsang.pdf

Speer, S. (2019). *Forgotten people and forgotten places: Canada's economic performance in the age of populism.* Retrieved 05 13, 2020, from https://macdonaldlaurier.ca/files/pdf/MLI_Speer_ScopingSeries1_FWeb.pdf

Statista. (2019). *Median age of the U.S. population 1960-2018 | Statista.* Retrieved 02 13, 2020, from https://www.statista.com/statistics/241494/median-age-of-the-us-population/

Statistics Canada. (2015). *Canada-United States Labour Productivity Gap Across Firm Size Classes.* Retrieved 03 11, 2020, from https://www150.statcan.gc.ca/n1/pub/15-206-x/2014033/part-partie1-eng.htm

Statistics Canada. (2016). *Economic Regions - Variant of SGC 2016 - Introduction - Definitions.* Retrieved 07 10, 2019, from http://www23.statcan.gc.ca/imdb/p3VD.pl?Function=getCET_Page&VD=318020&Item=318531

Statistics Canada. (2018). *Economic region (ER).* Retrieved 07 10, 2019, from https://www150.statcan.gc.ca/n1/pub/92-195-x/2011001/geo/er-re/er-re-eng.htm

Statistics Canada. (2019). *Table 1.1 Geographic areas by province and territory, 2016 Census.* Retrieved 05 07, 2020, from https://www12.statcan.gc.ca/census-recensement/2016/ref/dict/tab/t1_1-eng.cfm

Statistics Canada. (2019). *Temporary employment in Canada.* Retrieved 10 01, 2019, from https://www150.statcan.gc.ca/n1/daily-quotidien/190514/dq190514b-eng.htm

Statistics Canada. (2020). *Labour force characteristics by immigrant status, annual.* Retrieved 05 07, 2020, from https://www150.statcan.gc.ca/t1/tbl1/en/cv.action?pid=1410008301

Statistics Canada. (2020). *Labour Force Survey, April 2020.* Retrieved 05 12, 2020, from https://www150.statcan.gc.ca/n1/daily-quotidien/200508/dq200508a-eng.htm

Statistics Canada. (2020). *Labour Force Survey, March 2020.* Retrieved 04 21, 2020, from https://www150.statcan.gc.ca/n1/daily-quotidien/200409/dq200409a-eng.htm

Statistics Canada. (2020). *Labour Force Survey, May 2020.* Retrieved 06 09, 2020, from https://www150.statcan.gc.ca/n1/daily-quotidien/200605/dq200605a-eng.htm?HPA=1

The Conference Board of Canada. (2017). *Labour Productivity Growth.* Retrieved 02 13, 2020, from https://www.conferenceboard.ca/hcp/provincial/economy/labour-productivity.aspx

The Conference Board of Canada. (2017). *Unemployment Rate - Economy Provincial Rankings .* Retrieved 03 10, 2020, from https://www.conferenceboard.ca/hcp/provincial/economy/unemployment.aspx

Worldometer. (n.d.). *Australia Population (live).* Retrieved 02 13, 2020, from https://www.worldometers.info/world-population/australia-population/

Yssaad, L., & Ferrao, V. (2019). *Self-employed Canadians: Who and Why?* Retrieved 10 01, 2019, from https://www150.statcan.gc.ca/n1/pub/71-222-x/71-222-x2019002-eng.htm

Annex 2.A.

Annex Figure 2.A.1. Alberta: jobs at risk of automation

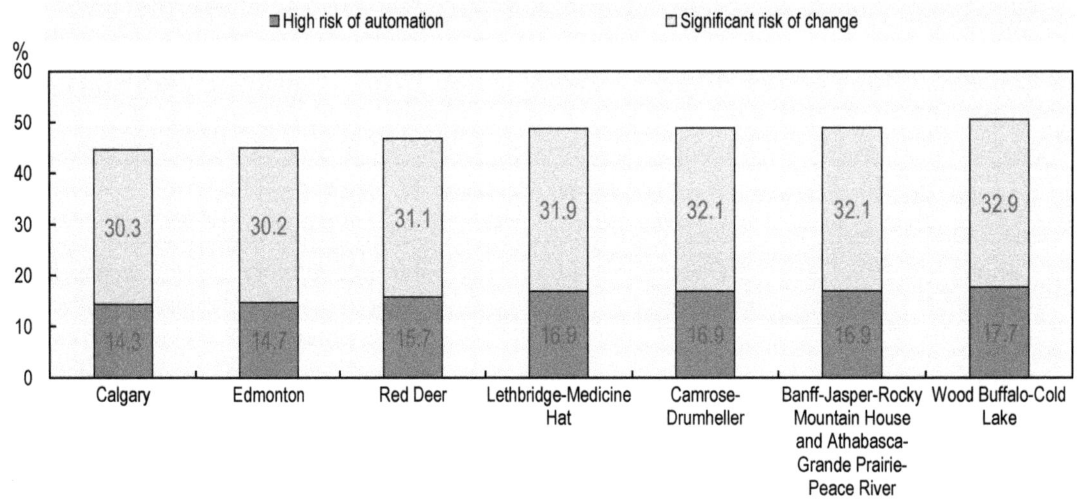

Source: OECD calculations on Labour Force Surveys.

Annex Figure 2.A.2. British Columbia: jobs at risk of automation

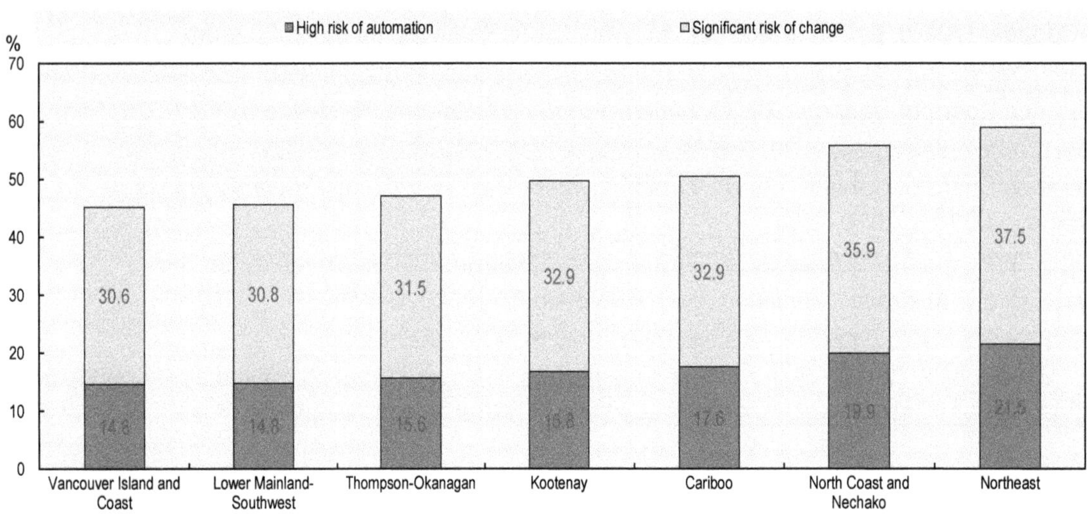

Source: OECD calculations on Labour Force Surveys.

Annex Figure 2.A.3. Manitoba: jobs at risk of automation

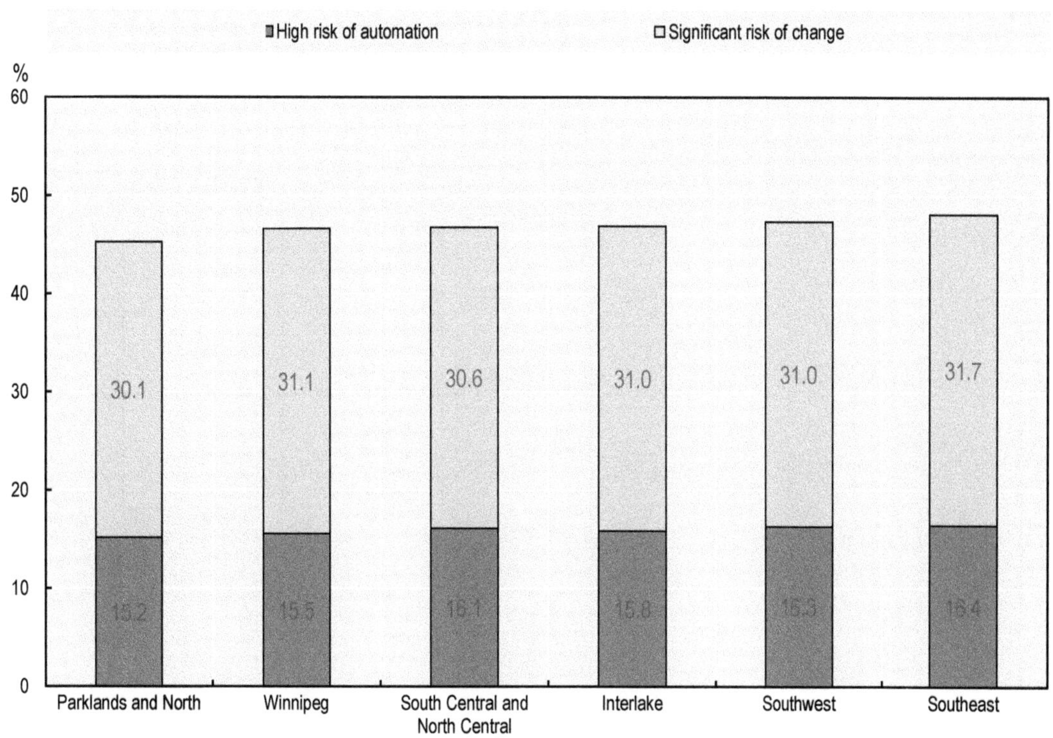

Source: OECD calculations on Labour Force Surveys.

Annex Figure 2.A.4. New Brunswick: jobs at risk of automation

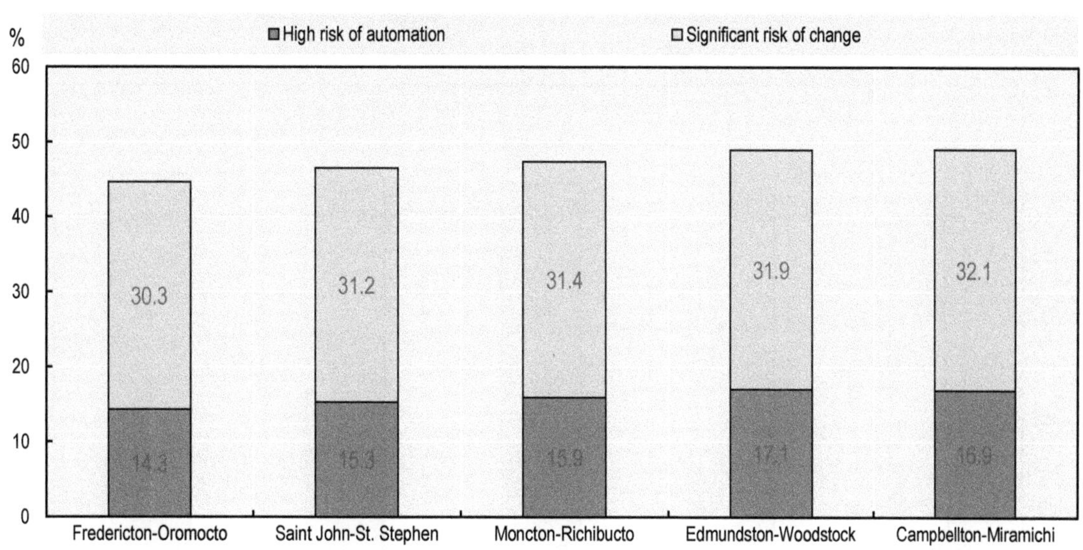

Source: OECD calculations on Labour Force Surveys.

Annex Figure 2.A.5. Newfoundland and Labrador: jobs at risk of automation

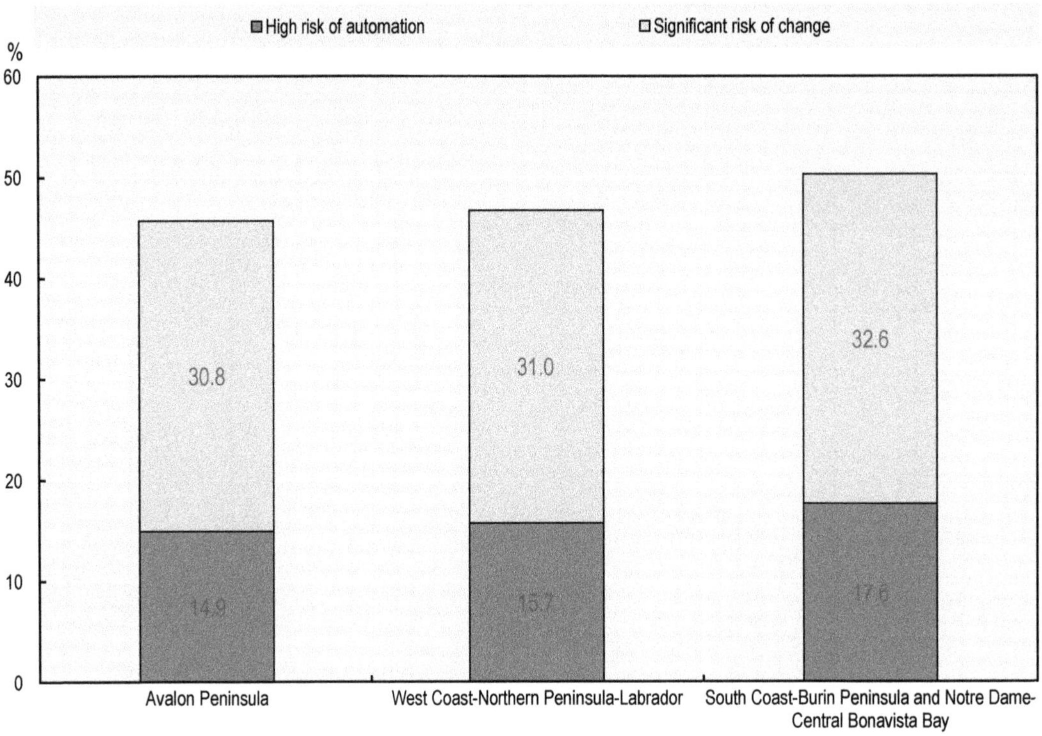

Source: OECD calculations on Labour Force Surveys.

Annex Figure 2.A.6. Nova Scotia: jobs at risk of automation

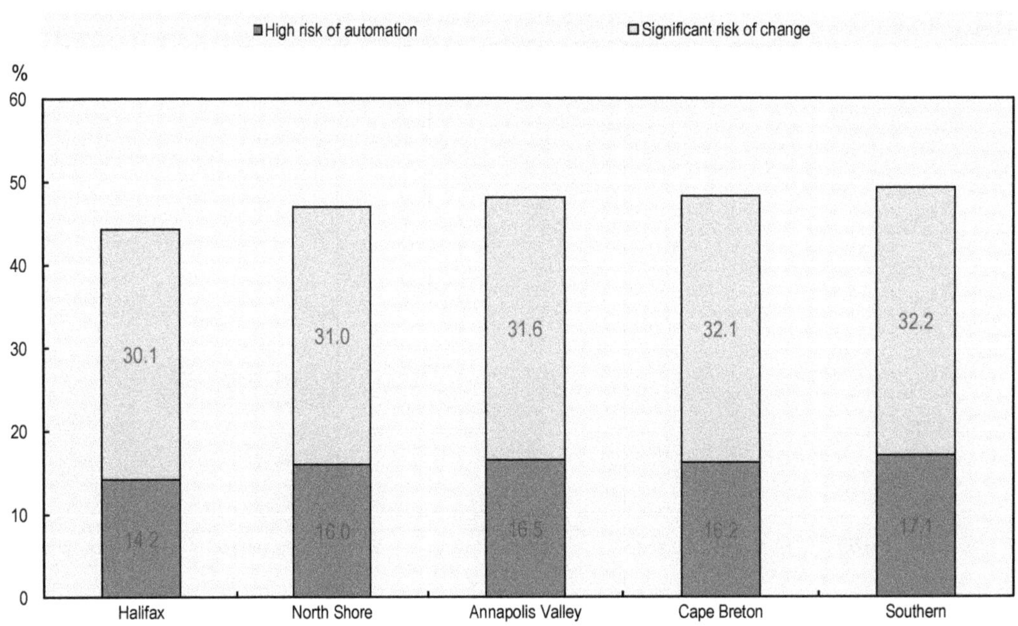

Source: OECD calculations on Labour Force Surveys.

Annex Figure 2.A.7. Quebec: jobs at risk of automation

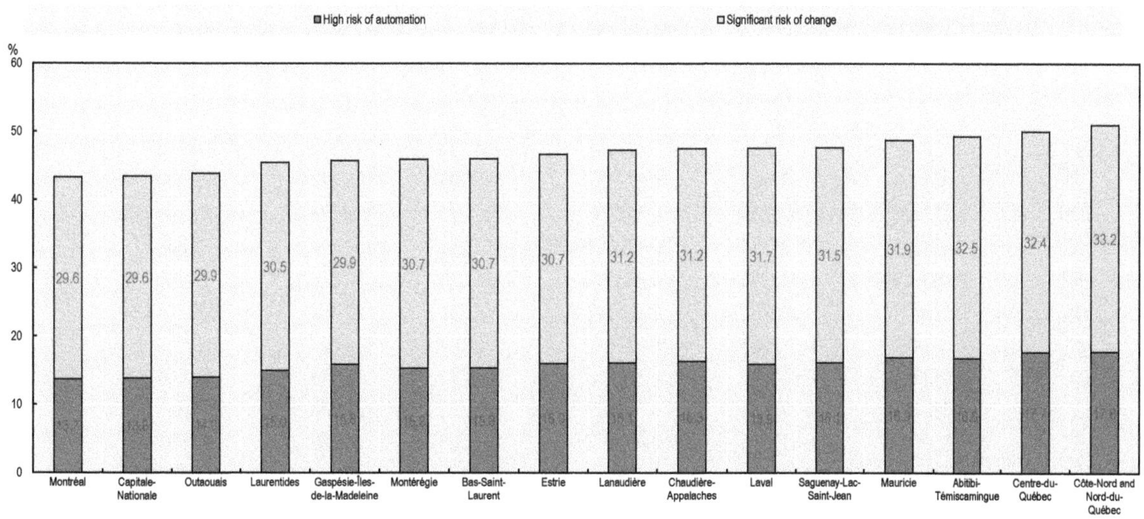

Source: OECD calculations on Labour Force Surveys.

Annex Figure 2.A.8. Saskatchewan: jobs at risk of automation

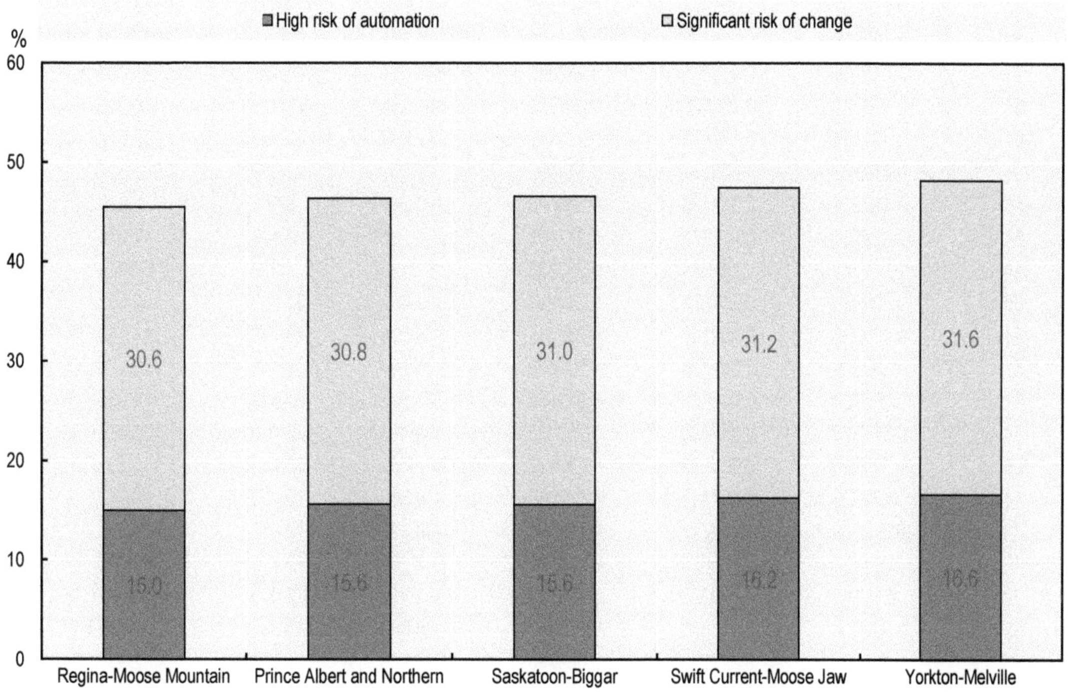

Source: OECD calculations on Labour Force Surveys.

Annex Table 2.A.1. Automation probabilities and calculations

Occupation (ISCO-08)	Mean probability of automation	High risk of automation	Significant risk of change	Total employment (Canada, 2018)	Workers at high-risk	Workers at significant risk
94	0.639117	0.3631	0.487006	104 137	37 813	50 715
93	0.618405	0.407734	0.372157	454 995	185 517	169 329
91	0.615125	0.306219	0.491768	349 923	107 153	172 081
96	0.595053	0.31844	0.472828	441 251	140 512	208 636
82	0.593685	0.380255	0.323469	81 045	30 818	26 216
75	0.589751	0.319752	0.395943	564 382	180 461	223 464
83	0.572421	0.272083	0.427021	656 147	178 526	280 189
44	0.569305	0.351238	0.351712	274 782	96 514	96 644
51	0.552404	0.247781	0.396458	838 392	207 738	332 387
62	0.550794	0.212313	0.461506	101 085	21 462	46 651
81	0.549266	0.331124	0.329114	332 842	110 212	109 543
41	0.549025	0.2108	0.468888	145 212	30 611	68 088
43	0.539582	0.236643	0.36636	316 871	74 985	116 089
74	0.539089	0.216449	0.359271	337 821	73 121	121 369
92	0.538197	0.161596	0.481661	79 952	12 920	38 510
52	0.537421	0.201836	0.427368	1 172 254	236 604	500 983
73	0.52306	0.205748	0.465147	356 794	73 410	165 962
72	0.512692	0.1924	0.381105	653 054	125 648	248 882
42	0.502638	0.098678	0.441922	531 371	52 434	234 825
71	0.48285	0.168879	0.288842	557 424	94 137	161 007
32	0.456921	0.133225	0.297774	591 338	78 781	176 085
61	0.453167	0.179475	0.261519	277 291	49 767	72 517
33	0.448923	0.09177	0.314997	2 101 552	192 859	661 982
35	0.432274	0.038125	0.345548	103 948	3 963	35 919
54	0.427346	0.12771	0.277001	206 765	26 406	57 274
25	0.41375	0.04984	0.293536	187 199	9 330	54 949
53	0.406935	0.116273	0.249298	331 662	38 563	82 683
24	0.406032	0.052149	0.255411	839 275	43 768	214 360
31	0.392399	0.092125	0.207638	626 934	57 756	130 176
21	0.385726	0.047153	0.219857	791 572	37 325	174 033
34	0.377875	0.051454	0.267228	435 794	22 423	116 456
26	0.370823	0.035738	0.237773	467 762	16 717	111 221
14	0.32979	0.037117	0.092083	416 382	15 455	38 342
12	0.312593	0.00717	0.090361	288 323	2 067	26 053
13	0.311814	0.025525	0.121197	501 288	12 795	60 755
22	0.31147	0.020256	0.115895	642 205	13 009	74 429
11	0.309954	0.013378	0.070402	65 887	881	4 638
23	0.2505	0.027889	0.089298	928 950	25 908	82 953

Note: occupations are ranked in descending order of mean risk of automation. Occupations are coded in ISCO-08, as this is the classification used in PIAAC. Conversion tables from NOC to ISCO-08 were used.
Source: OECD based on PIAAC and Labour Force Surveys.

3 Job polarisation and changing skills needs at the local level in Canada

Job markets are becoming increasingly polarised across the OECD as the employment share of middle-skill jobs has decreased, replaced by increases in the shares of either low or high-skill jobs. Communities in Canada are experiencing different job polarisation transitions, but the majority of regions are clearly shifting towards high-skill jobs. Prior to the COVID-19 outbreak, labour and skills shortages had been identified as significant labour market challenges in Canada. The ongoing crisis risks exacerbating these gaps, as workers across industries will have to adapt to rapidly changing conditions, and firms will have to learn how to match workers to new roles and activities. The pandemic is also making worker access to training and skills development and the use of skills in the workplace more important than ever. This chapter analyses how the demand and supply of skills is changing at the local level across Canada, with a special focus on the Province of Ontario.

In Brief

- **Labour markets have become increasingly polarised in Canada over the past two decades, as across most OECD countries, witnessing a decline in the employment share of middle-skill/middle-pay jobs**. Looking at the period 1995-2015, Canada experienced a similar degree of polarisation as the United States, with increases in the shares of low- and high-skill jobs. However, over 1998-2018, Canada saw a slight decline in the share of employment in low-skill jobs.
- **Between 2011 and 2018, all provinces in Canada have experienced a clear shift in employment shares towards high-skill jobs, but differences in job polarisation exist within provinces**. For example, in Ontario, while Kingston-Pembroke has experienced a clear polarisation trend over the last decade, in Muskoka-Kawarthas the employment share of middle-skill jobs increased between 2011 and 2018. The higher concentration of middle-skill jobs in some regions might pose challenges in the longer term, as middle-skill jobs often involve routine and repetitive tasks that could be subject to automation.
- **Job polarisation partly reflects increases in the supply of skills across Canada**. Canada leads the OECD in terms of educational attainment, with Ontario being the province with the highest share of tertiary graduates, albeit with regional differences. In Toronto and Ottawa, a notable share of the 25-64 aged population holds university certificates (40% and 37% respectively), while less than one in five achieves this level of education in Stratford-Bruce Peninsula (16%), Northeast (17%), Muskoka-Kawarthas (18%) and Northwest (19%).
- **The increasing sophistication of technology in the workplace is making some skill sets obsolete while increasing the demand for others, and these trends will likely be accelerated by COVID-19**. The 2018 ManpowerGroup Talent Shortage Survey reports that skills shortages represent an issue for 41% of employers in Canada. Shortages are affecting some sectors more than others, with manufacturing and retail trade emerging as the sectors suffering the most. COVID-19 is causing labour shortages of some essential workers, while dramatically accelerating the need for workers to have digital skills.
- **As labour markets face disruption caused by COVID-19, skills development opportunities will be crucial to prepare workers for the upturn** and provide them with the skills needed in the future of work. Getting the skills needed to respond to the trends with the future of work will require action on both the skills supply and demand sides. Workers will need to develop a combination of digital and non-digital skills as well as adaptability. Access to training will be crucial especially for vulnerable workers hit hard by the pandemic. At the same time, employers should make better use of the existing workforce skills and invest in the development of their workers' skills.

Introduction

OECD countries have experienced job polarisation over the past decades - that is a decrease in the employment share of middle-skill jobs and an increase in the share of low- and/or high-skill jobs. Section 3.1 presents trends in job polarisation in Canada and across regions in Ontario. Section 3.2 shows that job polarisation partly reflects increases in educational attainment in Canada. Section 3.3 discusses emerging skills shortages and mismatches across Canada, while section 3.4 presents actions on both the skills supply and demand side that could help reduce mismatches.

3.1. Job polarisation is shifting skills demand in Canada

3.1.1. The share of middle-skill jobs is declining in Canada and the OECD more generally

Labour markets across the OECD have become more polarised over the last decades, with declines in the share of employment in middle-skill jobs relative to jobs with higher or lower skill levels (OECD, 2017[1]). Middle-skill jobs include clerks, craft and related trades workers and machine operators and assemblers. On the other hand, high-skill jobs include professionals, manager and technicians, while low-skill jobs include service workers, shop and market sales workers and elementary occupations. Job polarisation has previously been widely documented by others in the United States (Autor, Katz and Kearney, 2006[2])and Europe (Goos, Manning and Salomons, 2009[3]). For almost all countries for which data is available this has resulted in a shift of employment towards high-skill occupations (OECD, 2019[4]). Looking at the period 1995-2015, Canada experienced a similar degree of polarisation as the United States. However, the decline in oil prices in 2014 resulted in lower demand for workers related to the resource sector. Over 1998-2018, Canada actually saw a slight decline in the share of employment in low-skilled jobs (OECD, 2020[5]).

Figure 3.1 illustrates that the share of employment in middle-skill jobs has decreased relative to in high- and low-skill jobs across the OECD over the last two decades.

While high-skill jobs are considered to be complemented by Information and Communication Technology (ICT), middle-skill jobs are typically substitutes. Technological developments and their capacity to replace routine jobs are identified as drivers of job polarisation, as the impact of technology on jobs varies across the skills distribution. Pioneering work looking at the impact of technological change and digitalisation on the tasks performed by workers at their jobs finds that within industries, occupations and education groups, computerisation is linked with reduced labour input of routine manual and routine cognitive tasks. On the other hand, it is associated with increased input of non-routine cognitive tasks (Autor, Levy and Murnane, 2003[6]). Middle-skill jobs, such as clerical and production jobs, typically entail routine tasks and are the ones easier to automate given the current state of technological developments. On the other hand, low-skill jobs tend to involve non-routine manual tasks, for example requiring manual dexterity, which are harder to automate.

Looking at the 2011-2018 period, the employment share of middle-skill jobs has declined, while there has been a clear shift towards high-skill jobs in all provinces. Between 2011 and 2018, the share of middle-skill jobs has decreased in all of Canada's provinces (see Figure 3.2). In addition, in all but New Brunswick, Saskatchewan and Newfoundland and Labrador, the share of low-skill jobs has also decreased, a trend that is particularly evident in provinces such as Alberta, Ontario and Nova Scotia. New Brunswick has experienced the largest shift in respective shares of total employment, undergoing the largest loss in middle-skill jobs across Canadian provinces in the last 10 years. Meanwhile, in Quebec, Alberta, and Ontario, high-skill jobs have grown to take up a larger part of the labour market since 2011, a trend that is more subdued in British Columbia.

Figure 3.1. Job polarisation has taken place across the OECD

Percentage point change in share of total employment, 1998 to 2018

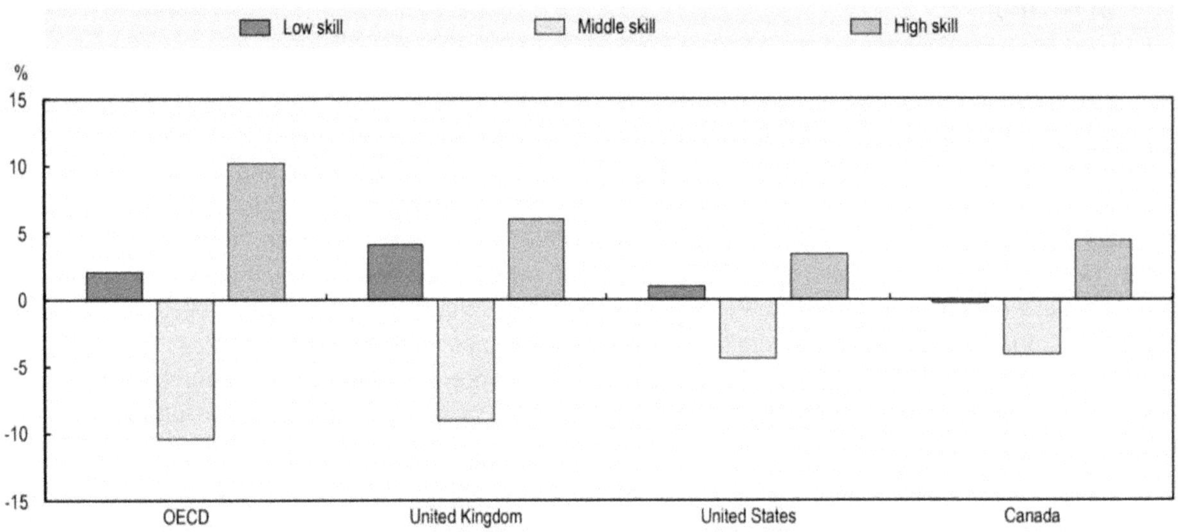

Note: High-skill occupations include jobs classified under the ISCO-88 major groups 1, 2, and 3. That is, legislators, senior officials, and managers (group 1), professionals (group 2), and technicians and associate professionals (group 3). Middle-skill occupations include jobs classified under the ISCO-88 major groups 4, 7, and 8. That is, clerks (group 4), craft and related trades workers (group 7), and plant and machine operators and assemblers (group 8). Low-skill occupations include jobs classified under major groups 5 and 9. That is, service workers and shop and market sales workers (group 5), and elementary occupations (group 9). Skilled agricultural and fisheries workers were excluded from this analysis.

Source: OECD (2020[5]), Workforce Innovation to Foster Positive Learning Environments in Canada, Getting Skills Right, OECD Publishing, Paris, https://dx.doi.org/10.1787/a92cf94d-en.

Figure 3.2. In all provinces in Canada, the share of middle-skill jobs has decreased and the share of high-skill jobs increased

Percentage point change in share of total employment, 2011 to 2018

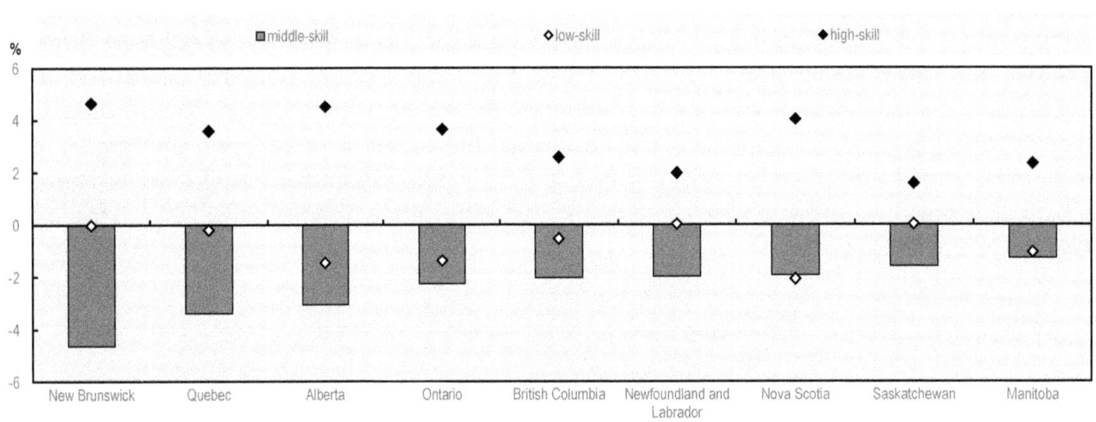

Note: TL2 regions (excluding Prince Edward Island, Yukon Territory and Northwest Territories & Nunavut).

Source: OECD calculations on Labour Force Surveys.

StatLink https://doi.org/10.1787/888934150082

3.1.2. Polarisation is mainly driven by occupational shifts within sectors across the OECD

Polarisation across the OECD occurs mostly as a result of occupational changes within individual industries (two-thirds of the change), while the reallocation of employment away from less polarised industries towards more highly polarised industries contributes the other third. The decline in the share of middle-skill occupations in total employment has affected almost all sectors of the economy across OECD countries. In most industries, these declines have been entirely offset by growth in top occupations. This is particularly the case for those sectors where the decline in middle-skill occupations has been the largest across the OECD, including manufacturing industries (such as "Pulp, paper, paper products, printing and publishing", "Chemicals and chemical products", and "Transport equipment manufacturing"), and services (such as "Finance and insurance", and "Real estate and business services"). Two services industries have experienced a clear shift of employment towards the bottom of the skill distribution ("Hotels and restaurants" and "Wholesale and retail trade; repairs") (OECD, 2017[1]).

The continued shift of employment from manufacturing to services accounts for the remaining one-third of job polarisation across the OECD (OECD, 2017[1]). Services jobs tend to be divided between high-skill professional and managerial jobs that require non-routine cognitive skills on one side, and low-skill jobs that require non-routine manual skills on the other (Goos and Manning, 2007[7]). Manufacturing instead provides more opportunities for middle-skill workers performing routine tasks. Routine exposures are highest in industries where core tasks follow "precise, well-understood procedures" (Acemoglu and Autor, 2010[8]), such as manufacturing, financial services, and transportation and storage. This reflects that these industries have traditionally had high concentrations of occupations with high routine tasks. For example, machine operators are pervasive in manufacturing; financial services have historically drawn on clerical workers (e.g. for data entry and accounting); and transportation and storage employs both elementary workers for manual labour, as well as clerical workers for logistics and communications (Das and Hilgenstock, 2018[9]).

Figure 3.3. Polarisation has taken place within many industries across the OECD

Percentage point change in share of total employment within industry for select OECD countries, 1995 to 2015

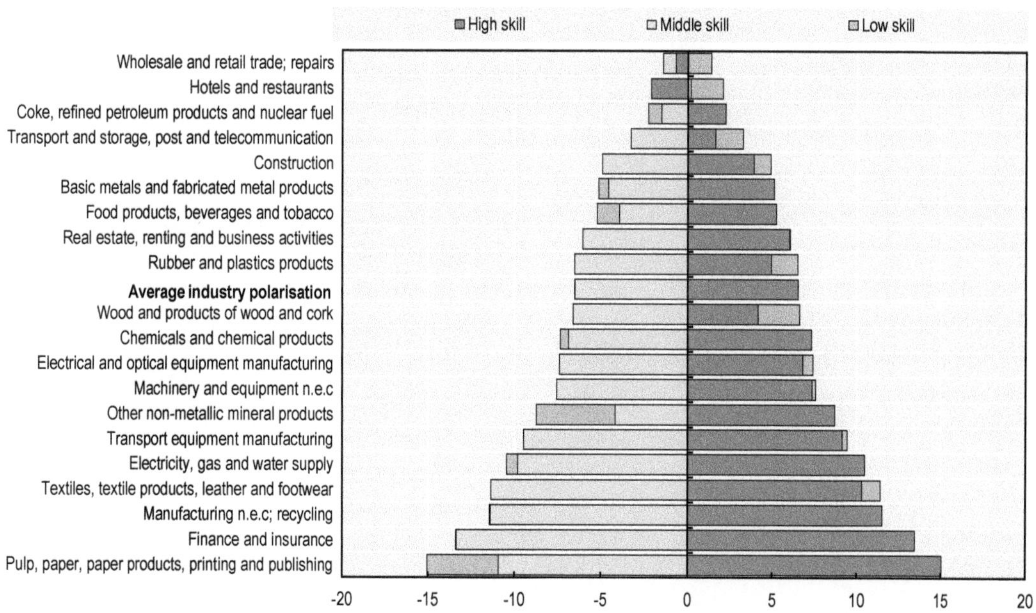

Source: OECD (2017[1]), OECD Employment Outlook 2017, OECD Publishing, Paris, https://dx.doi.org/10.1787/empl_outlook-2017-en.

3.1.3. Middle income workers are increasingly highly-skilled in Canada

Concerns around job polarisation are part of more general public concerns around growing inequalities and a shrinking share of workers attaining middle income. Middle-skill jobs were once considered a reliable ticket to a middle-class lifestyle, and even a springboard for social mobility for the next generation. However, recent research from the OECD suggests that this question is more complicated than a one-to-one relationship between a decline in middle-skill jobs and a shrinking middle class. In OECD countries, growth in high-skill occupations has outpaced growth in middle- and low-skill occupations, shifting the overall labour market distribution towards higher-skill jobs. The changing relationship between skills and income classes means that middle-skill workers are now more likely to be in lower-income classes than middle-income classes. The wage structure is also characterised by growing divides between top earners and everyone else, rather than growth at both ends of the wage scale (OECD, 2019[10]).

In Canada, the share of workers attaining middle income has declined by about 4% from the mid-1990s to the mid-2010s. On the other hand, the share of workers belonging to lower income levels has increased by about 5% and the share of those belonging to higher income has slightly decreased. Canada therefore belongs to a group of OECD countries that have witnessed a decline in the share of workers attaining middle income, but contrary to most countries in the same group, Canada has been characterised by a clear shift towards lower income levels (OECD, 2019[11]).

Middle-income workers are increasingly highly skilled and less middle-skilled. High-skill workers now outnumber the middle-skill in the middle-income class, in Canada as across most OECD countries (OECD, 2019[10]). In addition, the share of middle- and low-skill workers in low income has increased, while fewer medium- and low-skill workers achieve middle or upper income level. Similarly, the share of high-skill workers achieving upper and middle-income has decreased over the mid-1990s/mid-2010s period in Canada. At the same time, there has been an increase in the share of high-skill workers in low income classes (OECD, 2019[11]).

Figure 3.4. Middle-income workers are increasingly highly skilled and less middle-skilled

Changes in shares of middle-income workers with jobs in the different skill groups, mid-1990s to mid-2010s

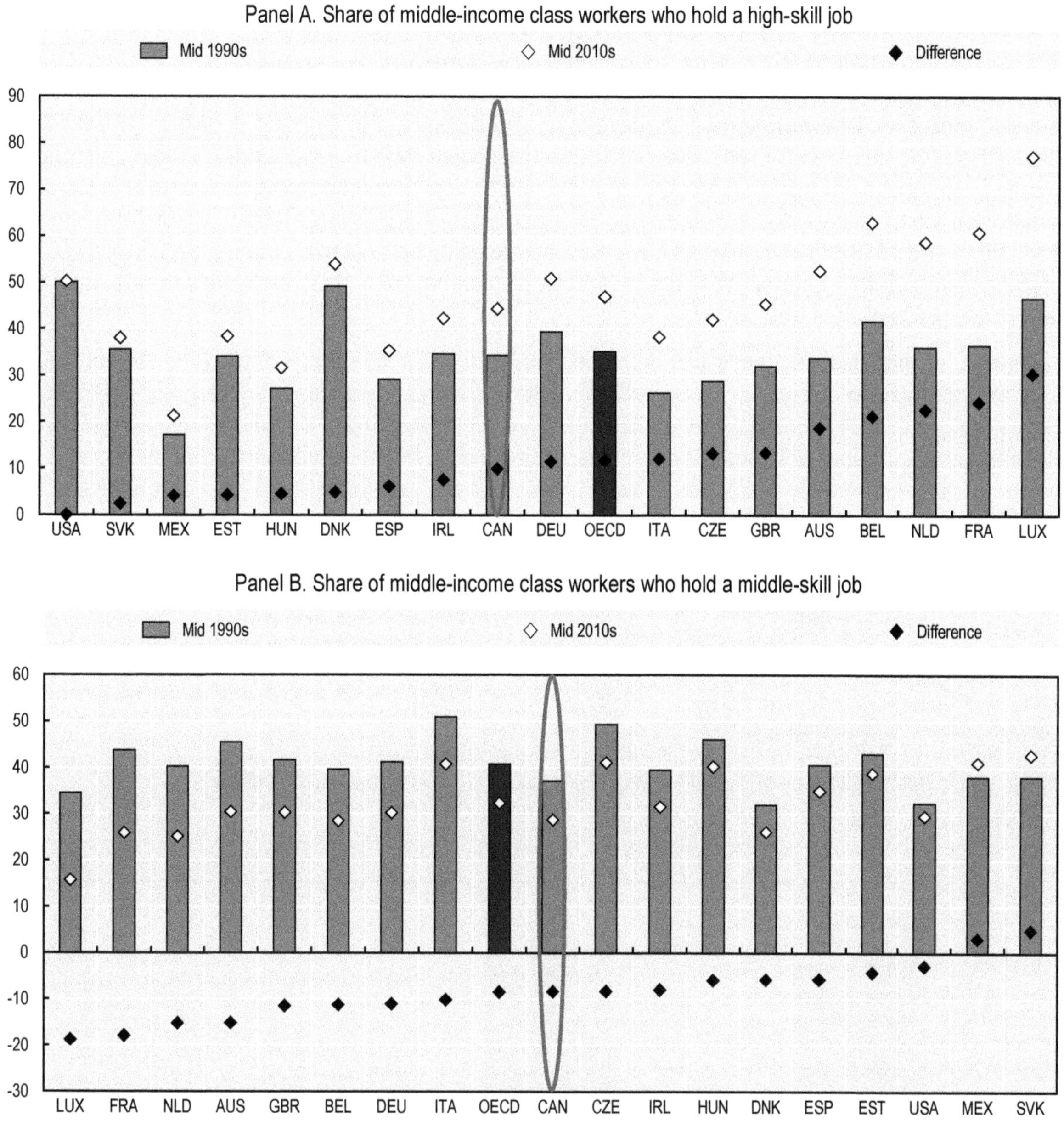

Note: The middle-income class comprises all individuals in households with net disposable income between 75% and 200% of the median household income in a given year and country. The income of reference is the household disposable income, corrected for household size with the OECD equivalence scale.

Source: OECD (2019[10]), Under Pressure: The Squeezed Middle Class, OECD Publishing, Paris, https://dx.doi.org/10.1787/689afed1-en.

3.1.4. In most Canadian regions, the employment share of middle-skill jobs is declining, but differences exist

The large majority of economic regions across Canada are experiencing declines in the employment share of middle-skill jobs (48 regions) and low-skill jobs (48 regions), and most regions are witnessing increases in the share of high-skill jobs (51 regions) (see Figure 3.5). However, the provincial job polarisation picture hides marked disparities among regions in Canada. In about 17 regions across Canada, the share of middle-skill jobs over total employment is increasing. As discussed in Chapter 1 of this OECD report, middle-skill jobs typically involve repetitive and routine tasks, which face a higher risk of being affected by automation. Northeast in British Columbia is the region that has witnessed the largest increase in the share of middle-skill jobs, which have increased by 14.9 percentage points as a share of total employment between 2011 and 2018. Middle-skill jobs have also increased by several percentage points in North Coast and Nechako in British Columbia (5.6 p.p.), Maurice in Quebec (5.1 p.p.) and Muskoka-Kawarthas in Ontario (3.6 p.p.) over the same period.

Disparities in job polarisation trends are more accentuated within some provinces (see Annex 3.A). In Alberta, all regions have lost low-skill jobs, while in other provinces the picture is mixed. For example, two out of five regions in New Brunswick and six out of sixteen regions in British Columbia have increased their employment shares in low-skill jobs. Regional disparities are even more pronounced in middle-skill jobs dynamics. In New Brunswick and Nova Scotia all regions have lost middle-skill jobs as a share of total employment, while almost half of the regions in Alberta, British Columbia and Ontario have experienced increases in the share of middle-skill jobs. The share of high-skill jobs has increased in most regions within provinces. Regional disparities in high-skill jobs are more visible in British Columbia, Newfoundland and Labrador, and Saskatchewan.

Figure 3.5. In most regions in Canada, the employment share of middle-skill and low-skill jobs is declining, while the share of high-skill jobs is increasing

Change in employment shares by skill level between 2011 and 2018, Canada economic regions

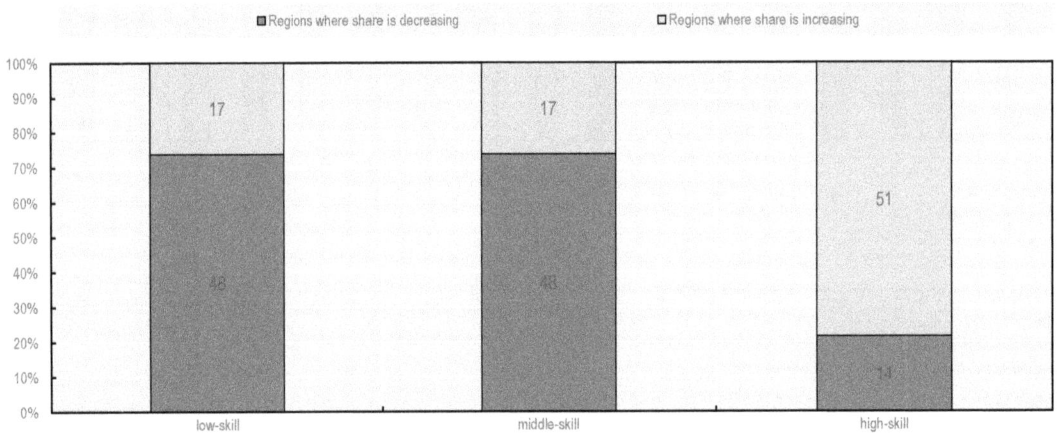

Note: Numbers in the bars denote the number of economic regions.
Source: OECD calculations on Labour Force Surveys.

Regional differences in job polarisation dynamics have also emerged in Ontario (see Figure 3.6). Kingston-Pembroke, Toronto and Ottawa have witnessed a substantial increase in the share of high-skill jobs and a steep decrease in that of middle-skill jobs. Similar dynamics have emerged in Kitchener-Waterloo-Barrie, Hamilton-Niagara Peninsula and Northeast. On the other hand, high-skill jobs have decreased as a share of total employment in Muskoka-Kawarthas, Northwest and London. Muskoka-Kawarthas has experienced a substantial increase in the share of middle-skill jobs over total employment. Stratford-Bruce Peninsula, Northwest, London and Windsor-Sarnia have also experienced increases in the share of middle-skill jobs.

Figure 3.6. Job polarisation across regions in Ontario

Changes in the shares of jobs over total employment by skill level, between 2011 and 2018

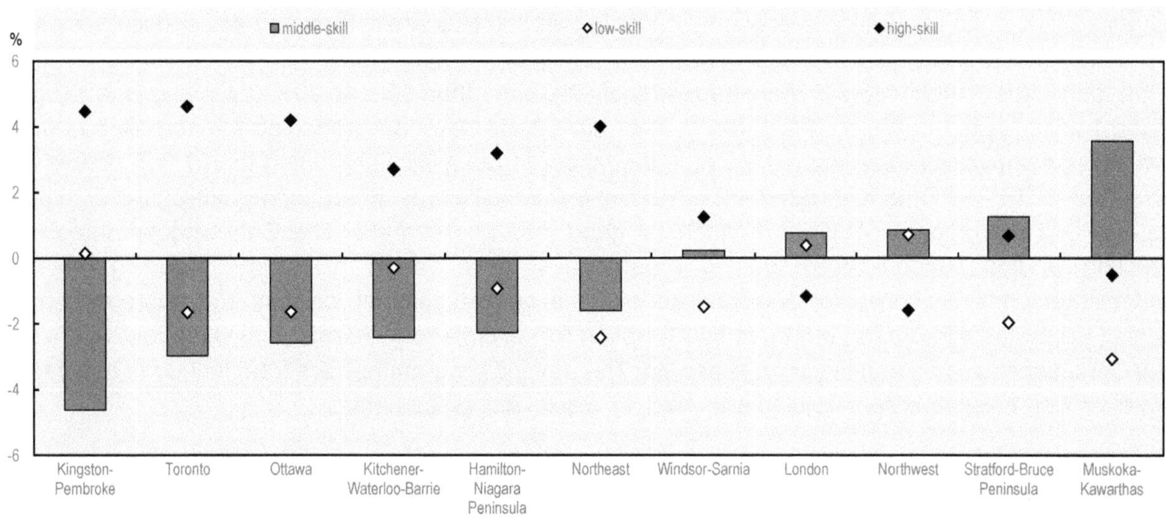

Source: OECD calculations on Labour Force Surveys.

StatLink https://doi.org/10.1787/888934150101

Box 3.1. Spotlight on London: an increasing demand for middle-skill jobs

London is among the regions in Ontario that have experienced an increase in the share of middle-skill jobs over 2011-2018. Wholesale and retail trade is the main sector of employment in the region, accounting for 16.1% of total employment in 2018. Manufacturing employment is among the highest across regions in Ontario, standing at 15% in the same year. Increases in the share of middle-skill jobs reflect a growing demand for middle-skill occupations in the region, which typically include skilled trade occupations. Considering the 2011-18 timeframe, transport and heavy equipment operation have created most new jobs (3 600). Jobs in processing and manufacturing machine operators as well as maintenance and equipment operation trades have also increased (3 200 new jobs each).

In addition, the demand for middle-skill workers such as trades workers is growing in London. It is estimated that in the London-area economy, most in-demand jobs are in the retail and service sectors, which are often low-paying. When it comes to well-paid jobs without enough people, skilled trades are at the top. Across Ontario, one in three tradespeople are older than 55, and 20% of Ontario jobs will be skilled trades-related in the next five years. Shortages have been accompanied by increases in the working age population reporting to be "not in the labour force", which amounted to 227 300 people in December 2018. The Ontario government is tackling these challenges by supporting pre-apprenticeship projects that will prepare people in London for good jobs and careers. The Ontario government is investing in four London-based training programmes for a variety of trades, including baker-confectioner, construction worker, brick and stone mason and educational assistant. Pre-apprenticeship training promotes careers in the trades as an option for all Ontario residents, including youth at risk, new Canadians, women and Indigenous people. The training programmes are free, last up to one year and often combine classroom training with an 8-12 week work placement.

Figure 3.7. What are the 10 occupations that have created most jobs in London?

Absolute changes in employment by occupation, 2011 to 2018

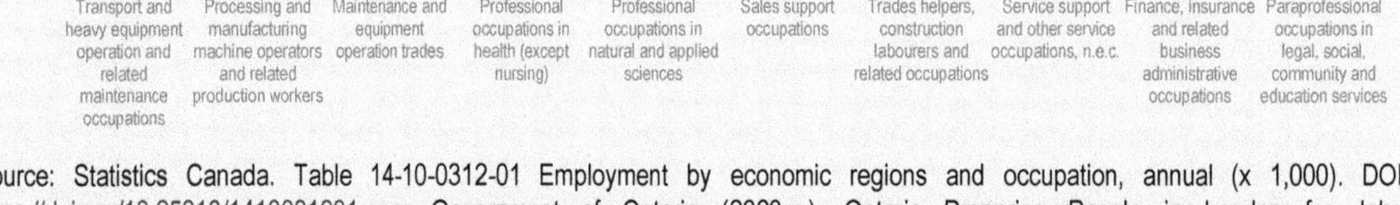

Source: Statistics Canada. Table 14-10-0312-01 Employment by economic regions and occupation, annual (x 1,000). DOI: https://doi.org/10.25318/1410031201-eng; Government of Ontario (2020[12]), Ontario Preparing People in London for Jobs, https://news.ontario.ca/mol/en/2020/01/ontario-preparing-people-in-london-for-jobs.html (accessed on 26 February 2020); The London Free Press (2020[13]), Begging for bodies: These are London's most in-demand jobs, trades, https://lfpress.com/news/local-news/begging-for-bodies-welders-and-machinists-among-londons-most-wanted-trades (accessed on 26 February 2020); worktrends.ca (n.d.[14]), Labour Market Facts for the London Economic Region - Interactive Tool, https://www.worktrends.ca/categories/london-economic-region (accessed on 26 February 2020).

3.2. Job polarisation partly reflects increases in the supply of skills in Canada

3.2.1. Canada outperforms OECD countries in educational attainment

The changes in the choice of occupational training in developed countries show that educational upgrading is a mechanism through which economies move away from learning routine cognitive tasks and manual tasks and towards learning non-routine cognitive and interactive tasks (Nedelkoska and Quintini, 2018[15]). Adults achieve higher levels of education in Canada than on average across the OECD (see Figure 3.8). About 57.9% of the 25-64 year-old population achieved tertiary education in 2018 in Canada, compared to 36.9% for the OECD average. Only 8.4% of the Canadian adult population attained only below upper secondary education in 2018 and 33.7% attained upper secondary education, compared to 21.1% and 42.4% for the OECD average. In addition, the supply of skills has been steadily expanding over the last decades in Canada. The share of tertiary educated adults has been consistently above the OECD average and OECD high-performing countries for decades (see Figure 3.9). Considering 2000 for example, already 40.1% of the Canadian population aged more than 25 attained tertiary education, compared to 22.3% on average across the OECD. Most tertiary education graduates mainly chose business administration and law, health and welfare as their fields of study, while few tertiary students choose services, agriculture and ICT as their specialisation (see Figure 3.10). Business administration and law are the main field chosen by tertiary education graduates across most OECD countries.

Colleges play an important role in preparing students for the labour market in Canada. A significant share of the Canadian population has college degrees, including both community colleges and polytechnics. Many community colleges and polytechnics in Canada offer both ISCED 5 (short-cycle tertiary) and ISCED 4 (post-secondary non-tertiary) programmes, including occupational preparation and adult education programmes. About 10.5% of Canadians hold post-secondary non-tertiary education and 26.1% hold short-cycle tertiary education, compared to 5.8% and 7.3% respectively for the OECD average in 2018.

The share of tertiary educated younger adults who have obtained a master's or a doctoral degree is below the OECD average. About 26% and 22% of 25-64 year-olds held short-cycle tertiary education and a Bachelor's or equivalent as their highest educational attainment in 2018, compared to the OECD averages of 7% and 17%. Only 10% have completed a master's or equivalent, compared to the OECD average of 13% (OECD, 2019[16]) .

Figure 3.8. Canada attains higher levels of tertiary education than on average across the OECD

Percentage of the 25-64 population with below upper secondary, upper secondary and tertiary education, 2018

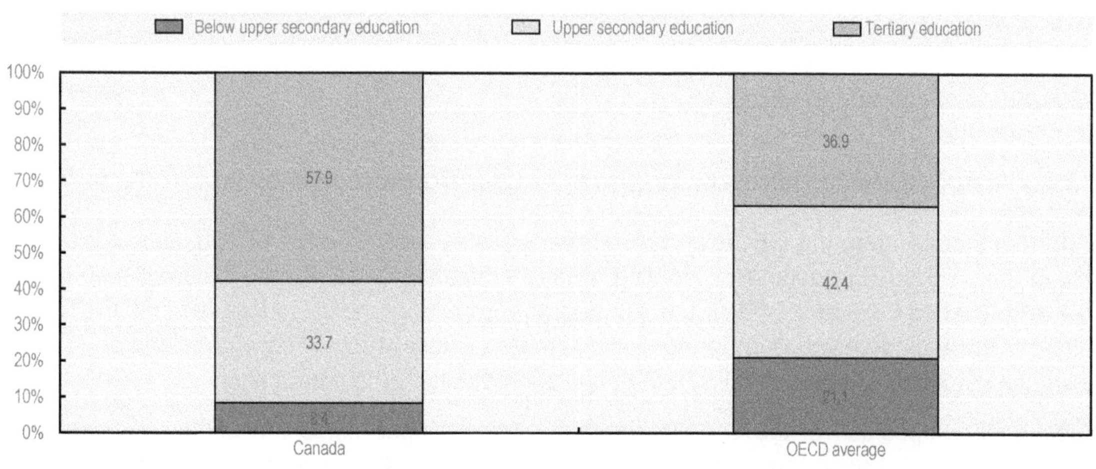

Source: OECD (2019), Adult education level (indicator). DOI: https://doi.org/10.1787/36bce3fe-en (Accessed on 13 May 2020).

Figure 3.9. Adult education levels have been on the rise across Canada and the OECD

Share of the population aged 25+ who attained tertiary education, 2000-18

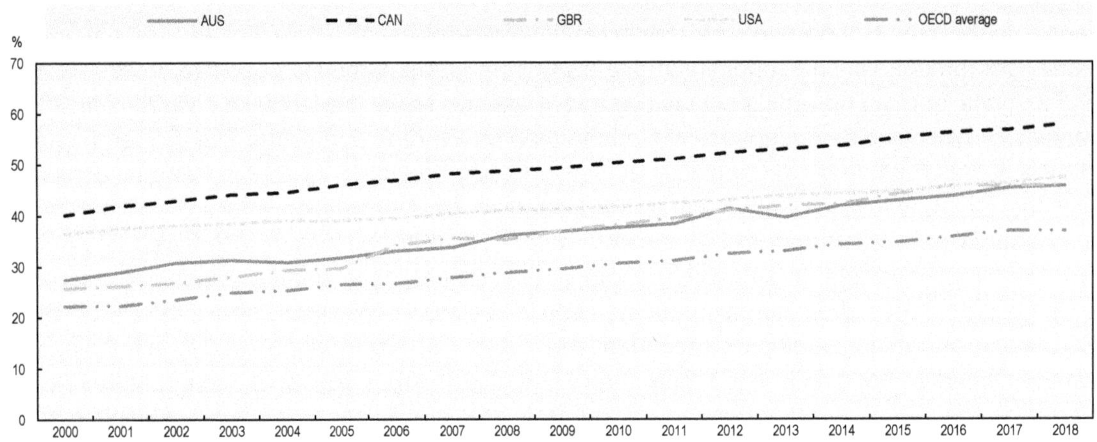

Source: OECD (2019), Adult education level (indicator). DOI: https://doi.org/10.1787/36bce3fe-en (Accessed on 17 July 2019).

Figure 3.10. Most tertiary education graduates in Canada have chosen business, administration and law as their field of study

Share of tertiary graduates by field in Canada, 2017

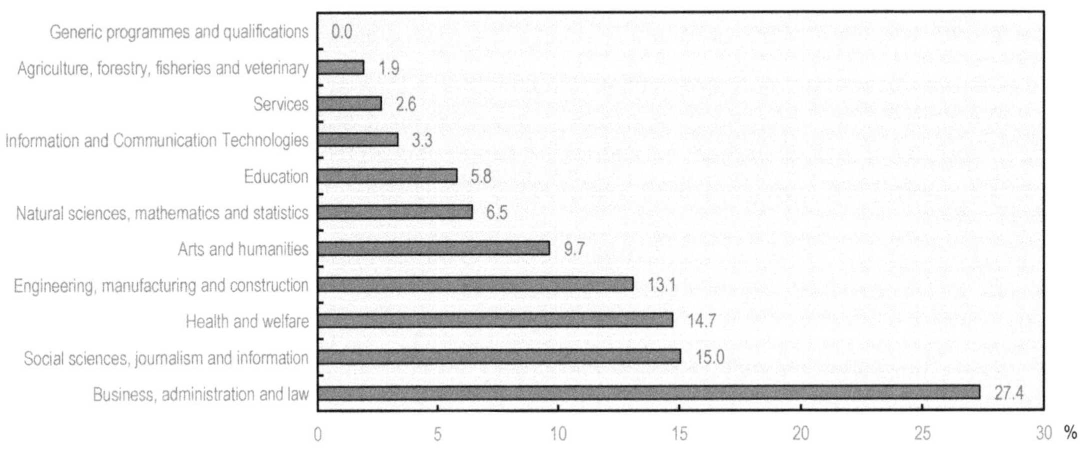

Source: OECD (2019), Education and a Glance database.

3.2.2. Educational attainment is higher in Ontario than on average in Canada

Ontario performs better than the OECD and the Canadian averages in terms of educational attainment, with 64% of the working age population holding tertiary education in 2018 (see Figure 3.11). In British Columbia and Quebec 56% and 54% of the working age population holds tertiary education. The skills composition of the workforce varies in Canada, with some provinces, such as Newfoundland and Labrador and Saskatchewan, where less than 50% of the population attains tertiary education.

The educational composition of the Ontario workforce has changed since the 2000s, with substantial increases in tertiary education attainment (see Figure 3.12). In 2000, almost 40% of the working age population attained high school and post-secondary non-tertiary education as their highest level of education, slightly below the share of those achieving tertiary education. At the same time, almost one in five in Ontario attained less than high school education in 2000. Over the recent decades the shares of working age people attaining high school or less has substantially decreased.

Figure 3.11. Tertiary education attainment is higher in Ontario than in other Canadian provinces and the OECD

Tertiary education attainment in Canada, Canadian provinces and the OECD average, 2018

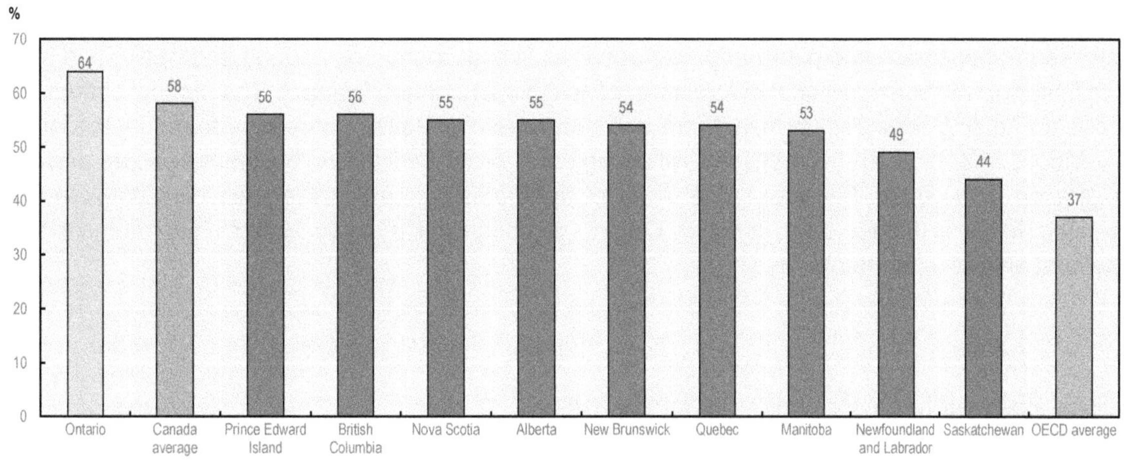

Note: Data does not include the territories.
Source: Statistics Canada. Table 37-10-0130-01 Educational attainment of the population aged 25 to 64, by age group and sex, Organisation for Economic Co-operation and Development (OECD), Canada, provinces and territories, https://doi.org/10.25318/3710013001-eng.

Figure 3.12. The educational composition of the Ontario workforce has changed over time

Percentage of the 25-64 year old population by highest educational attainment, 2000, 2010 and 2018

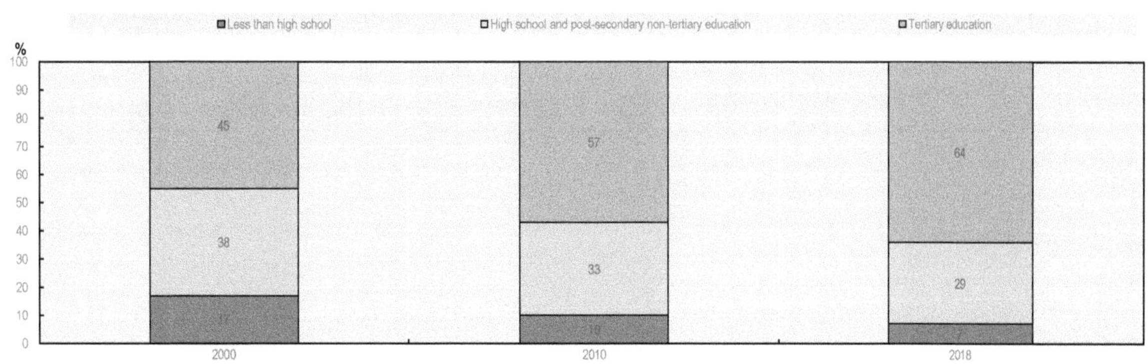

Source: Statistics Canada. Table 37-10-0130-01 Educational attainment of the population aged 25 to 64, by age group and sex, Organisation for Economic Co-operation and Development (OECD), Canada, provinces and territories, https://doi.org/10.25318/3710013001-eng.

3.2.3. The population in large urban centres holds higher levels of education in Ontario

While educational attainment has been consistently growing in Ontario, regions within the province achieve different levels of education (see Figure 3.13). In Toronto and Ottawa, the large majority of the 25-64-aged population have university certificates, diplomas or degrees at bachelor level or above (40% and 37% respectively). On the other hand, less than one person in five holds this level of education in Stratford-Bruce Peninsula (16%), Northeast (17%), Muskoka-Kawarthas (18%) and Northwest (19%). In Northwest and Stratford-Bruce Peninsula, more than 15% of people have no certificate, diploma or degree. The share of people attaining secondary education reaches almost 30% in Kingston-Pembroke, Muskoka-Kawarthas and Windsor-Sarnia. An element contributing to regional differences in educational attainment could be the fact that young people might move to Toronto and Ottawa to pursue studies, and remain there after finding jobs that fit their skills, which are more likely to be available where they went to school and in urban centres in general.

Among the 25-64 years olds holding post-secondary certificates, diplomas or degrees, most have degrees in business, management and public administration, architecture and engineering and health and related fields in Ontario, with some regional differences reflecting sectoral employment. The highest shares of 25-64 year-olds holding business, management and public administration degrees is found in Toronto and Ottawa (about 25% and 20% respectively), reflecting the availability of jobs in business services and public administration. In Kingston-Pembroke, the share of graduates with post-secondary certificates in health and related fields is higher than in other Ontario regions, which partly reflects the region's higher employment shares in the health field.

Figure 3.13. Largest urban areas have the highest share of university diplomas in Ontario

Educational attainment by economic region in Ontario, 2016

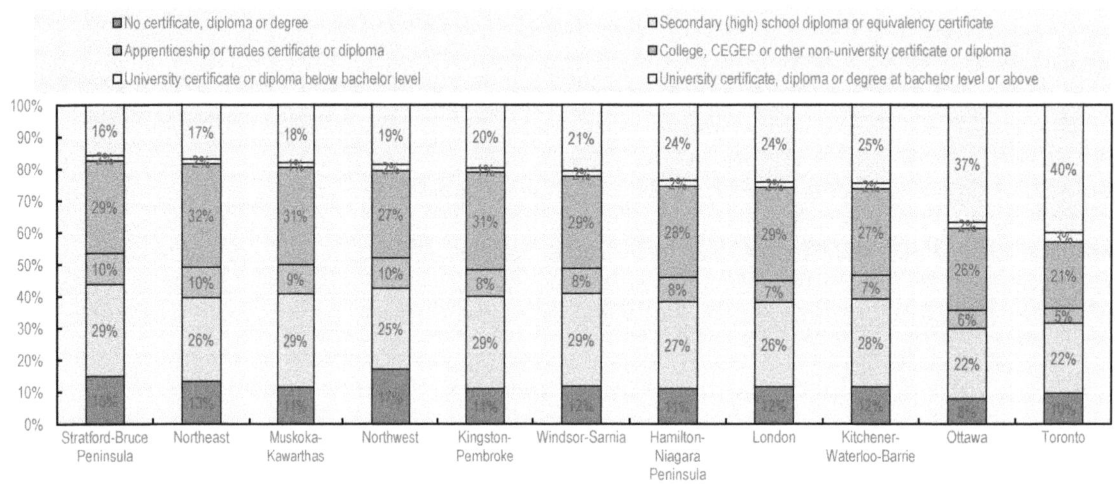

Source: OECD calculations on 2016 Census.

3.3. Canada is experiencing labour and skills shortages, which risk being exacerbated by COVID-19

3.3.1. Employers report labour shortages across Canada

The COVID-19 pandemic outbreak is likely to have lasting effects on the demand for labour in Canada as around the world. It has been suggested that the pandemic crisis could cause labour shortages in essential services and affect infrastructure in Canada (Tunney, 2020[17]). The agriculture sector is also reported to be experiencing labour shortages, as COVID-19 has led to delays in arrivals of temporary foreign workers, that the industry relies on (Sheldon, 2020[18]).

Prior to the COVID-19 outbreak, Canada was already facing labour shortages, as many employers struggled to fill open positions. Strong demand for workers is evident from the share of firms who report labour shortages that restrict their ability to meet demand. At 31%, this share is above the historical average (see Figure 3.14). The job vacancy rate, accounting for unfilled vacancies as a share of total occupied and vacant jobs, reached 3.5% in Q2 2019, reflecting tightening labour market conditions in Canada since 2016, when the rate stood at 2.4%. From a survey of about a hundred firms undertaken by the Bank of Canada to gather economic and business perspectives and sentiments for monitoring purposes, workforce ageing, changing worker preferences and difficulties attracting workers in rural areas were pointed out as main perceived challenges (Bank of Canada, 2019[19]). According to a survey by the Business Development Bank of Canada, 53% of small-and medium-sized enterprises say labour shortages will cause them to limit business investment (Matti, 2019[20]).

More than one in four employers in Canada report that the lack of applicants is the main reason why they cannot fill a position, according to the 2018 ManpowerGroup Talent Shortage Survey. The survey reports that shortages represent an issue for 41% of employers in Canada, and these are particularly challenging for large firms, who face twice as much difficulty filling roles than smaller ones (58% and 26% respectively). The share of companies reporting shortages in Canada is lower than the global average in 2018 (45%), and consistently below over the last decade. However, it has been increasing over the last years, suggesting that more and more companies are facing challenges filling positions in Canada. The lack of experience and of hard skills, as well as applicants expecting higher pay than offered are commonly cited reasons leading to shortage in Canada, reported by 19%, 17% and 12% of employers respectively (ManpowerGroup, 2018[21]).

Figure 3.14. A large share of firms reported labour shortages in Canada before COVID-19

Share of firms that report facing labour shortages that restrict their ability to meet demand, 2008 Q1 – 2019 Q4

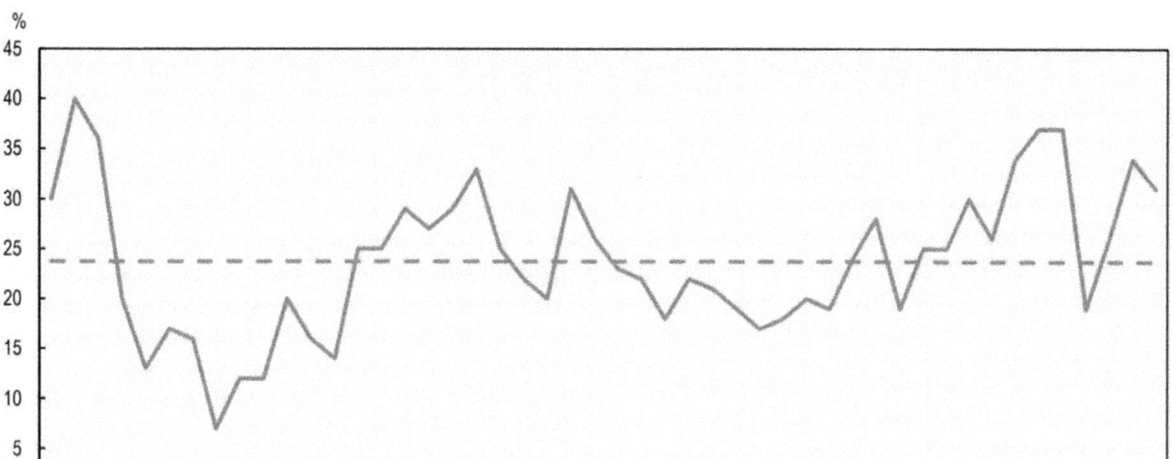

Note: The dotted line represents the historical average since 2008Q1.
Source: OECD (2020[5]), Workforce Innovation to Foster Positive Learning Environments in Canada, Getting Skills Right, OECD Publishing, Paris, https://dx.doi.org/10.1787/a92cf94d-en; Bank of Canada (2019[19]), *Business Outlook Survey—Autumn 2019*, https://www.bankofcanada.ca/2019/10/business-outlook-survey-autumn-2019/ (accessed on 23 January 2020).

Figure 3.15. The lack of applicants is the main reason employers cannot fill positions in Canada

Drivers of talent shortage, percentages, 2018

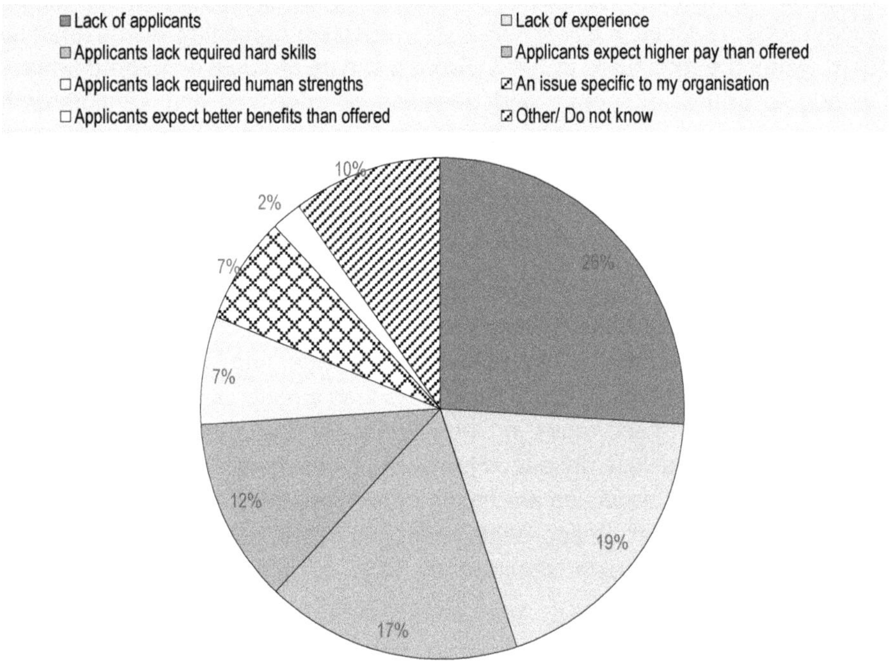

Source: ManpowerGroup (2018[21]), 2018 Talent Shortage - Solving the Talent Shortage: Build, Buy, Borrow and Bridge, https://manpowergroup.ca/campaigns/manpowergroup/talent-shortage/pdf/canada-english-talent-shortage-report.pdf (accessed on 1 August 2019).

3.3.2. Labour shortages are particularly critical in middle-skill occupations across Canada

Despite drops in employment shares linked to job polarisation, middle-skill jobs top the list when it comes to labour shortages in Canada. These include skilled trade occupations (e.g. electricians, welders and mechanics), sales representatives and drivers. Together with engineers and technicians, these occupations have consistently ranked among the top five hardest roles to fill in Canada for the past ten years (ManpowerGroup, 2018[21]). Consumerism drives demand for drivers and customer services representatives, while online retail activity continues to rise rapidly, together with jobs in logistics and last-mile delivery. Shortages in elementary occupations tend to be particularly accentuated in regions with rapid economic growth, historically in the mining or oil and gas industries (Komarnicki, 2012[22]). These are also the regions where the cost of living tends to be higher, and workers are therefore discouraged from moving there.

Labour shortages prevail in those sectors that typically face a higher risk of automation. Surveys undertaken with more than a thousand Canadian entrepreneurs by Business Development Canada show that manufacturing and retail trade are the sectors where the largest share of companies report difficulties in hiring (56% and 54% respectively) (Business Development Bank of Canada, 2018[23]). These sectors are followed by construction, health care, professional services and finance, insurance and real estate (see Figure 3.16). This could be linked to several factors, including insufficient participation in Vocational Education and Training (VET), relatively poorer pay and working conditions in some sectors. Automation and new technologies could represent an opportunity to tackle shortages and boost productivity in sectors at high risk of automation facing shortages, such as manufacturing and retail trade.

Figure 3.16. Labour shortages are mostly felt in manufacturing and retail trade across Canada

Percentage of respondents to the question "During the last 12 months, how easy has it been for your business to hire new employees?", 2018

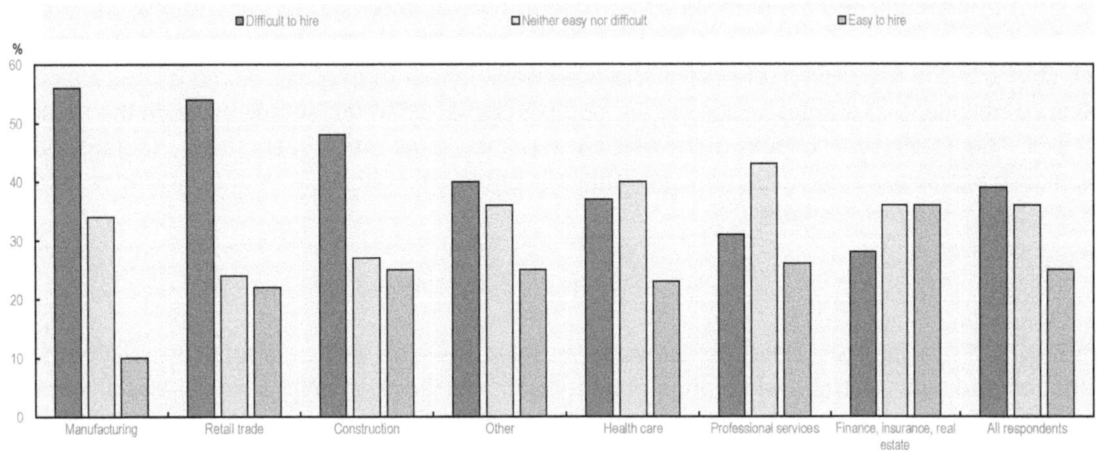

Note: Maru/Matchbox survey on Canada's labour shortage, 2018. Results exclude respondents who said, "I don't know" or "I prefer not to answer." Results are weighted by region and company size to reflect Canada's economy more accurately. n = 1 067.
Source: Business Development Bank of Canada (2018[23]), Labour Shortage in Canada: Here to stay, https://www.bdc.ca/en/documents/analysis_research/labour-shortage.pdf (accessed on 21 February 2020).

3.3.3. In addition, many workers lack the skills needed in the labour market in Canada

The mismatch between the supply and demand for skills may be exacerbated with the more rapid pace of change in the future of work. Mismatches can take the shape of skills shortages, when adequate skills are hard to find, or that of skill surpluses, when certain skills are in excess relative to the demand in the labour market. Skills mismatch can have a negative impact on productivity. Research for Canada shows that the impact of technological change and automation will mainly affect those with lower education level, and that individuals with a broad set of skills will be best-equipped to succeed in an era of increasing uncertainty and labour market changes (Morneau Shepell and Business Council of Canada, 2018[24]).

Changes related to digitalisation and automation have the potential to boost productivity, but they will also require workers to get new skills. Employer surveys conducted by Morneau Shepell and Business Council of Canada in 2017 look at how companies in Canada are adapting to changes in the demand for skills. The survey engaged 95 large Canadian private-sector employers, employing a total of more than 850 000 workers across Canada, specifically looking into the consequences for hiring practices linked to automation and technological developments. While hiring managers generally had a positive view of the impact of artificial intelligence and automation on the size of their workforce, they still cautioned that fast changes increase uncertainty in predicting longer-term trends. Companies also place higher expectations on new graduates, who need to be adaptable and able to acquire a mixed set of skills, and new partnerships are unfolding between businesses and education institutions to build work-integrated learning programmes (Morneau Shepell and Business Council of Canada, 2018[24]).

The COVID-19 pandemic crisis is also likely to make some skills more relevant in the future. COVID-19 has changed not only how people work but also how they consume, as well as basic patterns of movement and travel. The crisis has accelerated the levels of digitalisation to help reduce avoidable physical interactions. This has meant finding ways to reinvent work and, in some cases, a partial disruption of jobs and changes in the way workers perform them. The pandemic is setting up what could be lasting employment shifts that could require the large-scale re-skilling of workers. It is suggested that it will be crucial for employees to develop digital, higher cognitive, social and emotional, and adaptability and resilience in a post-COVID labour market (McKinsey & Company, 2020[25]).

The OECD Skills for Jobs database shows that some knowledge, abilities and skills are in shortage in Canada. The database defines skills as either hard-to-find (in shortage) or easy-to-find (in surplus) (see Box 3.2 for more information on the database). Skills shortages emerge when employers are unable to recruit staff with the necessary set skills in the accessible labour market and at the going rate of pay and working conditions. Skill surpluses arise in the opposite case, when the supply exceeds the demand for a given skill. The database also looks at the abilities and knowledge areas in shortage. Health services, fine manipulative abilities and resource management skills emerge respectively as the knowledge, abilities and skills most in shortage in Canada.

Box 3.2. Measuring skills mismatches through the OECD Skills for Jobs database

The OECD Skills for Jobs Database provides country-level (as well as subnational) information on shortages and surpluses of a wide range of dimensions, including cognitive, social and physical skills. Information is disaggregated into more than 150 job-specific Knowledge, Skills and Abilities and is available for 40 countries among OECD and emerging economies. Knowledge areas refer to the body of information that makes adequate performance of the job possible (e.g. knowledge of plumbing for a plumber; knowledge of mathematics for an economist). Skills refer to the proficient manual, verbal or mental manipulation of data or things (e.g. complex problem solving; social skills). Abilities refer to the competence to perform an observable activity (e.g. ability to plan and organise work; attentiveness; endurance).

Source: OECD (2018[26]), Skills for Jobs, https://www.oecdskillsforjobsdatabase.org/data/Skills%20SfJ_PDF%20for%20WEBSITE%20final.pdf (accessed on 3 October 2019).

Figure 3.17. Skills mismatches in Canada and the OECD

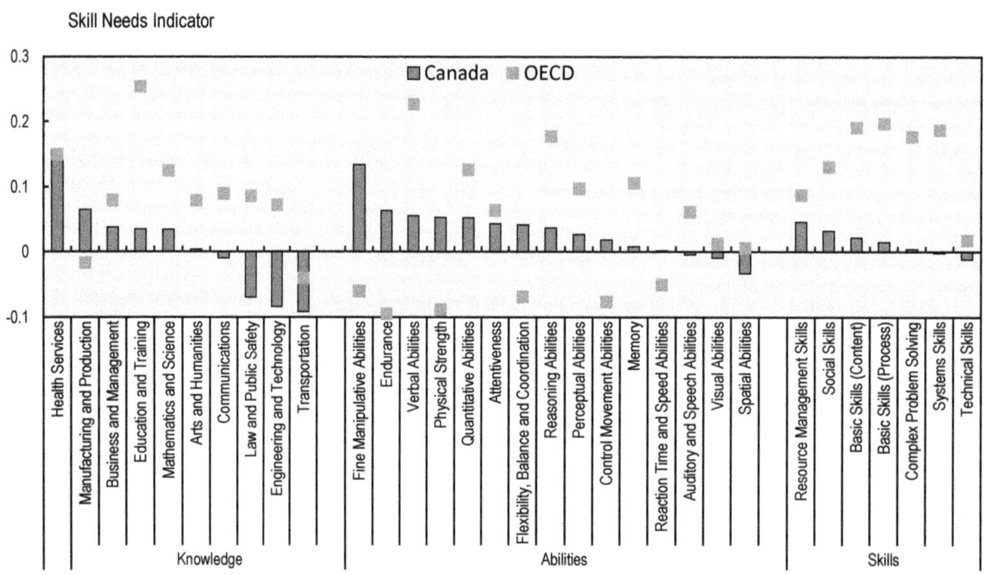

Note: Positive values indicate shortages while negative values indicate surpluses. The indicator is a composite of five sub-indices: wage growth, employment growth, growth in hours worked, unemployment rate and growth in under-qualification.
Source: OECD Skills for Jobs database (www.oecdskillsforjobsdatabase.org).

3.3.4. Skills shortages are affecting Ontario's labour market

Skills shortages are having profound impacts on Ontario's labour market. In 2013, it was estimated that skills shortages would cost the provincial economy about 4% of provincial GDP and they were projected to get worse without action to address them (The Conference Board of Canada, 2013[27]). The 2019 Business Confidence Survey, conducted by the Ontario Chamber of Commerce, shows that for 75% of members the ability to recruit and retain talent is a critical factor to organisational competitiveness (Ontario Chamber of Commerce, 2019[28]) (see Figure 3.18). Nearly half of respondents cited difficulty attracting or retaining staff as a reason for lacking confidence in the economic outlook of their organisations. Ontario Chamber of Commerce members also stressed that recruitment efforts are stifled by a supply/demand mismatch, driven in part by a deficit in areas such as skilled trades, emotional intelligence, design, communication, and STEM. While skills deficits are difficult to tackle over the short-term, a rebalancing of skills supply and demand might prove helpful over the longer term. A further challenge is however posed by the rapid pace of technological change in the workplace.

Ontario has been struggling with skills shortages for more than a decade. A study conducted by the Ontario Chamber of Commerce in 2017 showed that of the 62% of Ontario Chamber of Commerce members who attempted to recruit staff in the last six months of 2016, 82% of them experienced at least one challenge in doing so. The top challenge cited (by 60% of members) was finding someone with the proper qualifications. Employers also have a role to play in ensuring that workers develop the skills needed for job, providing training opportunities. The skills mismatch across Ontario is partly driven by credential inflation, defined as the process of inflation of the minimum credentials required for a given job and the simultaneous devaluation of the value of diplomas and degrees. The decisions of students to pursue qualifications in fields with limited employment opportunities results in an increase in the number of highly educated people working in positions where they are overqualified. This phenomenon ultimately leads to lesser-qualified people out of the labour market. Members of the Ontario Chamber of Commerce also emphasise that the possession of some skills and competencies, such as communication, emotional intelligence, creativity, design, interpersonal skills, entrepreneurship, technological skills and organisation awareness, are needed to succeed in the job (Ontario Chamber of Commerce, 2017[29]).

Figure 3.18. Recruiting and retaining talent is considered the main success factor to organisational competitiveness in Ontario

Percentage of respondents to "what extent do you agree or disagree that the following factors are critical to your organisation's competitiveness?", 2019

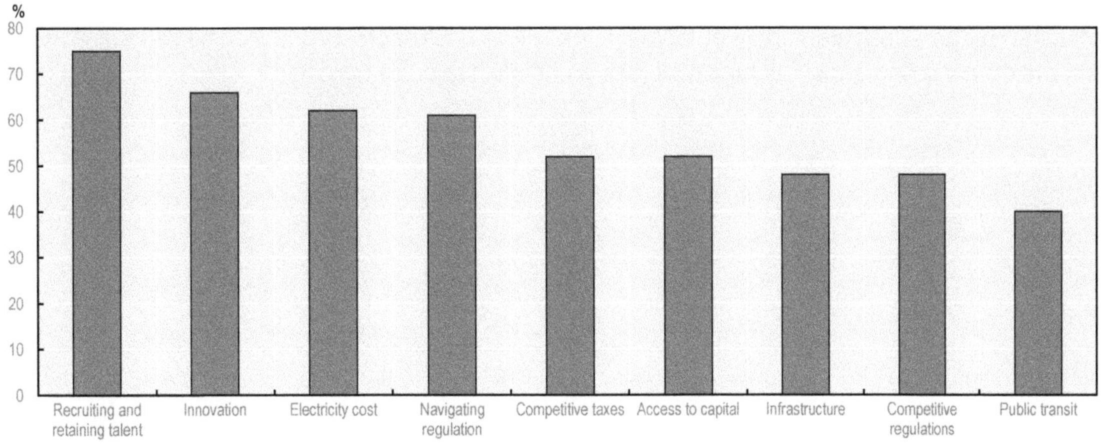

Source: Ontario Chamber of Commerce (2019[30]), Ontario Economic Report 2019, Ontario Chamber of Commerce, https://occ.ca/wp-content/uploads/2019-Ontario-Economic-Report.pdf (accessed on 9 July 2019).

3.3.5. Qualification mismatches are present in Ontario

While the skills provided by the education and training system need to correspond to those required by firms, it is also important to ensure that the labour market matches workers to jobs in which they can put their skills to the best use. Mismatches between workers skills and the demands of their jobs can have negative effects on different levels. At the individual level, they can affect job satisfaction and wages, at the firm level, they can increase job turnover and potentially reduce productivity, and at the macroeconomic level, they can increase unemployment and reduce growth through the waste of human capital and the implied reduction in productivity (OECD, 2018[31]). Qualification mismatches arise when workers have an educational attainment that is higher (over-qualification) or lower (under-qualification) than that required by their job. OECD research shows that while the share of 15-64 year-old workers who report being over-qualified is slightly lower in Canada than the OECD average (16.2% and 16.8% respectively), the opposite is true when looking at under-qualification (21.7% and 18.9%).

Qualification mismatches are spread in Ontario, although to a lesser extent than in other Canadian provinces (see Figure 3.19). In Saskatchewan, Manitoba and Quebec more than 30% of workers aged 25-64 are underqualified for the job, while less than 25% in Ontario and Newfoundland and Labrador. Over-qualification is higher in Newfoundland and Labrador (14.6%) and Nova Scotia (12.4%) compared to other provinces in Canada. Another type of skills mismatch is field of study mismatch, which occurs when workers who were educated in a particular field work in a different one. The 2016 General Social Survey shows that about 36% of Canadian adults are working in a different filed compared to the one in which they studied. Field of study mismatch is generated by both labour supply and demand factors, such as the saturation of a particular field in the labour market and the level of transferrable skills offered by specific fields of study. Linkages between education and the world of work can help provide students with skills needed in the labour market. For example, work-based learning offers useful solutions to the challenge of qualification mismatch as provision adjusts more or less automatically to the needs of the labour market (OECD, 2018[31]).

Looking at the occupational structure and educational attainment across regions in Ontario shows that most of them are in a high-skill equilibrium, although differences exist (see Figure 3.20). Ottawa and Toronto are in a high-skill equilibrium, as they are characterised by high educational attainment, high employment shares in high-skill occupations and high earnings. Also Hamilton-Niagara Peninsula, Kitchener-Waterloo-Barrie, Kingston-Pembroke and Northwest are in a high-skill equilibrium. On the other hand, London appears to be facing a skills surplus situation, suggesting that the supply of high-skill individuals is not met by high-skill jobs. The region experienced the least change within Ontario and the relative share of high-skill jobs has even declined slightly during 2011-18. Northeast is the only region in Ontario experiencing a skills deficit, suggesting that although the demand for high-skill jobs is present, this is not matched by an adequate supply of labour force. Finally, Stratford-Bruce Peninsula is in a low-skill trap: both the demand and supply of high-skill jobs and individuals are lacking.

Figure 3.19. Qualification mismatches are present in Ontario, although to a lesser extent than in other provinces

2016

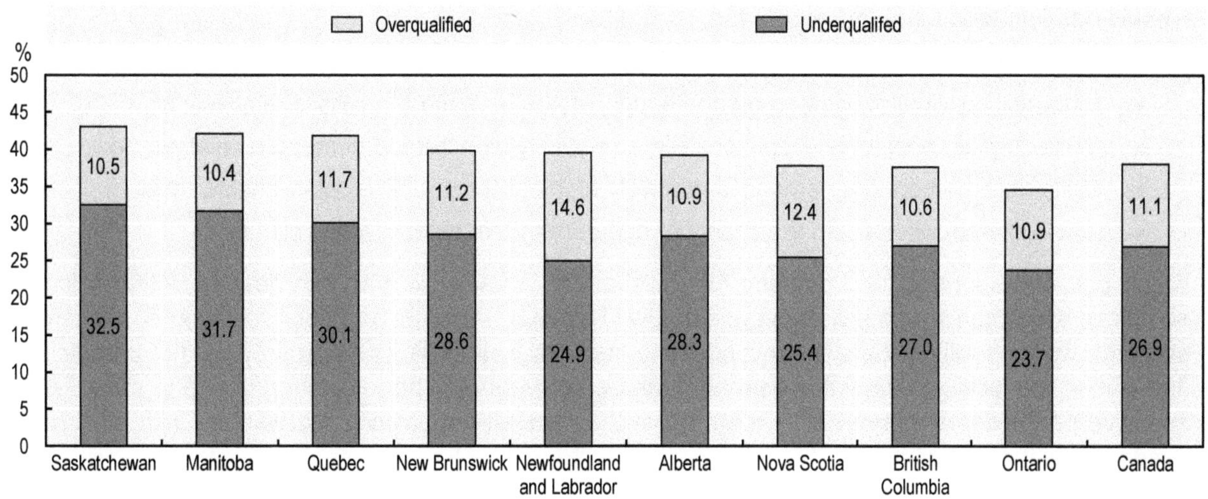

Source: OECD calculations based on Statistics Canada 2016 Census.

Figure 3.20. Most Ontario regions are in a high-skill equilibrium, but differences exist

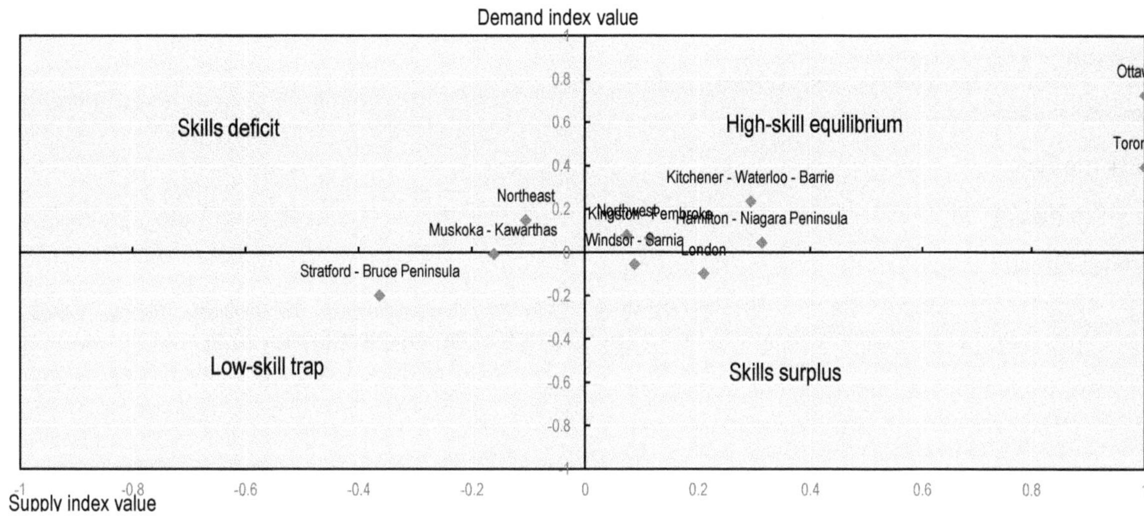

Source: OECD elaboration on Labour Force Survey, Statistics Canada.

StatLink https://doi.org/10.1787/888934150120

Box 3.3. A skills demand-supply classification

The OECD Local Economic and Employment Development (LEED) Programme has developed a typology designed to help understand the main different possible relationships between skills supply and demand at local (or regional) level. Local areas can fall into one of four categories:

- High-skill equilibrium, where both the supply of and demand for skills is relatively high;
- Skills surplus, where the supply of skills is relatively high but the demand is relatively low;
- Skills deficit, where the demand is relatively high but the supply is relatively low; and
- Low-skill trap, where both the supply of and demand for skills is relatively low.

When both the supply of and demand for skills is low, a low skills trap can develop within a local economy, which can create a vicious cycle or low investments in skills and poor quality jobs. In such a situation, workers will not have the incentives to upgrade their skills, knowing they will not be able to find jobs in the local economy that use them, and employers may be reluctant to move to more skill-intensive production and services, knowing that they are unlikely to find the workers with the skills needed to fill these positions.

The demand for skills is approximated using a composite index: percentage of the population employed in medium-high skilled occupations and earnings (weighted at .25 and .75 respectively). For building indices it is necessary to bring the variables in a common unit (scale) of measurement using a standardisation method. It was decided to use the inter-decile range method which compares the value of a region with the national median and is not influenced to a great extent by outliers. Using this formula, the supply and demand indices vary between -1 and 1. See the formula below:

(Xi -Xmed) / (X9th - X1st)

Where: Xi = value for TL3i

Xmed= median

X9th = 9th decile

X1st =1st decile

Source: Froy, F., S. Giguère and M. Meghnagi (2012[32]), Skills for Competitiveness: A Synthesis Report, OECD, http://www.oecd.org/cfe/leed/skills%20for%20competitiveness%20synthesis%20final.pdf (accessed on 11 July 2019).

3.4. Challenges related to COVID-19 and the future of work require action on both the skills supply and demand

3.4.1. Access to training opportunities is uneven in Canada

Despite boasting a higher training coverage than other countries across the OECD, access to training is uneven among segments of the population. Two-thirds of adults in Canada received some type of training in 2016, according to the 2016 General Social Survey. Participation rates in Canada are low among low-skill workers, low-waged workers, older workers, the unemployed, those working in SMEs and temporary workers (OECD, 2020[5]) (see Figure 3.21).

Canada displays one of the largest gaps in participation rates between high/middle-skill workers and low-skill workers. Adults with low skills often have limited opportunities to develop their skills further through education and training. Many risk being caught in a 'low-skills trap', in low-level positions with limited opportunities for development and on-the-job learning, and experiencing frequent and prolonged spells of unemployment (OECD, 2019[33]). Low-skill workers participate less than higher-skill workers in training, and this gap is larger in Canada than across the OECD (28 relative to 23 percentage points). The growing demand for high-level cognitive and complex social interaction skills suggest that low-skill workers in jobs that are intensive in repetitive or manual tasks are likely to suffer the most from changes related to the future of work (OECD, 2019[4]). Across the OECD, one of the main reasons for the participation gap of low-skill adults in training is that they find it more difficult to recognise their learning needs and hence are less likely to seek out training opportunities (OECD, 2019[33]).

Participation in training is also lower among Small and Medium-sized Enterprises (SMEs) and older workers in Canada. For SMEs, lack of time, limited information on training options, and lack of financial resources are often the typical barrier preventing training participation, in Canada as across many OECD countries. In addition, the share of workers who wanted to participate in training but did not because it was too expensive is higher within small than large firms. Training costs may be unaffordable for SME workers who on average earn lower wages and have fewer savings. Also, SME workers more often rely on their own private purse to pay for training, because they are less often beneficiary of employer-provided training, compared to large firms' workers. The participation gap between the prime age population (25-54) and older adults (55+) is larger in Canada relative to the OECD average (23 and 21 percentage points respectively). Older workers are likely to experience skills obsolescence unless they access training opportunities. Given the shorter period of time that older workers have to recoup the investment in training before retirement, they tend to receive less training than younger workers. Lower participation rates among older adults are often due to high inactivity among older people, low employer investment in the skills of older workers, and fewer incentives for older workers to improve their skills (OECD, 2014[34]).

Figure 3.21. Access to training is uneven across Canada

Percentage point differences in training participation rates between groups, Canada and OECD, 2012

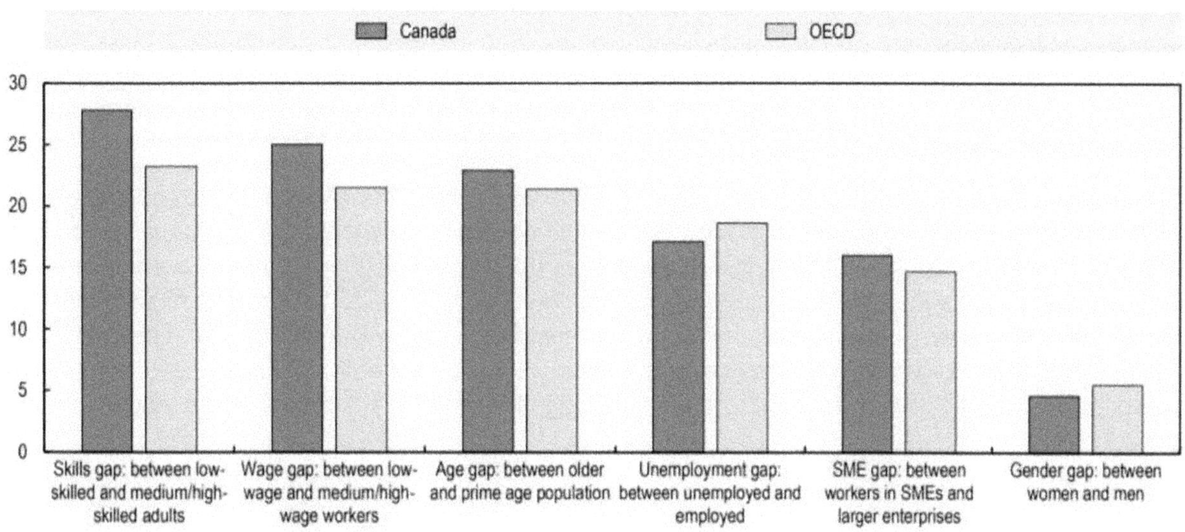

Note: Participation in formal and non-formal job-related education and training.
Source: OECD (2020[5]), Workforce Innovation to Foster Positive Learning Environments in Canada, Getting Skills Right, OECD Publishing, Paris, https://dx.doi.org/10.1787/a92cf94d-en.

3.4.2. COVID-19 makes skills development more important than ever, as it can prepare workers for the upturn

Investments today in lifelong learning and vocational training can ensure workers are ready for the upturn, while also supporting regions to make transitions to new economic opportunities. During the previous crisis in 2008, investments were aimed at helping individuals acquire skills in new and emerging sectors. However, such efforts were sometimes undermined by low firm demand and sub-optimal use of those skills in the workplace. Policy could focus on providing flexible forms of skills development to respond to the accelerated reallocation of labour in local economies, including greater access to e-learning opportunities that focus on the needs of the worker (especially those who are disadvantaged) while working with firms to promote workforce innovation and better human resources management practices. This tailoring and proximity to firms and workers will be an essential asset for the recovery (OECD, 2020[35]).

Closing gaps in access to training will be particularly important, given the uneven impacts of COVID-19 across the skills spectrum. Low-skill, low-wage, and young people may be the most vulnerable to job losses as they are employed in the sectors most at risk today, they are less likely to hold jobs that allow them to telecommute, and are more likely to be on temporary contracts. These same groups are also more likely to hold jobs at higher risk of automation, a process that firms may accelerate in light of the pandemic (OECD, 2020[35]). Going forward, it will be crucial to ensure that these categories of workers can access skills development opportunities to prepare for the upturn and transition into new jobs.

3.4.3. Digital skills are in need across Canada

COVID-19 is pointing out the importance of digital skills in the labour market. The crisis has accelerated the adoption of digitalisation in the workplace, to help reduce avoidable physical interactions. This has meant finding ways to reinvent work and, in some cases, a partial disruption of jobs and changes in the way workers perform them (McKinsey & Company, 2020[25]).

Digital skills were in high-demand across sectors in Canada already before the COVID-19 outbreak. The Brookfield Institute for Innovation + Entrepreneurship (BII+E) has developed a taxonomy of digital skills and explored patterns in digital skill demand across Canada and Ontario. It has drawn on six years of online job postings data from Burning Glass Technologies (Burning Glass), including about three million job postings recorded for Ontario over this period, representing over 40% of online job postings in Canada. Digital skill demand in Canada is not monolithic. Digital skills vary widely, and can be understood as belonging to four clusters (see Box 3.4).

Digital skills are more in demand in Ontario than across Canada. A weighted average of the share of digital skills across almost 1 000 occupational groups reveals that while an online job posting in Canada typically consists of 13% digital skills, in Ontario, this share is over 16% (or 25% higher than the Canadian share). This difference is seen across all four digital skill clusters. The ten digital skills that show up most frequently in Ontario are the same 10 digital skills that show up most frequently in Canada overall. These include baseline digital skills, such as proficiency using the Microsoft Office suite, in particular Excel, as well as more specialized digital skills such as SQL, a querying language, and Java, a programming language (see Table 3.1).

Box 3.4. Digital skill clusters in Canada

In ascending order of digital intensity, these are: Workforce Digital Skills, Data Skills, System Infrastructure Skills, and Software/Product Development Skills. BII+E identified these clusters by first delineating between digital and non-digital skills based on the occupational contexts in which skills are demanded, including whether they consistently and uniquely show up in digital occupations as defined in BII+E's previous work, and on Burning Glass's existing categorisation of software skills. BII+E then used graph theory and network analytics techniques to identify clusters of digital and non-digital skills.[1]

Workforce Digital Skills (997 skills): This skill cluster is the least digitally-intensive, comprising skills ranging from those associated with general office tasks to those associated with specific professions, such as use of architectural and engineering-based software to augment job tasks and business processes. Prominent skills in this cluster include Microsoft Excel, Word, PowerPoint, and Office (741 191, 296 992, 266 792, and 621 690 mentions respectively). This cluster also includes skills associated with general-use design software, such as Adobe Photoshop (53 855 mentions), as well as basic data analysis skills (mentioned 60 256 times) and use of tools such as SAS (21 130 mentions).

Data Skills (507 skills): This skill cluster is focussed primarily on data gathering and analysis, especially in large-scale enterprise analytics. The skills in this cluster are important across the economy and have a wide variance in their digital intensity. Prominent skills include "Data Modeling" (20 252 mentions), "Big Data" (13 173 mentions), "Business Intelligence" (35 361 mentions), and familiarity with data analytics tools, such as Apache Hadoop (10 509 mentions), Tableau (9 121 mentions), and R (4 132 mentions). This cluster can be further divided into basic data skills, which intersect with the Workforce Digital Skills cluster, and two groups of advanced data skills: Data Infrastructure, which intersects with the System Infrastructure cluster; and AI/Machine Learning skills, which intersect with the Software/Product Development cluster.

System Infrastructure Skills (985 skills): This cluster consists of skills related to digital infrastructure management, ranging from setting up and managing cloud computing services to general IT support. Prominent skills include proficiency with specific platforms such as VMWare (25 319 mentions) or Windows Server (21 094 mentions), and general support skills such as 'system administration' (33 459) and 'hardware and software installation' (23 940 mentions).

Software/Product Development Skills (1 109 skills): This skill cluster pertains to the generation of new digital products, both web- and software-based. Prominent skills include proficiency in programming languages, such as Java (112 680) and Python (43 137 mentions), and general skills such as 'software development' (133 681 mentions), 'software engineering' (47 775 mentions), and 'web development' (41 184 mentions). Some technical design skills, pertaining specifically to web development, are also a part of this cluster. On average, skills in this cluster are the most digitally-intensive.

Source: Vu, V., R. Willoughby and C. Lamb (2019[36]), I, Human: Digital and soft skills in a new economy, https://brookfieldinstitute.ca/wp-content/uploads/I-Human-ONLINE-FA.pdf (accessed on 24 January 2020).

Table 3.1. Top digital skills for Ontario

Skill	Number of Job Postings
Microsoft Excel	382 851
Microsoft Office	306 588
Microsoft PowerPoint	149 155
Microsoft Word	145 048
SQL	100 167
Software Development	76 120
Spreadsheets	73 447
Java	68 847
Technical Support	64 084
SAP	62 525

Source: Vu, V., R. Willoughby and C. Lamb (2019[36]), I, Human: Digital and soft skills in a new economy, https://brookfieldinstitute.ca/wp-content/uploads/I-Human-ONLINE-FA.pdf (accessed on 24 January 2020).

Digital skill demand varies across local economies in Ontario. When comparing the three focus jurisdictions — London, Kitchener, and Hamilton — to other provincial jurisdictions, including Ottawa, Toronto, and Waterloo, it is clear that the digital skills employers are seeking differ depending on the jurisdiction. In all local economies, demand for employees with the ability to use the Microsoft Office suite is high, but beyond this, important differences arise. For example, demand for skills from the Software/Product Development cluster is significantly higher in Waterloo, while in Hamilton, no skills from this cluster rank among the top 10 in-demand digital skills for this region. All of the top 10 digital skills asked for in Hamilton are general workforce digital skills. In Kitchener, skills from both the Software/Product Development and Data clusters are in high demand. Interestingly, however, SAP, which appears in both the national and provincial top 10 list, is the 29th most requested skill, while other software and product development skills, such as "Software Engineering," "Linux," and "C++," appear more often. For London, skills from the Software/Product Development cluster appear less often, with JavaScript appearing as the 13th most commonly requested skill, and Java as the 17th most requested. Workforce digital skills such as "Spreadsheets," "Word processing," and "Technical Support" appear more frequently.

Table 3.2. Top digital skills in Kitchener

Skill	Number of Job Postings
Microsoft Excel	5 388
Microsoft Office	4 988
Microsoft Word	2 306
Microsoft PowerPoint	1 633
SQL	1 557
Software Development	1 310
Spreadsheets	1 071
Java	1 027
JavaScript	986
Technical Support	961

Source: Vu, V., R. Willoughby and C. Lamb (2019[36]), I, Human: Digital and soft skills in a new economy, https://brookfieldinstitute.ca/wp-content/uploads/I-Human-ONLINE-FA.pdf (accessed on 24 January 2020).

Table 3.3. Top digital skills in London

Skill	Number of Job Postings
Microsoft Excel	13 830
Microsoft Office	13 251
Microsoft Word	5 444
Microsoft PowerPoint	4 393
Spreadsheets	2 564
Technical Support	2 409
SQL	2 118
Word Processing	1 889
Software Development	1 879
SAP	1 639

Source: Vu, V., R. Willoughby and C. Lamb (2019[36]), I, Human: Digital and soft skills in a new economy, https://brookfieldinstitute.ca/wp-content/uploads/I-Human-ONLINE-FA.pdf (accessed on 24 January 2020).

Table 3.4. Top digital skills in Hamilton

Skill	Number of Job Postings
Microsoft Excel	7 539
Microsoft Office	6 143
Microsoft Word	3 305
Microsoft PowerPoint	2 204
Spreadsheets	1 601
Word Processing	1 202
Microsoft Outlook	1 026
Technical Support	938
Telecommunications	886
SAP	869

Source: Vu, V., R. Willoughby and C. Lamb (2019[36]), I, Human: Digital and soft skills in a new economy, https://brookfieldinstitute.ca/wp-content/uploads/I-Human-ONLINE-FA.pdf (accessed on 24 January 2020).

3.4.1. Digital skills are important, but not in isolation

While digital skills are in need across Ontario, this is not in isolation. BII+E has identified some trends shaping Canadian labour markets, whereby employers are seeking digital and non-digital skills in combination, i.e. "hybrid jobs". Canadians across the economy require a skillset that includes general workforce digital skills and a suite of soft skills. Despite a growing narrative around the importance of learning to code, for most Canadians, foundational digital skills alongside a suite of non-digital skills — in particular, interpersonal skills — are critical foundations to be competitive in the labour market. General workforce digital skills, while less digitally-intensive, show up in roughly one third of all job postings in Canada. This includes the baseline digital skills that most Canadian workers need, the most predominant of which are those found in the Microsoft Office Suite. It also includes occupation-specific software, such as business intelligence software and SAS. The most common skills appearing alongside workforce digital skills are communication and organisational skills. Other soft skills likely to appear alongside workforce digital skills include interpersonal skills, such as 'teamwork', 'collaboration', and 'customer service'; project management skills, such as 'budgeting' and 'planning'; and more general skills and aptitudes, such as 'problem-solving' and 'detail-orientedness'.

For highly technical workers, digital skills are necessary, but they should be complemented by non-digital skills. Roles requiring a high proportion of skills from the Software/Product Development and Systems Infrastructure skills clusters are not only the most digitally-intensive, but also the most hybrid. This means that in addition to digital skills, employers look for non-digital skills from different domains at a higher intensity compared to other roles. For these highly-digital roles, employers are looking for particularly dynamic candidates, with technical domain knowledge augmented by many non-digital skills; in particular, those that pertain to communications, teamwork, problem solving, and project management, reflecting the creative and collaborative nature of these roles. For current and prospective workers in these fields, strong digital skills are necessary, but insufficient. It is perhaps just as critical to enhance one's interpersonal, creative, and problem-solving skills and abilities.

For many professionals in creative sectors, design-oriented digital skills are essential. In many core creative roles, from advertising professionals to video game designers, employers are looking for candidates with a strong overlap in non-digital communications, marketing, and/or design skills, as well as design-oriented digital tools. The digital skills that are in-demand for these creative professionals pertain to graphic design, web development, and marketing/communications. For these workers, the tools from the Adobe Creative Suite are requested most often. Many of these jobs also require digital skills that relate to marketing and communications — the ability to use social media platforms were among the most commonly requested. Digital marketing management tools and general web development skills are also in high demand. From an employer perspective, the core creative practices, which include non-digital communications, marketing, and design skills, remain the most important elements of the job; but, in many cases, these need to be augmented by specific digital skills and abilities.

Data skills are highly in-demand and act as connectors between less and more digitally-intensive occupations. Data is becoming an indispensable component of our economy. For workers, data skills are not only some of the most in-demand digital skills, but can also serve as a link between less and more digitally-intensive roles. One area of upgrading that offers promise is advancement from Microsoft Excel to SQL. Microsoft Excel is the single most in-demand digital skill in Canada, and as a spreadsheet programme is applicable across the economy. SQL, a database querying software, is much more digitally-intensive, but is also the fifth most requested digital skill in Canada. While these skills sit within two distinct clusters, with different levels of digital intensity, they also form a strong connection with one another. There are many instances in which an employer asks for both Excel and SQL in the same job posting. An individual who is proficient at Excel and seeking to become more competitive in digitally-intensive roles may consider learning SQL. However, these kinds of job transitions will also likely require skill and credential upgrading in other areas (Vu, Willoughby and Lamb, 2019[36]).

Previous OECD work has also stressed the importance of expanding entrepreneurial education in Canada, to develop skills and confidence in potential entrepreneurs and increase their likelihood to innovate and succeed (OECD, 2017[37]). There are many examples of the use of entrepreneurship education tools in Canadian schools. However, some provinces (notably Quebec and Ontario) are forging ahead of others and some activities are limited on the ground, such as contacts between inspiring role models and students; school trips to local business incubators and enterprises; summer camps for successful participants of entrepreneurship competitions; and online competitions and virtual firm games. At tertiary level, almost all institutions offer a few entrepreneurship courses and extra-curricular activities such as workshops, business competitions and mentoring. Some jurisdictional apprenticeship authorities in Canada deliver an Achievement in Business Competencies (Blue Seal) Program, a credential to help certified skilled trades workers succeed in business. However, the proportion of students reached is limited and many of the activities depend on the efforts of a few individuals rather than institutionalised processes.

3.4.1. Improving the use of skills in the workplace is an opportunity for Ontario

Having a workforce with the right skills is not sufficient to achieve growth and foster productivity. For economies to grow and individuals to succeed in the labour market, skills need to be put to productive use at work (OECD, 2016[38]). Traditionally, workforce development initiatives have focused on the supply side of labour markets: job search, matching, skills development, and addressing employment barriers faced by vulnerable groups. However, there is increasing recognition of the value of demand-side efforts, including engaging employers in making optimal use of their employees' skills (OECD/ILO, 2017[39]).

While Ontario achieves high levels of literacy proficiency compared to most provinces, it scores in the average when it comes to reading skills use at work. Better using skills in the workplace represents an opportunity for Ontario, as the use of reading skills at work strongly correlates with output per hour work, even accounting for average proficiency scores in literacy and numeracy, suggesting that the frequency with which skills are used at work is important in itself (OECD, 2016[38]). In addition, workers who use their skills more frequently also tend to have higher wages, even after accounting for differences in educational attainment, skills proficiency and occupation. Effective skills use is also traditionally linked to higher job satisfaction.

Promoting the emergence of high-performance work practices could be a means to putting skills into good use in Ontario. The term "high performance work practices" (HPWP) refers to a set of human resources practices that are shown to be associated with greater skills use and informal learning. HPWPs include aspects of work organisation and job design (such as teamwork, autonomy, task discretion, mentoring, job rotation, applying new learning), as well as management practices (such as employee participation, incentive pay, training practices and flexibility in working hours). In Canada, 28% of firms employ some type of high-performance work practice on a weekly basis, which is just ahead of the OECD average (25%), but behind top performers Denmark (41%), Sweden (41%), and New Zealand (34%) (see Figure 3.23). The use of HPWP is more common among large firms than in SMEs and high-skill workers are more likely to be engaged in HPWP than less-skill workers (OECD, 2019[40]). Some sectors are more likely to employ HPWPs (see Figure 3.24). Over 35% of firms in information and communications, utilities and professional, scientific and technical services employ HPWP, while less than 20% of firms in primary industry (agriculture, forestry, fisheries) and transportation and storage do. Further, there is variation in the likelihood of employing HPWPs across firms in different provinces and territories (see Figure 3.25). Firms in the central and western provinces of Canada are more likely to participate in HPWPs on a weekly basis than those in the eastern provinces, which likely reflects differences in industry composition across provinces and territories. Looking specifically at literacy and reading skills across Canada, Ontario emerges as one of the provinces with the highest performance in literacy proficiency, after Yukon, Prince Edward Island and Nova Scotia. However, looking at the reading at work indicator, Yukon, Alberta, Nova Scotia, British Columbia, Saskatchewan and Northwest Territories show higher scores than Ontario.

Figure 3.22. Literacy proficiency and reading at work across Canada

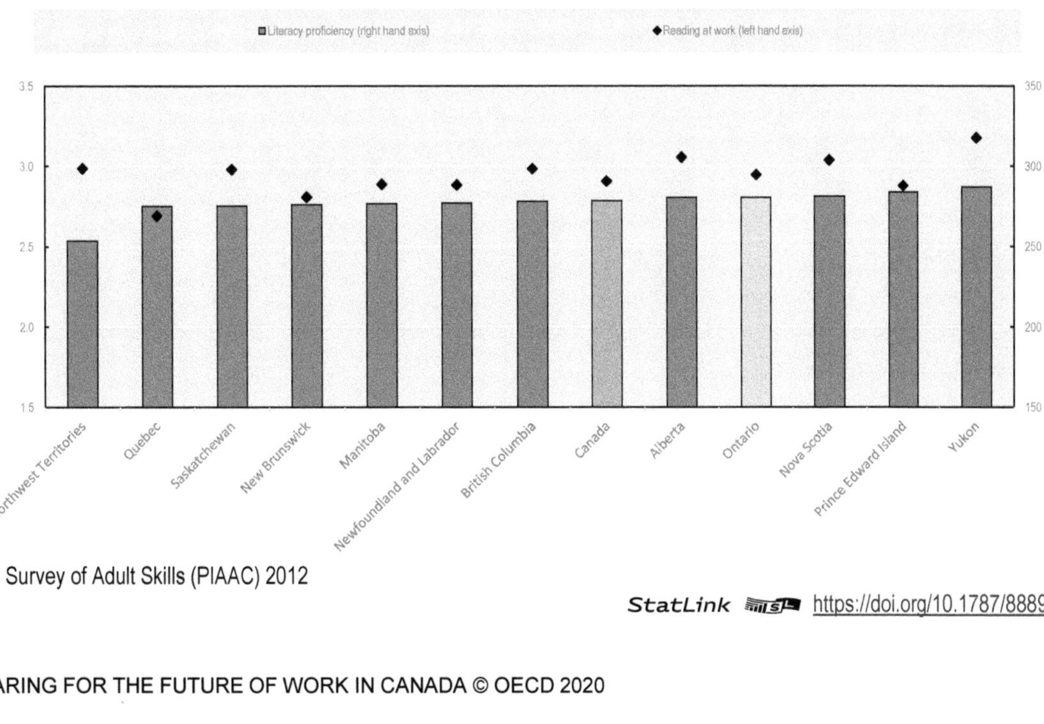

Source: Survey of Adult Skills (PIAAC) 2012

StatLink https://doi.org/10.1787/888934150139

Figure 3.23. More employers in Canada employ some type of HPWP than on average across the OECD, but less than best performing countries

Share of jobs that employ some type of HPWP on a weekly basis, 2012

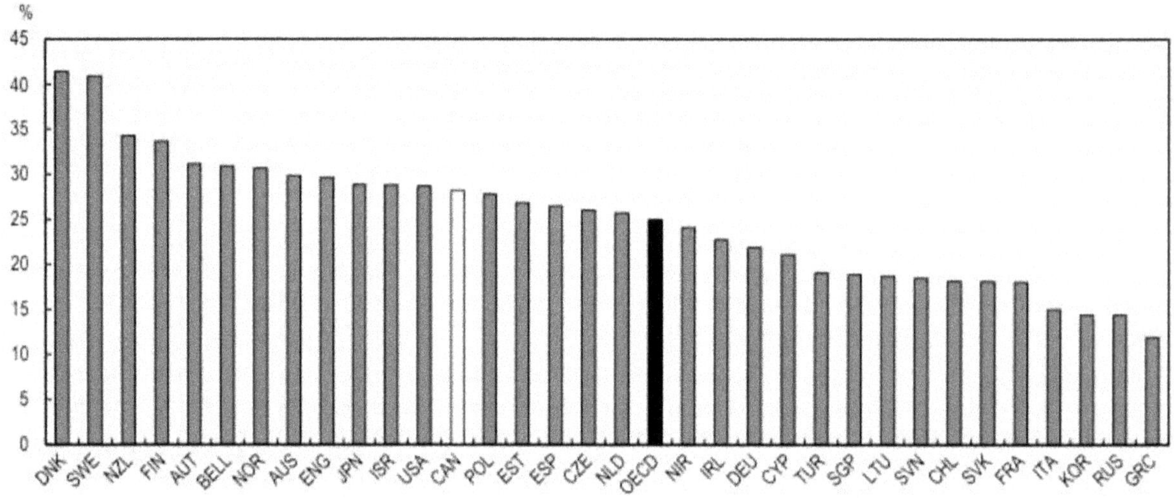

Source: OECD (2020[5]), Workforce Innovation to Foster Positive Learning Environments in Canada, Getting Skills Right, OECD Publishing, Paris, https://dx.doi.org/10.1787/a92cf94d-en.

Figure 3.24. The adoption of HPWP varies across sectors in Canada

Share of jobs that employ some type of HPWP on a weekly basis, 2012

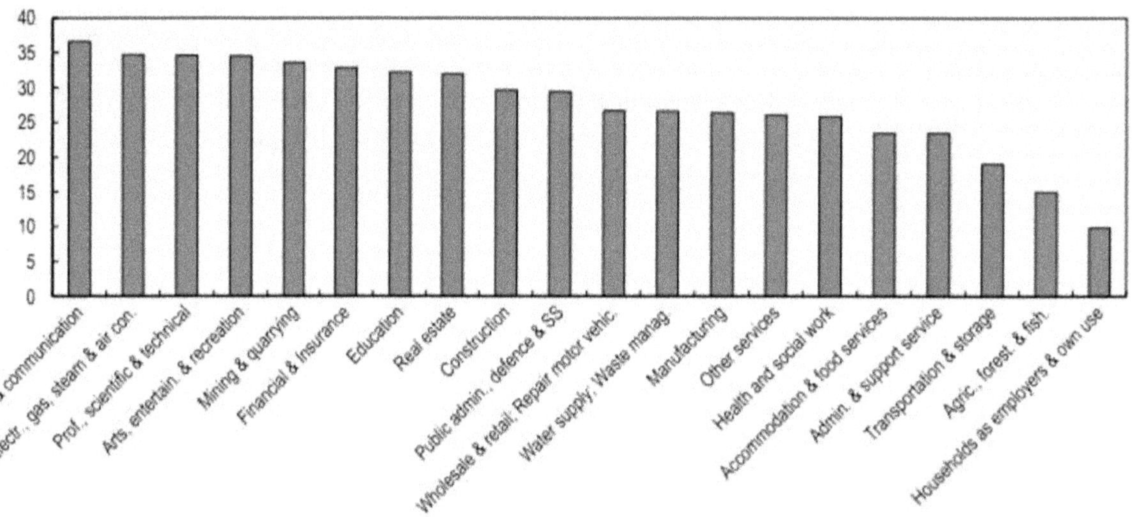

Source: OECD (2020[5]), Workforce Innovation to Foster Positive Learning Environments in Canada, Getting Skills Right, OECD Publishing, Paris, https://dx.doi.org/10.1787/a92cf94d-en.

Figure 3.25. The adoption of HPWP varies across provinces and territories in Canada

Share of jobs that employ some type of HPWP on a weekly basis, 2012

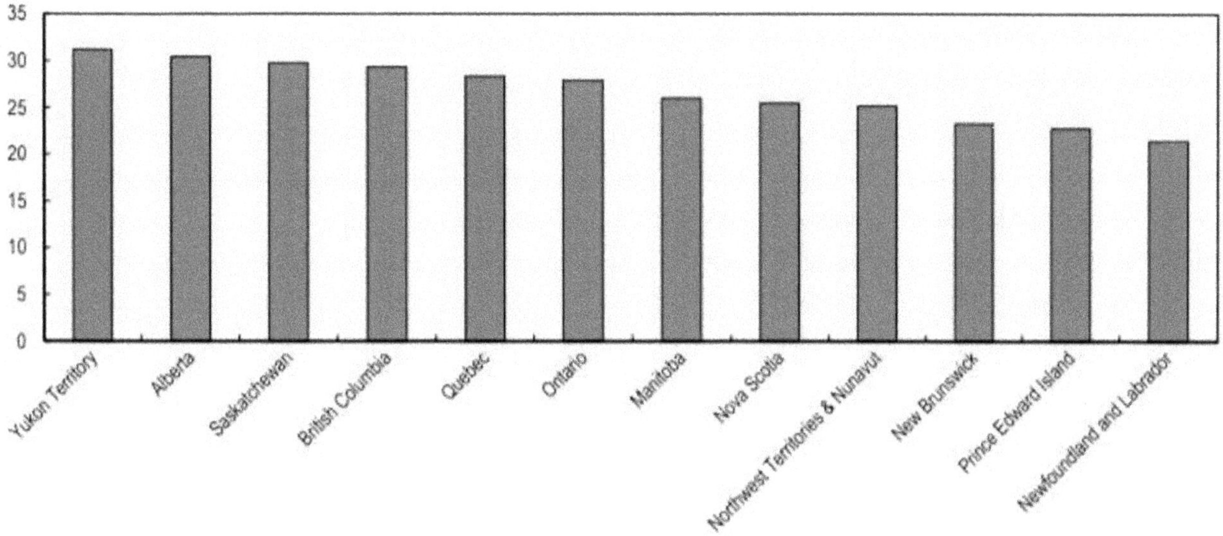

Source: OECD (2020[5]), Workforce Innovation to Foster Positive Learning Environments in Canada, Getting Skills Right, OECD Publishing, Paris, https://dx.doi.org/10.1787/a92cf94d-en.

Conclusion

Job polarisation has led to a hollowing-out of the employment share of middle-skill jobs in Canada as in most OECD countries. The share of middle-skill jobs has declined in all Canadian provinces, but this masks substantial differences within provinces. For example, in 5 out of 11 Ontario regions the relative importance of middle-skill jobs over total employment has increased over recent years. Dynamics in job polarisation partly reflect trends in the supply for skills across Canada. In Ontario, large urban centres attain higher levels of education than other regions. Polarisation takes place at a moment when labour shortages and skills mismatches are having a profound impact on labour markets across Canada. The ongoing COVID-19 pandemic is likely going to exacerbate labour and skills shortages going forward, and is making skills development and skills use crucially important. More employers than ever require workers to have digital skills. At the same time, workforce training and skills development, as well as a better use of skills in the workplace, represent an opportunity to make better use of the available workforce. The next chapter outlines examples of policies and programmes being implemented in Canada with a special focus on the Province of Ontario to prepare people, places and firms for the future of work.

Note

[1] In BII+E's *I, Human* report, "skills" is used as a catch-all for skills, abilities, knowledge, and other elements required for workers to be successful in a job.

References

Acemoglu, D., & Autor, D. (2010). *Skills, Tasks and Technologies: Implications for Employment and Earnings.* NBER Working Papers Series. Retrieved 02 20, 2020, from http://www.nber.org/papers/w16082

Adalet McGowan, M., & Andrews, D. (2017). Skills mismatch, productivity and policies: Evidence from the second wave of PIAAC. In *OECD Economics Department Working Papers.* OECD Publishing, Paris. doi:https://dx.doi.org/10.1787/65dab7c6-en

Autor, D., Katz, L., & Kearney, M. (2006). *The Polarization of the U.S. Labor Market.* National Bureau of Economic Research, Cambridge, MA. doi:10.3386/w11986

Autor, D., Levy, F., & Murnane, R. (2003). *The Skill Content of Recent Technological Change: an Empirical Exploration*.* Retrieved 02 20, 2020, from https://economics.mit.edu/files/11574

Bank of Canada. (2019). *Business Outlook Survey—Autumn 2019.* Retrieved 01 23, 2020, from https://www.bankofcanada.ca/2019/10/business-outlook-survey-autumn-2019/

Breemersch, K., Damijan, J., & Konings, J. (2017). Labour Market Polarization in Advanced Countries: Impact of Global Value Chains, Technology, Import Competition from China and Labour Market Institutions. In *OECD Social, Employment and Migration Working Papers.* OECD Publishing, Paris. doi:https://dx.doi.org/10.1787/06804863-en

Business Development Bank of Canada. (2018). *Labour Shortage in Canada: Here to stay.* Retrieved 02 21, 2020, from https://www.bdc.ca/en/documents/analysis_research/labour-shortage.pdf

Canadian Federation of Independent Business (CFIB). (2019). *Labour shortages are holding back the construction sector: Here's what governments and businesses can do.* Retrieved 03 12, 2020, from https://www.cfib-fcei.ca/en/media/labour-shortages-are-holding-back-construction-sector-heres-what-governments-and-businesses

Das, M., & Hilgenstock, B. (2018). *The Exposure to Routinization: Labor Market Implications for Developed and Developing Economies.* Retrieved 02 20, 2020, from https://www.imf.org/en/Publications/WP/Issues/2018/06/13/The-Exposure-to-Routinization-Labor-Market-Implications-for-Developed-and-Developing-45989

Froy, F., Giguère, S., & Meghnagi, M. (2012). *Skills for Competitiveness: A Synthesis Report.* OECD. Retrieved 07 11, 2019, from http://www.oecd.org/cfe/leed/skills%20for%20competitiveness%20synthesis%20final.pdf

Goos, M., & Manning, A. (2007). Lousy and Lovely Jobs: The Rising Polarization of Work in Britain. *Review of Economics and Statistics, 89*(1), 118-133. doi:10.1162/rest.89.1.118

Goos, M., Manning, A., & Salomons, A. (2009). Job Polarization in Europe. *American Economic Review, 99*(2), 58-63. doi:10.1257/aer.99.2.58

Government of Ontario. (2020). *Ontario Preparing People in London for Jobs.* Retrieved 02 26, 2020, from https://news.ontario.ca/mol/en/2020/01/ontario-preparing-people-in-london-for-jobs.html

Komarnicki, E. (2012). *Labout and Skills Shortages in Canada: Addressing Current and Future Challenges.* Report of the Standing Committee on Human Resources, Skills and Social Development and the Status of Persons with Disabilities. Retrieved 01 23, 2020, from http://publications.gc.ca

ManpowerGroup. (2018). *2018 Talent Shortage - Solving the Talent Shortage: Build, Buy, Borrow and Bridge.* Retrieved 08 01, 2019, from https://manpowergroup.ca/campaigns/manpowergroup/talent-shortage/pdf/canada-english-talent-shortage-report.pdf

Marcuse, P. (1989). 'Dual city': a muddy metaphor for a quartered city. *International Journal of Urban and Regional Research, 13*(4), 697-708. doi:10.1111/j.1468-2427.1989.tb00142.x

Matti, M. (2019). *Canada's skilled labour shortage: What does it mean and what can employers do about it?* Retrieved 03 12, 2020, from https://www.ctvnews.ca/canada/canada-s-skilled-labour-shortage-what-does-it-mean-for-workers-and-employers-1.4623996

May, B. (2019). *Labour Shortages and Solutions in the GTHA Construction Industry: Report of the Standing Committee on Human Resources, Skills and Social Development and the Status of Persons with Disabilities.* Retrieved 03 12, 2020, from https://www.ourcommons.ca/Content/Committee/421/HUMA/Reports/RP10492157/humarp17/humarp17-e.pdf

McKinsey & Company. (2020). *To emerge stronger from the COVID-19 crisis, companies should start reskilling their workforces now.* Retrieved 05 13, 2020, from https://www.mckinsey.com/business-functions/organization/our-insights/to-emerge-stronger-from-the-covid-19-crisis-companies-should-start-reskilling-their-workforces-now

Morneau Shepell and Business Council of Canada. (2018). *Navigating change 2018: Business Council Skills Survey.* Retrieved 10 07, 2019, from https://thebusinesscouncil.ca/wp-content/uploads/2018/04/Navigating-Change-2018-Skills-Survey-1.pdf

Nedelkoska, L., & Quintini, G. (2018). Automation, skills use and training. In *OECD Social, Employment and Migration Working Papers.* OECD Publishing, Paris, https://dx.doi.org/10.1787/2e2f4eea-en

OECD. (2014). Education at a Glance 2014: OECD Indicators, https://dx.doi.org/10.1787/eag-2014-en

OECD. (2016). Skills Matter: Further Results from the Survey of Adult Skills. In *OECD Skills Studies.* OECD Publishing, Paris. doi:https://dx.doi.org/10.1787/9789264258051-en

OECD. (2017). OECD Employment Outlook 2017. doi:https://dx.doi.org/10.1787/empl_outlook-2017-en

OECD. (2017). SME and Entrepreneurship Policy in Canada. In *OECD Studies on SMEs and Entrepreneurship.* OECD Publishing, Paris. doi:https://dx.doi.org/10.1787/9789264273467-en

OECD. (2018). *Good Jobs for All in a Changing World of Work: The OECD Jobs Strategy.* OECD Publishing, Paris. doi:https://dx.doi.org/10.1787/9789264308817-en

OECD. (2018). *Skills for Jobs.* Retrieved 10 03, 2019, from https://www.oecdskillsforjobsdatabase.org/data/Skills%20SfJ_PDF%20for%20WEBSITE%20final.pdf

OECD. (2018). *Skills for Jobs: Canada country note.* Retrieved 10 03, 2019, from https://www.oecdskillsforjobsdatabase.org/data/country_notes/Canada%20country%20note.pdf

OECD. (2019). Education at a Glance 2019: OECD Indicators, https://dx.doi.org/10.1787/f8d7880d-en

OECD. (2019). *Getting Skills Right: Engaging low-skilled adults in learning.* Retrieved 02 25, 2020, from http://www.oecd.org/employment/emp/engaging-low-skilled-adults-2019.pdf

OECD. (2019). Getting Skills Right: Future-Ready Adult Learning Systems. In *Getting Skills Right.* OECD Publishing, Paris. doi:https://dx.doi.org/10.1787/9789264311756-en

OECD. (2019). *Job polarisation and the work profile of the middle class.* OECD. Retrieved 07 08, 2019, from https://www.oecd.org/els/emp/Job-polarisation-and-the-work-profile-of-the-middle-class-Policy-brief-2019.pdf

OECD. (2019). OECD Employment Outlook 2019: The Future of Work. doi:https://dx.doi.org/10.1787/9ee00155-en

OECD. (2019). *Under Pressure: The Squeezed Middle Class.* OECD Publishing, Paris. doi:https://dx.doi.org/10.1787/689afed1-en

OECD. (2020). *From pandemic to recovery: Local employment and economic development .* Retrieved 05 12, 2020, from https://read.oecd-ilibrary.org/view/?ref=130_130810-m60ml0s4wf&title=From-pandemic-to-recovery-Local-employment-and-economic-development

OECD. (2020). Workforce Innovation to Foster Positive Learning Environments in Canada. In *Getting*

Skills Right. OECD Publishing, Paris. doi:https://dx.doi.org/10.1787/a92cf94d-en

OECD/ILO. (2017). *Better Use of Skills in the Workplace: Why It Matters for Productivity and Local Jobs.* OECD Publishing, Paris. doi:https://dx.doi.org/10.1787/9789264281394-en

Ontario Chamber of Commerce. (2017). *Talent in transition: Addressing the Skills Mismatch in Ontario.* Retrieved 10 03, 2019, from https://occ.ca/wp-content/uploads/Talent-in-Transition.pdf

Ontario Chamber of Commerce. (2019). *Ontario Economic Report 2019.* Ontario Chamber of Commerce. Retrieved 07 09, 2019, from https://occ.ca/wp-content/uploads/2019-Ontario-Economic-Report.pdf

Ontario Chamber of Commerce. (2019). *Unlocking Ontario's Economic Potential.* Retrieved 02 21, 2020, from http://occ.ca/wp-content/uploads/Unlocking-Ontarios-Economic-Potential.pdf

Salvatori, A., & Manfredi, T. (2019). Job polarisation and the middle class: New evidence on the changing relationship between skill levels and household income levels from 18 OECD countries. In *OECD Social, Employment and Migration Working Papers.* OECD Publishing, Paris. doi:https://dx.doi.org/10.1787/4bf722db-en

Sheldon, M. (2020). *'We need all hands on deck': Canadian farmers struggle with labour shortfall due to COVID-19.* Retrieved 05 13, 2020, from https://www.cbc.ca/news/canada/farm-labour-foreign-workers-covid-19-1.5535727

The Conference Board of Canada. (2013). *The Need to Make Skills Work: The Cost of Ontario's Skills Gap.* Retrieved 02 21, 2020, from https://www.conferenceboard.ca/e-library/abstract.aspx?did=5563

The London Free Press. (2020). *Begging for bodies: These are London's most in-demand jobs, trades.* Retrieved 02 26, 2020, from https://lfpress.com/news/local-news/begging-for-bodies-welders-and-machinists-among-londons-most-wanted-trades

Tunney, C. (2020). *Pandemic could affect food supplies, power grids, telecommunications, says government document.* Retrieved 05 13, 2020, from https://www.cbc.ca/news/politics/labour-shortages-emergency-food-power-1.5531583

Vu, V., Willoughby, R., & Lamb, C. (2019). *I, Human: Digital and soft skills in a new economy.* Retrieved 01 24, 2020, from https://brookfieldinstitute.ca/wp-content/uploads/I-Human-ONLINE-FA.pdf

worktrends.ca. (n.d.). *Labour Market Facts for the London Economic Region - Interactive Tool.* Retrieved 02 26, 2020, from https://www.worktrends.ca/categories/london-economic-region

Annex 3.A.

Annex Figure 3.A.1. Disparities in job polarisation are wide within some provinces

Changes in employment shares by skill level, 2011 to 2018

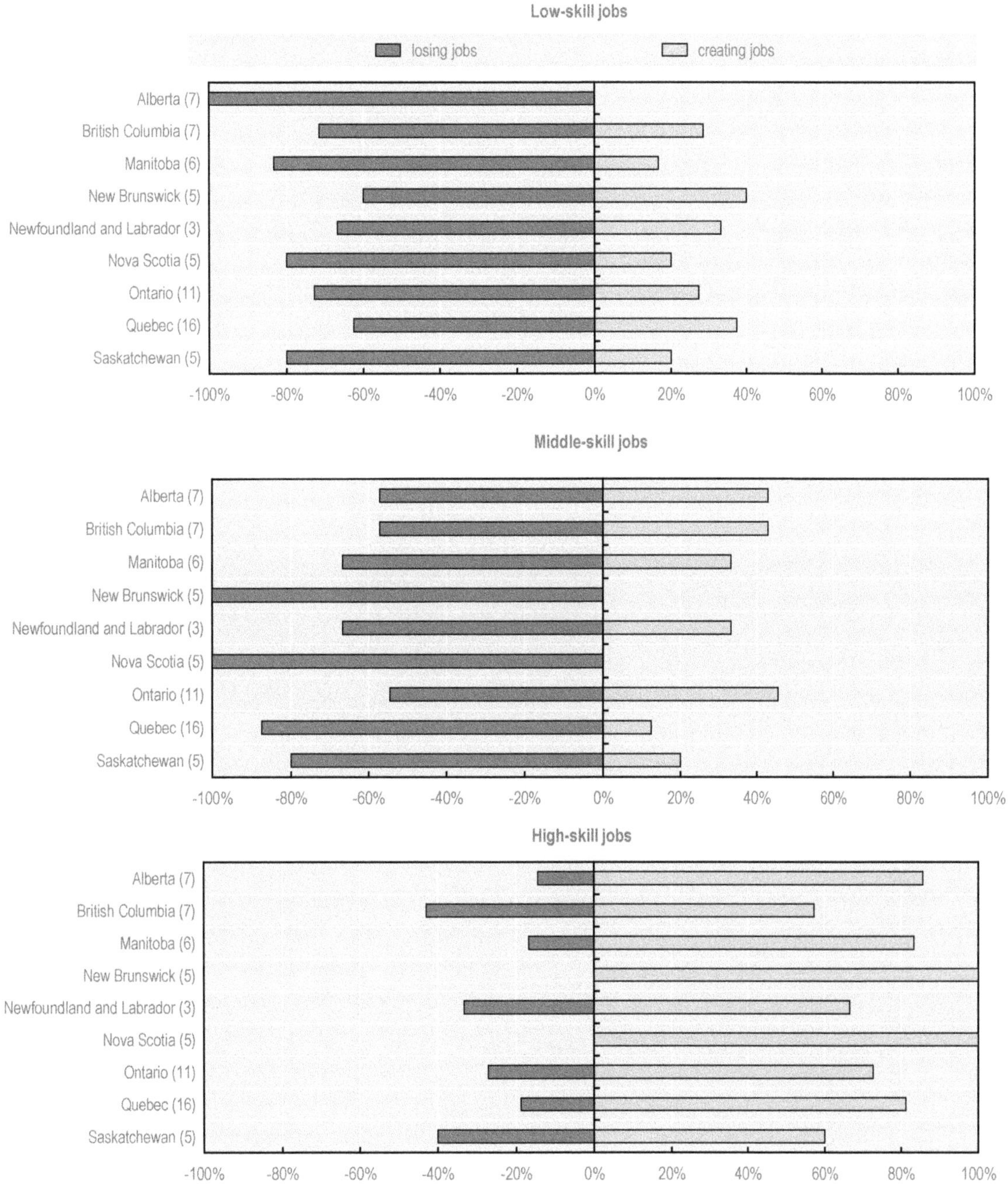

Notes: The number in parenthesis shows the number of regions in each province.
Source: OECD calculations based on Labour Force Surveys.

StatLink https://doi.org/10.1787/888934150158

4 Future-proofing people, places and firms in Canada

COVID-19 is having profound impacts on communities in Canada as around the world. Challenges associated with COVID-19 and the future of work will diverge by local economy, depending on the profile of the local labour market. This chapter provides a framework for understanding how current technological developments differ compared to previous waves. It also outlines examples of policies and programmes being implemented in Canada, with a special focus on the Province of Ontario, to prepare workers for the upturn, while addressing the specific challenges facing people, places and firms in keeping pace with the future of work.

In Brief

The different impacts of the future of work, likely exacerbated by COVID-19, require a people, places and firms-based policy response

- **COVID-19 is having profound impacts on communities across Canada**. The Government of Canada has put in place a series of measures aiming to provide income support to workers who have lost their job and segments of the population hit particularly hard by the pandemic.
- **The pandemic hits at a time when technology is re-shaping the way people live and work.** In the new wave of technological developments, machines are learning over time and accumulating knowledge. Automation is likely to replace tasks within jobs rather than entire jobs, enabling greater competition in the global skills market and creating demand for new skills.
- **COVID-19 and the future of work will affect people, places and firms differently**. Both federal, provincial and territorial governments in Canada are taking action. In 2019, the Government of Canada launched Future Skills to help ensure Canada's skills policies and programmes are "future fit". Future Skills aims to ensure jobseekers, workers and employers continue to have access to skills development programmes that meet their evolving needs and better position them for success into the future. This public policy will be critical in nudging people, places, and firms to think more critically of future employment and skills development opportunities.
- **The Province of Ontario has been at the forefront of designing innovative policy responses to help people, places, and firms make transitions**. Programmes such as Second Career and the Canada-Ontario Job Grant are providing skills training opportunities linked to growing and emerging sectors of the Canadian economy. These programmes will be even more crucial to help workers develop skills which could help them find jobs once the pandemic is over.
- **SMEs often struggle more than larger companies in accessing the skills they need and developing their workforce talent**. As SMEs account for substantial shares of employment across Canada and within the Province of Ontario, targeted strategies to ensure SMEs invest in preparing their workforce for future changes in the labour market are needed.

Introduction

COVID-19 is disrupting communities across Canada as in the whole world. This happens at a time when technology was already changing the way people live and work. This report has demonstrated that the impact of new technologies will vary by place depending on the occupational profile of the local labour market. As some people and firms will also be more affected by technological developments than others, the uneven impact of automation and digitalisation requires targeted policy responses. Sections 4.1 and 4.2 of this chapter provide a conceptual framework for analysing the impact of new technologies on jobs and skills in Canada. Sections 4.3 and 4.4 provide information on new actions that are being taken to prepare for the future of work at the federal and provincial level in Canada. Section 4.5 focuses on the needs of small and medium sized enterprises, which require more customised solutions to participate in workforce development programmes.

4.1. A changing world of work requires re-thinking traditional policy approaches

4.1.1. COVID-19 is posing unprecedented challenges to communities in Canada as around the world

COVID-19 is having a widespread impact across communities in Canada. While considered necessary for reducing the risk of spreading COVID-19, confinement measures are putting unprecedented pressure on local labour markets and economies. COVID-19 is causing dramatic losses in employment. Total employment declined by 10% in all Canadian provinces between February and April 2020, led by Quebec (-18.7%, or -821 000 jobs). Employment also dropped sharply from February to April in each of Canada's three largest census metropolitan area (CMAs). Montréal recorded the largest decline (-18.0%; -404 000), followed by Vancouver (-17.4%; -256 000) and Toronto (-15.2%; -539 000). COVID-19 is impacting vulnerable workers the most. In April, employment losses continued to be more rapid in jobs offering less security, including temporary and non-unionized jobs. Between February and April, the number of people aged 15 and older living in economic families (which includes people living alone) where no one is employed has increased by 23.5% (+1 655 000) (Statistics Canada, 2020). As of May, the gradual easing of COVID-19 restrictions has been accompanied by initial rebounds in employment. Employment rose by 290 000 (+1.8%), while the number of people who worked less than half their usual hours dropped by 292 000 (-8.6%). Combined, these changes in the labour market represented a recovery of 10.6% of the COVID-19-related employment losses and absences recorded in the previous two months (Statistics Canada, 2020).

4.1.2. COVID-19 is hitting at a time when new technological developments are changing the way people live and work

New technologies including automation have disrupted the existing order ever since the invention of the wheel. In modern history, the big disruption came from the industrial revolution in the mid-19th century but waves of disruption have followed every few decades ever since. Each wave of new technology altered the existing pattern of jobs and skills. Despite fears, technological innovations have always given rise to new jobs that provided employment, while the productivity growth from automation has been an important driver of rising living standards (OECD, 2018). However, automation has also posed challenges: the labour saving effect linked to automation can be sudden, whereas it might take considerable time until new jobs are created that replace the lost jobs. At the same time, the skill profiles of jobs lost to automation and the skill profiles of the jobs replacing them are not necessarily the same.

In the current wave of technological disruption, the concept of "smart" machines is rapidly changing what we produce and how we produce using technologies such as artificial intelligence (AI), self-learning machines (SLMs), algorithm-based technologies, and digital fabrication. This newer wave of technology is qualitatively different from previous generations of automation. Because these machines can "learn" over time they can acquire and accumulate knowledge to enhance their ability to make accurate decisions. Given the ability of this wave of technology to disrupt the existing order, policy needs to investigate ways to mitigate the adverse effects while taking advantage of the opportunities offered by these new technologies. Hosanagar (2019) argues that only a better, deeper, more nuanced understanding of algorithmic thinking can prepare us to meet the full challenge of these adaptive technologies, pointing out that algorithms function a lot like their programmers who are, after all, human.

4.1.3. Several other forces have affected people's lives over the past decades

These new technologies are emerging at a time when several other forces are shifting the context for people around the world. New technologies, together with globalisation and population ageing are having profound impacts on the type and quality of jobs available and the skillsets they require. The number of manufacturing jobs in advanced economies has decreased and an increasing number of the remaining jobs requires workers to have new skills. Meanwhile, new jobs have emerged that did not exist in the past, requiring new skills, such as data scientists, social media managers and web developers. Both technological change and globalisation have created new jobs, like big data managers, robot engineers, social media managers and drone operators – all occupations that did not exist a generation ago. In addition, entirely new jobs may be created in the future as a result of innovations, either to complement machine capabilities within existing occupational categories (e.g. new types of teachers who blend in-class and computer-based learning) or in entirely new fields (e.g. social media managers, internet of things architects, AI experts, user-experience (UX) designers, etc.) (OECD, 2019). Environmental degradation and environmental sustainability are also identified as trends that will profoundly shape the future of work, given the tight link between economic activity and the natural environment (International Labour Organization, 2018).

Much anxiety surrounds the future of work. Doomsday scenarios are unlikely to materialise, but there are some risks (OECD, 2019). In the absence of policy interventions, disruptive changes might lead to greater inequality, environmental unsustainability and the exclusion of certain groups of people, which would eventually threaten the prosperity that comes from economic growth. Shaping a future of work that is more inclusive and rewarding calls for a whole-of-government approach that targets interventions on those who need it most. Such a policy agenda would need to cover education and skills, public employment services and social protection, but also labour market regulation, taxation and even housing, transport, competition law and industrial policy (OECD, 2019).

While COVID-19 is likely to accelerate the speed of automation, it could lead to a slowdown of globalisation and a delocalisation of production and industry jobs. Disruptions in global supply chains and shortages in equipment or pharmaceuticals produced abroad have opened up new questions in the debate about the pros and cons of globalisation. Production activities could be re-shored, especially in relation to priority goods in health care. Shorter food production could be promoted. There are opportunities for local economies to diversify economic activity and restore middle-skill jobs, but this trend could also negatively affect local economies specialised in tradable goods (OECD, 2020).

4.2. Technological disruption, jobs and skills

Little is known about the shape and extent of the impacts of new technologies on people's work, which limits the scope for predictions. Notwithstanding such uncertainty, some trends have emerged already that can guide policy responses for the future. In this context, COVID-19 is likely to accelerate the adoption of technologies in the workplace. To reduce their exposure to any potential future social distancing and confinement measures, more firms could decide to invest in technology to automate the production of goods and services. In addition, the adoption of automation in the workplace tends to accelerate in times of economic crises, as firms replace workers performing routine tasks with a mix of technology and better-skilled workers.

4.2.1. New technologies are more likely to replace tasks within jobs than entire jobs

A process of creative destruction is under way, whereby certain tasks are either taken over by new technologies or offshored, and other, new ones, are created (OECD, 2019). Automation is often portrayed as an intelligent robot that would replace a given job in its entirety, with the idea of a driverless car as the best example of such fear. An entire job, the driver, would be replaced by technology that would allow a car to drive from point A to point B without the help of a human driver. In reality, this scenario in which a current job done by a human being is taken over by a robot is likely to be the exception, not the rule. In the case of the vast majority of jobs, technology is likely to automate a few tasks or several tasks but not all the tasks.

These trends make promoting effective adult education and training a much needed policy intervention to provide workers with re-skilling and up-skilling opportunities (OECD, 2019). He and Guo (2018) simulate the application of automation to the financial sector in China to conclude that while 23% of jobs in this sector would be cut or modified, the remaining 77% of jobs would be enhanced in their efficiency through the use of these technologies. Bughin (2018) supports this assessment of the effect of automation by pointing out that the trend in reduction of labour/output ratio, around 1% per annum, has not changed in recent years and is unlikely to change between now and 2030.

Workers affected by technology need to be helped to move quickly to new jobs through effective and timely employment services, as well as prevention and early intervention measures. Adequate income support tied to incentives and support for active job search is also critical in reducing the individual and social costs of these adjustment processes, and can play a stabilising role in the current context of uncertainties about the future of work. Tackling gaps in income support, which typically serves as the main gateway to labour market reintegration measures, may require extending support for jobseekers with intermittent, low-paid or independent employment (OECD, 2019).

Automation's impact on jobs can be considered in several steps. First, automation will lead to a redefinition of tasks and jobs. The second step is to consider the skills needed for the tasks and whether these skills could be supplied by imparting training to the job incumbent or if there is a need to hire new employees. This describes a job-centric approach to considering automation's impact and the related policy response. A complementary approach is to focus on the worker as opposed to the job. A worker-centric analysis would factor in both the extent of automation disruption as well as the current skills, education and ability of the worker to adapt to the demands of the new technology.

4.2.2. Automation will have an impact across the skill spectrum, although some jobs will be more affected than others

Over the last two decades, employment in manufacturing has decreased by 20% across the OECD, while employment in services has grown by 27%. Labour markets have become more polarised, with increasing shares of low-skill and high-skill jobs, while middle-skill jobs have been hollowed out. Skill-biased technological change has been the main driver behind these trends. While manufacturing is considered a sector at high risk, so are many service sectors. Health, education and the public sector may face lower risks of facing disruption due to automation, but they typically employ many people across the OECD. Changes are likely to affect many workers (OECD, 2019).

It is therefore expected that the impact of automation would be felt across the entire spectrum of jobs ranging from low-skill to the highest-skill jobs. Every job and worker would need to adapt to these technologies to some extent. For jobs that have a relatively small share of tasks at risk of automation, some training on how to incorporate those technologies into their current jobs would be needed. While the need for such training, either formal or non-formal, would be felt all across the skill spectrum, the amount of training needed would vary based on workers' skills. Low-skill workers would particularly benefit from increased access to training, as occupations requiring no specific skills and training have the highest risk of being automated. However, they typically face more challenges than higher-skilled workers in accessing training, also due to the nature of their employment.

For occupations where the share of tasks threatened by automation is in the mid-range, some jobs would need to be combined to form new job descriptions. Workers in these occupations will need to be re-deployed across locations and possibly, employers and industries. The number of jobs and people in this category can be expected to be smaller than the first category. Lastly, the share of tasks affected by automation would be large, in some jobs that would be mostly low-to-middle-skill in nature. These jobs could be gradually eliminated and the people in it would need an exit strategy from their existing job.

Figure 4.1. A model of jobs disruption and policy responses

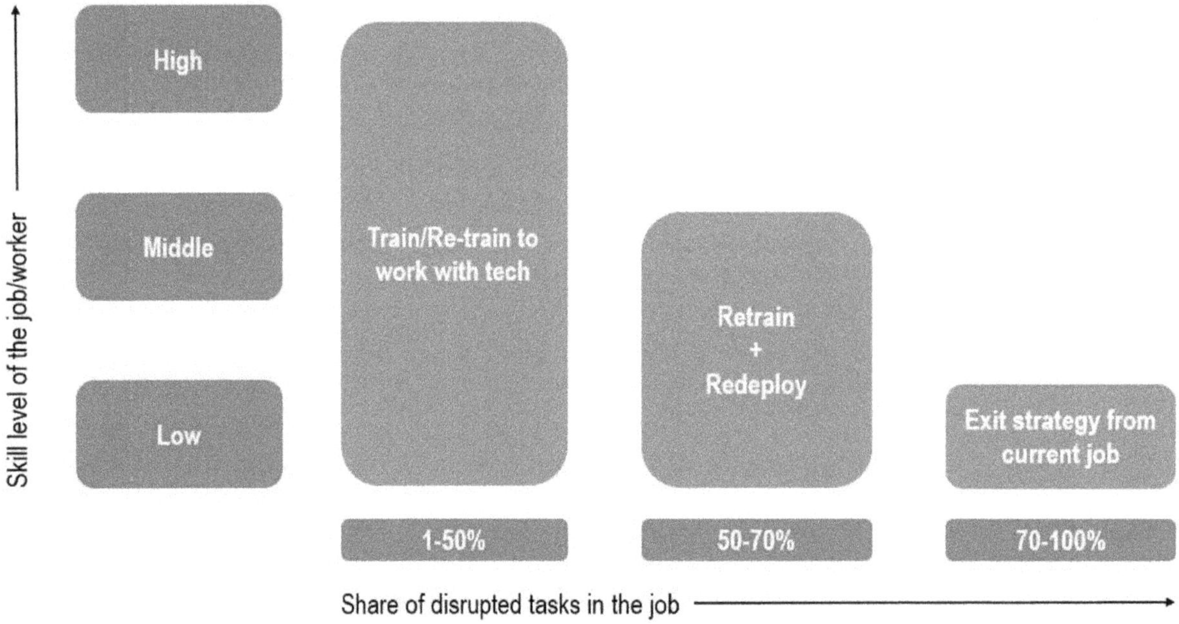

Note: The figure presents a simplified illustration based on the authors' elaboration and model.
Source: Authors' elaboration.

4.2.3. COVID-19 and new technologies make adult education and training even more relevant

Maintaining the skills acquired in youth will not be sufficient for workers to adapt to labour market developments linked to COVID-19 and the future of work. Instead, workers will need to acquire and develop skills in demand in the labour market that will allow them to transition to new tasks throughout their working lives. Career transitions, especially when they occur in mid- or late-career, are often far from being smooth. Technological development has also led to increased competition between workers around the world. Online labour platforms enable firms to call on workers elsewhere with a variety of skill levels, possibly at the expense of investing in the skills of their employees (OECD, 2019). Sending radiology scans overseas for a detailed analysis and report, is a good example of this effect of new technology. These trends suggest that more repetitive tasks performed by higher skill professionals and technicians can also be disrupted by newer forms of automation.

In a labour market disrupted by COVID-19, new technologies and global integration, among other measures, it is important to increase investment in people's capabilities. This approach goes beyond simply investing more in human capital to a broader concept of meaningful and inclusive development that leaves no one behind. Investments in lifelong learning would enable people to acquire skills, re-skill and up-skill, many times over the life course. Action on the adult learning front is a priority, as in view of the scope and speed of changes taking place, marginal adjustments are unlikely to be sufficient, and a substantial overhaul of adult learning policies is needed to make adult learning systems future-ready for all (OECD, 2019). It should also be recognised that some people might not wish to continue learning and policy and programme responses should therefore consider how different kinds of barriers, including resistance and disinterest, may be addressed.

A recent study identifies individual and firm level factors that hinder career transitions (Lamb, Vu, & Huynh, 2019). At the individual level, health, age, gender, financial resources, geography, unemployment spells and "mindset" are factors that can hinder or facilitate transitions. At the firm level, educational credentials, social and cultural capital are relevant factors in determining success in career transitions. The study examined career transitions in two clusters where jobs have declined in recent years: clerks from the financial services sector and motor vehicle technicians. It found that in the case of clerks from banks and insurance companies, over 90% of their knowledge and skills made them eligible to bid for jobs in three areas where jobs have been growing: financial sales, human resources and executive assistants. In the case of motor vehicle technicians, whose numbers have been declining, 84-87% of their knowledge and skills fit with technicians in mechanical engineering and electrical engineering, where jobs have been growing. Therefore, while pathways are feasible this information regarding knowledge and skills overlap need to be studied, developed and disseminated to employers and jobseekers alike. These are the areas where new policies and programmes can help smoothen career transitions that are likely to become increasingly necessary.

4.2.4. Technological disruption requires local partnerships for adult education and training

The costs of skill formation in the wake of automation disruption can vary based on the extent of disruption. At the low end, on-the-job training for people whose jobs are likely to experience minimal change can be delivered relatively inexpensively. However, skill development costs rise rapidly when the required response entails re-training and re-deployment, and it is much higher if people return to school later in life. Much of the accumulated evidence on automation to date suggests that the need for skill development across the entire economy will become increasingly acute. Given that disruption is likely to affect workers in some occupations and sectors more than others, and these not equally distributed within countries, skills development policies need to be responsive to place-specific characteristics and challenges.

Adult education and training entails a partnership among three parties: governments, employers and individuals. Two fundamental questions need to be answered before any investment can be made: who decides who will receive a certain level of skill development and who will pay for it? The sharing of this decision and the related costs vary over the life course. Governments assume a large portion of costs of early and higher education as well as the costs of education later in life.

Governments in Canada spend significantly on skills development but it is unlikely that they would increase their spending many-fold from current levels. Spending on education tends to be front-loaded, being concentrated on childhood, adolescence and young adulthood. Adult learning in the Canadian system occurs in a number of ways including training on-the-job, formal classroom training, retraining as also returning to school to enhance one's qualifications or to change one's skill sets to enter new career paths. A relevant policy issue in this context is to find ways to increase investment in skill development. Each party to this decision faces some constraints but also some creative ways to lever each other's investments to increase the overall investment. While individual (and family) spending on skills development has gone up considerably in recent decades, individuals often lack information about their options in a fast-changing market for skills. Employers are generally adverse to investment in training unless they have some assurance that they can capture the returns to training. As the Canadian labour market is a relatively flexible market in which talent moves freely across regions, industries and employers, employers are not keen to spend on development of generic skills.

Effective adult education and training requires adequate financing, including incentives for both individuals and employers. Training subsidies, tax incentives and loans, as well as paid training leaves and individual training accounts, can be instrumental in incentivising individuals to contribute to the financing of adult learning. Even small, incremental investments by governments and employers can provide better labour market information and counsel to the individual who, in turn, would be willing to increase their investment in developing their skill sets. Many firms, and especially SMEs, face challenges to financing training, which may lead to under-investments. Two typical types of financial incentives for employers widespread across OECD countries are subsidies and tax incentives: the former include subsidies for workplace training of employees and subsidies to take on and train the unemployed, while the latter include reductions/exemptions in social security contributions. In addition to the training costs, firms face indirect expenses such as continued wage payments during training periods. Some OECD countries have put in place job rotation schemes to help firms find a temporary replacement worker (usually an unemployed person) during the training period to tackle challenges related to foregone productivity during worker absence for training purposes (OECD, 2019).

Box 4.1. Towards a local approach to the future of work: Lesson from Southampton, United Kingdom (UK)

The city of Southampton in the UK recently carried out an extensive inquiry on the future of work in the city. It considered the potential impact of artificial intelligence, robotics and other digital technologies on the Southampton economy, identifying good practices being implemented elsewhere and policies to potentially introduce in the city. Building on the inquiry, the City Council has designed an action plan, to ensure the city and its residents stay ahead of the curve in the digital age.

The inquiry, led by a panel comprised of elected officials, was held between September 2018 and March 2019, to consider how the city could maximise the opportunities created by artificial intelligence (AI), automation and technological changes. At the same time, it aimed to identify and mitigate potential disruption to the local economy, particularly for workers in sectors that are most likely to see the greatest increase in the level of use of AI, automation and technological advancement.

As part of the inquiry, advice and insights from experts as well as local practitioners in other cities were gathered. These were undertaken alongside extensive analysis conducted by a dedicated team at the council to develop a robust business case to shape the city's future growth. The inquiry identifies the ingredients available in the city and potentially allowing the tech sector to grow and become more vibrant, and institutions and partnerships that could help advance the city's objectives. A resulting action plan identifies main actions the city plans to undertake in response to the inquiry on the future of work. These include for example the development of a city-wide skills strategy and the update of education curricula to enrich the offer of digital skills, as well as the analysis of the current skills offer of education providers in the city. As part of the strategy, the city also plans to map existing platforms facilitating lifelong learning across Southampton and find ways to improve access, improve rates of progression and increase job outcomes.

Source: Southampton City Council (Getting Southampton ready for the AI revolution, 2019), Getting Southampton ready for the AI revolution, https://www.southampton.gov.uk/news/article.aspx?id=tcm:63-418034 (accessed on 3 February 2020); Southampton City Council (2019), Executive response to the Future of Work in Southampton Inquiry.

4.2.5. Automation creates significant demand for new skills

Lastly, automation is creating demand for some skills and thus creating new jobs even as it disrupts the existing ones (OECD, 2019). Automation's threat is accompanied by new opportunities that need to be harnessed to create prosperity. Jobs requiring new skills such as big data management, robot engineering and drone operation did not exist a generation ago. Appropriate policy response to the introduction of automation needs to consider how those new skills would be made available to workplaces. Workplaces can also be themselves the generators of new skills, as workers innovate on the job and build new skillset. Specific skills could also be taught on the job and integrated into training programmes.

One important issue pertinent to this assumption is a discussion about the rate at which automation would create demand for new skills and jobs. Notably, the period of automation in agriculture, from the 1880s to the 1920s, saw rapid growth in demand for labour in factories to manufacture cars and other consumer items. During the current round of automation in the last two decades, although the global economy and the number of jobs have grown, automation by itself does not appear to have created enough demand for skilled jobs to compensate for the well-paid skilled jobs that it replaced, resulting in stagnation in employment and wages (Acemoglu & Restrepo, 2019). Acemoglu and Restrepo (Acemoglu & Restrepo, 2019) argue that it is necessary to acknowledge that the type of automation adopted would determine if skilled and better-paid jobs would be created in the coming rounds of automation.

While some types of automation would not result in big increases in productivity, other types of automation could spur productivity growth and lead to growing demand for skilled labour. Many new technologies do not increase labour productivity, but are explicitly aimed at replacing it by substituting cheaper capital (machines) in a range of tasks performed by humans. Historically, as automation technologies were being introduced, other technological advances simultaneously enabled the creation of new tasks in which labour had a competitive advantage. This generated new activities in which human labour could be reinstated into the production process and contributed to productivity growth as new tasks improved the division of labour. The episode of agricultural mechanisation, which started in the second half of the 19th century, vividly illustrates this pattern (Acemoglu & Restrepo, 2019). Looking at the United Kingdom during the industrial revolution in the second half of the 18th century, labour-saving innovations raised profitability of other inputs and therefore the demand for workers producing them. The burgeoning wealth of those profiting from these innovations increased demand for new products and services in a range of sectors, such as more solicitors, accountants, engineers, tailors, gardeners, which created more jobs. In the current wave of automation however there is uncertainty around whether similar dynamics will emerge (Banerjee & Duflo, 2019).

Among other things, meeting the challenge of rapidly developing skills needed to create, adopt and manage these technologies, means that a more agile response from skills development institutions is necessary (OECD, 2019). Colleges and universities or private training providers could shorten the lead time needed to design and offer new courses, while employers bear some of the effort. Funders of these activities such governments and the private sector need a more agile ability to assess quickly what the market needs and how best to mobilize resources, both financial and human, to meet those demands. Any complacency in this regard is likely to result in missed opportunities for creating prosperity. The world today is far more connected and competitive. If the need for new skills is not addressed properly, those opportunities will be grabbed by others, forcing the laggards to the second-tier of progress and prosperity.

4.3. Preparing Canadians for a changing labour market

4.3.1. Both federal and provincial governments are providing support to families and workers during the COVID-19 crisis

The Government of Canada is taking action to support Canadians and businesses facing hardship as a result of the global COVID-19 outbreak. For example, the Canada Emergency Response Benefit (CERB) provides temporary income support for workers who have stopped working or are earning less than CAD 1 000 in a month due to COVID-19. It grants a payment of CAD 2 000 for a 4-week period for up to 16 weeks. The Canada Emergency Wage Subsidy (CEWS) on the other hand targets employers, providing a 75% wage subsidy to eligible employers for up to 12 weeks, retroactive to March 15, 2020, as a result of COVID-19. Temporary financial support is also being provided for post-secondary students and graduating high-school students (Government of Canada, 2020). Box 4.2 provides an overview of the measures by taken by the federal government in Canada to respond to COVID-19.

Provincial governments are complementing federal efforts, also by focusing on skills development. For example, Ontario has taken steps to support people and families by planning to invest CAD 3.7 billion in support of people and jobs. Measures include among others 200 million in new funding to provide temporary emergency supports for people in financial need and funding to municipalities and other service providers to respond to local needs (e.g. food banks, homeless shelters, churches and emergency services); committing CAD 100 million in funding through Employment Ontario for skills training programmes for workers affected by the COVID-19 outbreak; working with the federal government to find ways to support apprentices and enable businesses to continue to retain these skilled trades workers during the COVID-19 outbreak (Government of Ontario, 2020).

Box 4.2. Federal responses to COVID-19 in Canada

Measures adopted by the Government of Canada to respond to the pandemic crisis include policies and programmes in support of individuals, businesses and specific sectors. Examples of measures targeting individuals include:

- Individuals and families: providing temporary wage top-up for low-income essential workers, increasing the Canada Child Benefit, providing extra time to file income tax returns and delaying mortgage payment;
- People facing loss of income: Canada Emergency Response Benefit (CERB);
- Indigenous people: supporting immediate needs in Indigenous communities, Indigenous communities public health needs and post-secondary students;
- People who need it the most: improving access to essential food support, supporting people experiencing homelessness and women and children fleeing violence, delivering essential services to those in need;
- Seniors: including through support to the delivery of items and personal outreach and providing essential services to seniors;
- Youth, post-secondary students and recent graduates: Canada Emergency Student Benefit (CESB), expanding existing federal employment and skills development programmes, including the Youth Employment and Skills Strategy and Student Work Placements programmes, as well as new temporary flexibilities for the Canada Summer Jobs program to allow employers to support up to 70 000 job placements for youth in 2020-21.

A range of programmes have been adopted to support business and workers, including:

- Avoiding layoffs and rehiring employees: implementing the Canada Emergency Wage Subsidy (CEWS), and a temporary 75% wage subsidy for up to 24 weeks;
- Access to credit: among others, by establishing a Business Credit Availability Program (BCAP) to provide additional support through the Business Development Bank of Canada (BDC) and Export Development Canada (EDC);
- Creating new jobs and opportunities for youth: as mentioned above, as part of the supports for youth, students and recent graduates, the Government of Canada announced an additional CAD 153.7 million in funding for the Youth Employment and Skills Strategy to create over 6 000 job placements and supports for youth in high-demand sectors such as agriculture, technology, health and essential services, as part of its response to address the economic impacts of COVID-19 on student and youth employment;
- Taxes and tariffs: providing more time to pay income taxes;
- Support for workers not covered or eligible for Employment Insurance: Canada Emergency Response Benefit (CERB);
- Indigenous businesses: allocating funding for Indigenous SMEs and Financial Institutions;
- Supporting financial stability: for example through the Bank of Canada's actions and by launching an Insured Mortgage Purchase Program.

Finally, the Government of Canada has also taken measures in support of sectors particularly affected by the crisis. These measures generally aim at protecting workers, ensuring the continuity of supply chains and waiving payments. Interested sectors include agriculture, agri-food, aquaculture and fisheries; culture, heritage and sport sectors; air transportation; tourism; and energy.

Source: Government of Canada (Canada's COVID-19 Economic Response Plan , 2020), *Canada's COVID-19 Economic Response Plan*, https://www.canada.ca/en/department-finance/economic-response-plan.html#businesses (accessed on 14 May 2020).

4.3.2. More action is being taken at the federal level to prepare for the future of work

In the area of labour market policy, Employment and Social Development Canada (ESDC) manages a number of programmes and services that are designed to help people prepare for work. Prominent examples include loans/grants for students and apprentices as well as Indigenous programs, and youth/student/WIL initiatives. ESDC also administers the Employment Insurance programme, which is a national programme, funded through employer and employee contributions, that offers temporary financial assistance to qualified workers who have lost their job (OECD, 2014). In terms of activation policies, the centrepiece of the federal government's policies and programmes is covered through the Labour Market Development Agreements (LMDAs) and Workforce Development Agreements (WDAs), which are bilateral agreements negotiated with the Provinces and Territories.

Each year, the Government of Canada invests over CAD 2 billion through the Labour Market Development Agreements and about CAD 1 billion through the Workforce Development Agreements, for a combined investment of around CAD 3 billion a year. The former are geared towards training and employment assistance for individuals who qualify for Employment Insurance. The relatively new Workforce Development Agreements seek to help individuals who are further removed from the labour market, unemployed, underemployed, and seeking to up-skill to either find a good job or reorient their career. This agreement would include funding for skills training for individuals who are generally not qualified for Employment Insurance.

Outside of these agreements, ESDC runs a number of programmes aimed at skills development in general, with some specialised programmes aimed at targeted population segments, such as Indigenous People, immigrants, persons with disabilities and older workers (OECD, 2014) (OECD, 2018). While the development of employment and skills policies takes place at both the federal and provincial level in Canada, the federal government has introduced a number of programmes designed to respond to the future of work. For example, Future Skills is part of the Government's plan to ensure that skills development policies and programmes are prepared to meet changing needs. The Canadian Government is investing CAD 225 million over four years, starting in 2018, and CAD 75 million per year thereafter, to:

- examine major trends that will have an impact on national and regional economies and workers;
- identify emerging skills that are in demand now and into the future;
- develop, test and evaluate new approaches to skills development; and
- share results and best practices across public, private and not-for-profit sectors to support broader use of innovative approaches across Canada.

As part of Future Skills, the Future Skills Council provides advice to the Minister of Employment, Workforce Development and Disability Inclusion on emerging skills and workforce trends. The Council identifies and promotes priorities for action of pan-Canadian significance relating to skills development and training. The council plays a role in mobilising action across sectors on the issues of pan-Canadian significance they identify. Future Skills also includes the Future Skills Centre, which is an independent innovation and applied research centre that has been set-up to develop, test and measure new approaches to skills development. Future Skills places a focus on addressing the needs of disadvantaged groups, such as Indigenous People, persons with disabilities, workers with low income, immigrants and youth (see Box 4.3) notably by applying a gender-based analysis plus (GBA+) approach recognising that different approaches are needed to meet the needs of a diverse population geographically and demographically. Future Skills places a strong emphasis on ensuring the evidence produced by the Centre and the Council is widely disseminated.

Box 4.3. Testing local approaches through the Future Skills Centre in Canada

The Future Skills Centre is investing in local community-based projects that are testing innovative approaches to skills across Canada. Currently, there are 46 innovation projects and 4 strategic initiatives that have been funded. Sixteen of these projects are operational. In addition, the Centre is launching a new call for innovation proposals in response to the COVID crisis. Each project will be evaluated using tools and approaches aligned to their unique goals and local context but using a unique evaluation framework to ensure consistency and reliability of the Future Skills Centre's project findings. Some examples of innovative projects that have been funded include:

- *Up-skilling displaced workers in Kitchener and Toronto*: Mold-making and injection-molding companies in the Kitchener-Waterloo and Greater Toronto Areas report a severe shortage of experienced, skilled workers to fill job vacancies. The Work-Based Learning Consortium (WBLC) is partnering with Canadian Association of Mold Makers to explore how to up-skill displaced workers, providing them with the training required to fill vacancies in the mold-making trade and injection-molding occupations in the Greater Toronto Area (including Oshawa) and the Kitchener-Waterloo areas. The Future Skills Centre is investing CAD 873 300 in this 20-month project. The programme will evaluate the effectiveness of a model to help transition 24 mid-career workers into new careers. The model is a worked-based learning competency-based and circumvents traditional CV and qualification-based recruitment approaches and has proven successful in other population groups. The project will take place in two stages: 1) Competencies for the target job will be mapped, candidates who have been displaced (or are at risk of being displaced) will be identified and referred for interviews; and 2) successful candidates will go through digitally-delivered classroom learning to acquire the basic theoretical knowledge and on-the-job training to obtain an industry-recognised credential.
- *Dementia training for mid-career workers in London*: Personal Support Workers (PSWs) are a vulnerable group of health care providers – they are mostly female, over the age of 40, mid-career, and often with English as a second language. Many PSWs have transitioned from other careers and have multiple jobs. Few have received adequate dementia skills development training. Researchers at Western University's Sam Katz Community Health and Ageing Research Unit developed 'Be EPIC', a two-day dementia-specific skill development program. The training programme teaches PSWs to use person-centred communication, incorporate social history of clients into care routines, and use the environment when caring for people living with dementia. The Future Skills Centre will invest CAD 418 717 over two years to test, and evaluate the effectiveness of the Be EPIC training programme in different context. Be EPIC will engage 48 participants in an urban setting (London, Ontario) and a rural setting (Northumberland County, Ontario). By leveraging virtual reality technology, the programme allows PSWs who are culturally and linguistically diverse to gain the skills necessary to relate to people living with dementia and provide quality care.
- *Digital competencies project*: Due to rapidly shifting digital skills needs, a mismatch exists between the skills of many post-secondary graduates and the technical skills required by employers. These digital skills often include a combination of innovation, entrepreneurship, an understanding of the technology adoption processes, and soft skills, including communications, creativity, and adaptability. The Future Skills Centre will invest CAD 1.24 million in a two-year project led by the Information Technology Association of Canada (ITAC), which explores new approaches to defining digital competencies and creating new pathway opportunities into digital roles for non-STEM graduates, internationally-educated professionals, and high-potential workers without traditional credentials. This subsidised project delivers skills training in a heavily-blended approach for digital and professional competencies. ITAC, along with member

companies and partners, will work to define a set of in-demand, innovative digital competencies. Using this knowledge, the curriculum will be developed and tested for alternative pathways into digital roles. Rigorous skills testing and aptitude assessments will be a key component of this project. This project will target 370 job seekers and employers in Ontario, Alberta, British Columbia, and Nova Scotia.

Source: Examples summarised from Future Skills Centre (Innovation Projects, 2020), *Innovation Projects*, https://fsc-ccf.ca/innovation-projects/.

4.3.3. Actions are also being taken to provide support to individuals making labour market transitions

Individual learning schemes are training schemes attached to individuals (rather than to a specific employer or employment status), which are at their disposal to undertake continuous training along their working lives and at their own initiative. The goal of these schemes is to boost individual choice and responsibility concerning training. A characteristic of such schemes that has made them attractive, given the current changes and disruption in the labour market, is their ability to make training rights "portable" from one job or employment status to the other, thereby linking trainings to individuals rather than to jobs. The OECD has recently undertaken a review of the existing individual learning schemes, developing recommendations on how such schemes should be developed to ensure they are effective (see Box 4.4).

Box 4.4. Designing effective Individual Learning Schemes

A rise in non-standard work across the OECD and an increased fragmentation of worker careers have generated new challenges for training policies, at a time when structural changes are increasing the need for re- and up-skilling. Policy makers are searching for new solutions to the challenges related to the future of work, and individual learning schemes have received renewed attention. Individual learning schemes can take different forms, consisting for example of individual saving accounts for training (where the individual can accumulate resources for further training), individual learning accounts (where rights for training are accumulated over a certain period of time) or voucher schemes (supporting training through direct governmental payment to individuals). The OECD has articulated some principles that should guide the development and design of individual learning schemes, to ensure they attain the desired targets. These include:

- Targeting individual learning schemes could help improve participation of low-skill workers.
- Funding should be substantial if the scheme is expected to make a significant difference to training outcomes.
- Individual learning schemes should be kept simple in order to maximise participation.
- Individual learning schemes need to be accompanied by other measures to boost participation among under-represented groups.
- Guaranteeing training quality becomes even more important in the case of individual learning schemes; and
- The way individual learnings schemes are financed has important implications for redistribution and the predictability of funding.

Source: (OECD, 2019), Individual Learning Accounts: Panacea or Pandora's Box?, OECD Publishing, Paris, https://doi.org/10.1787/203b21a8-en.

The Government of Canada has recently announced the Canada Training Benefit (CTB), a programme aiming to help workers re-skill and up-skill in a changing world of work. The CTB would give workers a refundable tax credit on their income tax and benefit return to help offset tuition costs for training, provide income support during training, and offer job protection so that workers can take the time they need to keep their skills relevant and in-demand. The CTB complements existing skills development programmes in Canada, such as Labour Market Development Agreements (LMDAs) and Workforce Development Agreements (WDAs), and fills a gap identified by the 2018 Horizontal Skills Review which found that unemployed Canadians receive a broad range of supports to acquire or develop new skills but that working adults in mid-career could benefit from more support (Department of Finance, 2019). The benefit would includes:

- A new, non-taxable Canada Training Credit to help Canadians with the cost of training fees paid to a university, college, or other educational institution for courses at a post-secondary level or occupational skills courses. Eligible Canadian workers between the ages of 25 and 64, earning between CAD 10 000 and the top of the third tax bracket (around CAD 150 000 in 2019) would accumulate a credit balance at a rate of CAD 250 per year, up to a lifetime limit of CAD 5 000. The credit could be used to refund up to half the costs of taking a course or enrolling in a training program.
- A new Employment Insurance Training Support Benefit to provide workers with up to four weeks of income support, paid at 55% of average weekly insurable earnings, to be taken within a four-year period when they require time off work to train;
- A new leave provisions under the Canada Labour Code that would allow workers whose employers are in the federally regulated private sector to take time away from work to pursue training and receive the EI Training Support Benefit without risk to their job security.

Box 4.5. How are individual training schemes being implemented in other countries?

Compte Personnel de Formation, France

Among individual learning schemes, the French *Compte Personnel de Formation* (CPF) is frequently cited as an interesting new approach which could boost participation in the new world of work, and the only example of individual learning account in the world. Introduced in 2015 to replace an earlier training account (*Droit Individuel à la Formation*), the CPF is available for all labour force participants and it is financed through a compulsory training levy on firms.

The CPF is a virtual, individual account in which training rights are accumulated over time. It is virtual in the sense that resources are mobilised if training is actually undertaken. As part of the programme, individuals get EUR 500 per year, capped at EUR 5 000 in the standard case, and training programmes are required to deliver a certificate.

The CPF has involved 627 205 participants in 2018 or 2.1% of the labour force.

SkillsFuture Credit, Singapore

Introduced in 2016, the SkillsFuture Credit is a lifetime voucher available to all citizens aged 25 and above, and it is financed through general taxation. Eligible Singaporean citizens receive an opening credit of SGD 500, without time limits, and the government provides periodic top-ups. The credit can be used on top of existing government course subsidies to pay for a wide range of approved skills-related courses, including online courses, subsidised or approved by SkillsFuture Singapore. These include selected courses offered by Ministry of Education-funded institutions, including the Institute of Technical Education, polytechnics, autonomous universities, Singapore University of Social Sciences, LASALLE College of the Arts and Nanyang Academy of Fine Arts. The SkillsFuture Credit has involved 431 000 participants over 2016-18 and 146 000 in 2018, respectively 12% and 4% of the labour force.

Source: OECD (2018), Economic Outlook for Southeast Asia, China and India 2019: Towards Smart Urban Transportation, OECD Publishing, Paris, https://doi.org/10.1787/saeo-2019-en.; SkillsFuture (2019), SkillsFuture: 2018 Year In Review, https://www.skillsfuture.sg/NewsAndUpdates/DetailPage/a35eccac-55a5-4f37-bd2f-0e082c6caf70 (accessed on 14 January 2020).

4.4. The Province of Ontario is focusing on supporting labour market transitions

4.4.1. Employment Ontario is under reform to make it more responsive to individual workers and firms

Employment Ontario is the employment and training system primarily managed by the Ministry of Labour, Training and Skills Development. It was created through the integration of a variety of federal and provincial programmes through the 2007 Canada-Ontario Labour Market Development Agreement. Employment Ontario is responsible for policy directions for employment and training; setting standards for occupational training, particularly for trades under the Trades Qualification and Apprenticeship Act; managing provincial programmes to support workplace training and workplace preparation, including apprenticeship, career and employment preparation, and adult literacy and basic skills; and, undertaking labour market research and planning.

Employment Ontario is currently at the frontlines of providing workers with skills development opportunities in light of COVID-19. The Government of Ontario has committed CAD 100 million in funding through Employment Ontario for skills training programmes for workers affected by the COVID-19 outbreak (Government of Ontario, 2020).

Employment services are delivered in part through a network of 170 contracted service providers with over 400 service delivery locations across Ontario (OECD, 2014). The Ministry manages the delivery of programmes and services through four regional branches and a network of local offices. Through Employment Ontario, individuals have access to client service planning and co-ordination; resource and information; job search; job matching, placement and incentives; and, job training and retention services. In general, two levels of service are provided: unassisted and assisted. For unassisted services (i.e. self-services), any person entering an employment service provider office will have access to job search assistance, such as filling out applications or completing a curriculum vitae. Assisted services are provided to individuals who require more intensive services in finding a job. While service providers have considerable latitude in organising counselling and placement services for training programmes, they recommend courses for clients to a training consultant (any provincial government employee) who reviews and approves the application.

The Ontario government has recently announced that it is moving ahead with the reform of the employment services system by introducing new Service System Managers in three prototype regions across the province. This approach will aim to create an efficient employment service to meet the needs of all people, including those on social assistance or with a disability; be more responsive to local labour market needs; and deliver results for job seekers, employers and communities (Ontario Government, 2020). The new employment services model was first implemented in three prototype regions: Region of Peel, Hamilton-Niagara and Muskoka-Kawarthas. A new competitive process open to any public, not-for-profit and private sector organization was launched to select Service System Managers for the three prototype regions (Ontario Government, 2020).

4.4.2. Ontario has an established structure of local boards that work at the community level

Workforce Planning Ontario, a network of workforce planning boards launched in 1994 has the mandate to connect stakeholders within the labour market. Workforce Planning Ontario include a network of 26 Workforce Planning Board areas covering four regions across the province. Each Workforce Planning Board gathers intelligence about the supply of labour and the demand of skills within their local labour market by working with employers to identify and meet their current and emerging skills needs. The primary role of Workforce Planning Boards is to help improve understanding of and coordinate local responses to labour market issues and needs.

As an example, established in 1997, Workforce Planning Hamilton (WPH), a non-profit, is one of 26 Local Boards in Ontario. Its Board is governed by members drawn from business, labour, education, and community representatives from various groups such as women, aboriginal peoples, persons with disabilities, visible minorities, and francophone, among others. WPH undertakes the following activities:

- Profile the trends, opportunities, and priorities of Hamilton's labour market
- Identify skills shortages and future training requirements
- Share research with the community to promote labour force planning and training
- Undertake projects and partnerships that address labour force issues

WPH conducts, as do other Workforce Planning Boards in Ontario, the annual Employer One survey, which queries employers in the region regarding their current and future hiring needs. Results are published on their website. In 2019, 326 employers completed the survey, an increase of almost 50 employers from the previous year.

In addition to the Workforce Planning Boards, the Ontario government announced the establishment of Local Employment Planning Council pilots. These councils were announced in 2015 with the goal of promoting place-based approaches to workforce development, while generating and analysing local labour market information. The ministry is piloting LEPCs in eight communities: Durham, London-Middlesex-

Oxford-Elgin (see Box 4.6), Ottawa, Peel-Halton, Peterborough, Thunder Bay, Timmins, and Windsor. Both the Workforce Planning Boards as well as the Local Employment Planning Council pilots conduct localised research and actively engage organisations and community partners in local labour market projects. However, their role is mostly limited to gathering and disseminating labour market information – they generally do not manage or delivery employment and skills development programmes.

The Ontario Ministry of Labour, Training and Skills Development is making active efforts to ensure that the local boards have access to critical programme information to inform their local labour market planning. For example, the Ministry shares aggregate activity reports on a number of government programmes, such as Apprenticeships, Employment Services, Literacy and Basic Skills, Ontario Employment Assistance Services, Second Career, and the Youth Job Connection programme. The data is shared with the Local Boards, Local Employment Planning Councils, and other regional networks to identify potential gaps or duplications in service within their catchment areas and provide insight into better engaging disadvantaged groups.

Going forward, evaluating the work of the Workforce Planning Boards, and using the findings of the evaluations of the Local Employment Planning Councils pilot project in informing decision-making, and taking corrective action where needed, could help ensure their effectiveness. In January 2017, the councils began reporting labour market information to the Ministry on a quarterly basis. The Ministry had concerns with the information provided and the councils' ability to build local labour market information capacity. For example: some reports/products contained limited analysis and interpretation; considerable number of reports repackaged Statistics Canada data with little analysis and did not appear to add to the body of evidence on local labour market needs; engagement with employers was uneven across the councils. While some councils were relatively strong in engaging employers, in most cases there was limited involvement with employers; issues with data collection techniques such as using open-ended survey questions that were difficult to analyse and interpret, and sampling methods and response rates were unclear.

The Higher Education Quality Council of Ontario (HEQCO) is an agency of the Government of Ontario that brings evidence-based research to the continued improvement of the post-secondary education system in Ontario. As part of its mandate, HEQCO evaluates the post-secondary sector and provides policy recommendations to the Ministry of Colleges and Universities to enhance the access, quality and accountability of Ontario's colleges and universities. The Council reports to the Ontario Minister of Colleges and Universities and must prepare an annual report, which it submits to the Minister for tabling in the Legislative Assembly of Ontario (Higher Education Quality Council of Ontario). HEQCO recently completed two large-scale trials involving more than 7 500 students at 20 Ontario universities and colleges to measure literacy, numeracy and critical-thinking skills in entering and graduating students. Findings include that one-quarter of graduating students score below adequate on measures of literacy and numeracy. Based on the findings, HEQCO recommends that such assessments be implemented across all institutions and involve all students, rather than just a sample, and that they be integrated into programme requirements (Higher Education Quality Control of Ontario, 2018).

Box 4.6. Local actions being taken by the Local Employment Planning Council in London, Ontario

In December 2015, the Elgin Middlesex Oxford Workforce Planning and Development Board was selected by the Ministry of Training, Colleges, and Universities to pilot the Local Employment Planning Council (LEPC) project for the London Economic Region, which includes Middlesex, Oxford and Elgin County. Activities are governed by a Central Planning Table that is comprised of stakeholders in the London Economic Region from a variety of sectors. In addition, there are several working groups: 1) Employer Engagement, 2) Service Planning, and 3) Intergovernmental /Inter-ministerial partnerships. The LEPC aims to create a network of employers, service providers, educators and government officials to address the needs of the local workforce. The LEPC supports the following activities:

- Labour Market Information and Intelligence: The LEPC aims to expand the current understanding of local labour market issues while improving access to labour market information resources.
- Integrated Planning: The LEPC aims to serve as a central point of contact and facilitator for linking employers, service providers, and other levels of government to identify and respond to labour market and workforce development challenges and opportunities.
- Service Coordination for Employers: The LEPCs aims to act as a hub for connecting employers, industry associations, sector groups and other employer groups with appropriate employment and training services to address their workforce development needs. Working with local employment and training service providers, including those outside the Employment Ontario network such as Ontario Works Employment Assistance and Ontario Disability Supports Program – Employment Supports, the LEPC co-ordinates services to employers, such as job development and job placements.
- Research and Innovation: The LEPC collaborates with community stakeholders to develop projects related to the research and piloting of innovative approaches to addressing local labour market issues.
- Sharing Best Practices and Promising Approaches: The LEPC works with provincial and community organisations, including other LEPCs, to identify and share local best practices that could inform action.

The LEPC also sets bi-annual local development strategies for the economy and the labour market of the London Economic Region. Among the innovative initiatives proposed by the LEPC, there is a section of the council's website that is devoted to reality checks. The LEPC has reached out to local businesses to find out what may be stopping people from finding work and businesses from finding employees. It has then collected a list of statements on the current situation of the labour market in London as well as national and global trends, marking them as "facts" and "myths" providing explanations and resources to educate the community about the regional labour market.

Source: Local Employment Planning Council (2020), *Local Employment Planning Council website*, http://www.localemploymentplanning.ca/ (accessed on 14 January 2020); Oxford Workforce Development Partnership (2018), *Local Employment Planning Council (LEPC): London Economic Region (LER)*.

Box 4.7. Establishing local boards or facilitators: How do other OECD places do it?

Many OECD countries are looking for opportunities to promote more place-based responses to employment and skills training. The type and nature of local response varies with some countries providing more autonomy to the local level in actively deciding on the management and delivery of programmes and services.

United States

There are over 600 Workforce Investment Boards (WIBs) that are responsible for providing employment and training services within a specific geographic area. The number of WIBs within each state varies by population, geographic size and a state's approach to providing services. The federal legislation, the Workforce Investment and Opportunity Act requires that at least 50% of the WIB members come from local firms in a community, which helps to ensure that each board is demand driven.

Australia

Australia has recently established Employment Facilitators which are contractors of the Department of Education, Skills and Employment with an on the ground presence that work with displaced workers and other job seekers to connect them with training, job opportunities and other supports. Employment Facilitators aim to establish strong connections with firms in their region, while also working with local employment service and training providers to improve connections between job seekers and those firms looking for workers.

United Kingdom

There are 38 Local Enterprise Partnerships (LEP) currently operating within England. A LEP plays a central role in deciding local economic priorities and undertaking activities to drive economic growth and create local jobs. A LEP is overseen by a Board which is led by a business Chair and its board members are local leaders of industry (including SMEs), educational institutions, and from the public sector.

Source: OECD (2020), "Better using skills in the workplace in the Leeds City Region, United Kingdom", OECD Local Economic and Employment Development (LEED) Papers, No. 2020/01, OECD Publishing, Paris, https://doi.org/10.1787/a0e899a0-en; OECD, (2019), Indigenous Employment and Skills Strategies in Australia, OECD Reviews on Local Job Creation, OECD Publishing, Paris, https://doi.org/10.1787/dd1029ea-en; and OECD (2014), Employment and Skills Strategies in the United States, OECD Reviews on Local Job Creation, OECD Publishing, Paris, https://doi.org/10.1787/9789264209398-en.

4.4.3. Helping communities make labour market transitions into growing sectors

In general, an important strength in the Ontario education and training system are the strong linkages that exist across local institutions. These linkages translate into collaborations across education, industry, government and community organisations. Local boards such as workforce planning boards and economic development boards provided focal points for problem-solving at the local level. As an example of such collaborations, Communitech is an unusual community organisation that formed in response to the emergence of a digital technology hub in the Kitchener-Waterloo area. It combines resources from several local organisations to offer a range of services for enterprises in the region. One such service is to help fast-growing tech companies find mid-career talent in other industries.

Communitech has been working with employers to develop career paths that would take mid-career people from industries more vulnerable to disruption to the technology-driven firms and industries. Demand for certain skills in technology firms has been growing even as some other sectors have been declining. This therefore creates a scenario that could help re-allocate labour from one sector to another. These transitions are however not necessarily smooth, as it is not immediately apparent how people from industries more vulnerable to disruption could easily port their skills to technology-driven newer firms. From a survey of employers in the Kitchener-Waterloo-Cambridge region, Communitech in collaboration with the Brookfield Institute of Ryerson University, identified a set of seven job families that were in high demand in the tech sector but could be found also in other industries. These job clusters were software development, artificial intelligence, data science, sales and marketing, production management, user experience, and business management skills for the tech sector (Tibando & Do, 2018).

These job families are then used to identify potential talent for recruitment from other industries. Communitech uses these job families to offer employers a range of services to recruit. The survey revealed that tech employers in the region have been successful in talent acquisition from other industries at the mid-career level. Survey findings also suggest that mid-career workers holding a wide range of jobs in older industries are an under-utilised opportunity for tech employers.

Box 4.8. Increasing awareness of the importance of digital technology at the local level: Communitech, Kitchener, Ontario

Communitech was founded in 1997 by a group of entrepreneurs committed to making the Kitchener-Waterloo Region a global innovation leader. Today, Communitech is a public-private innovation hub that provides resources to more than 1 400 companies — from start-ups to scale-ups to large global players. Communitech's work shows that there is an opportunity for tech employers to seek out people making or considering mid-career transitions and help is available to firms who reach out. A major takeaway from local networks is that institutional linkages need to be dense and strong at the local level to facilitate efficient and agile response to changing demands of the marketplace. Without these networks, local institutions risk being isolated and unable to mobilise resources in a co-ordinated way to solve skills development challenges.

Communitech provides tools to enhance talent strategy from the recruitment process through to employee engagement and development; a platform for firms to exchange ideas on innovation; consulting help in a variety of ways including Peer2Peer groups; marketing products in domestic and international markets; as well as help to tech workers about their own careers.

Source: Communitech (Communitech website),, http://www.communitech.ca/ (accessed on 14 January 2020).

4.4.4. Supporting mid-career workers especially in the manufacturing sector to develop new skills, while ensuring other workers are not left behind

This OECD report has demonstrated that the manufacturing sector is particularly vulnerable to job losses as a result of automation. Automation provides both threats and opportunities – on the one hand, some communities with a strong manufacturing sector will continue to face a risk of losing jobs to automation. The opportunity is that automation enables local firms to offset potential skills shortages and become productive over time.

From 2008 to 2019, the manufacturing employment share in Ontario fell from about 13.4% of total employment to slightly more than 10%. One of the government responses to this change was the introduction of the Second Career programme in Ontario by the Ministry of Labour, Training and Skills Development. Second Career is for laid-off unemployed workers for which skills training is the most appropriate intervention to transition them into high-skill, demand occupations in the local labour market. The programme is targeted to recently laid-off unemployed workers to get new skills. Eligible participants can received up to CAD 28 000 for costs include tuition; books; manuals, workbooks or other instructional costs transportation; basic living allowance (maximum CAD 410 per week); and childcare. Individuals receive occupationally-specific skills training or literacy and basic skills training to prepare them for more advanced training.

Looking at the local level in Ontario, the City of Hamilton is known as the "rust belt" of Ontario because of the strong presence of manufacturing jobs. The manufacturing sector represents 12.4% of the city's employment. The city has focused on building an Advanced Manufacturing cluster to build on its manufacturing history. This includes the following:

- The establishment of a McMaster Automotive Resource Centre – This new, 70 000 sq. ft. facility allows private and public sectors to collaborate to develop, design and test hybrid technology. The facility includes a state-of-the-art commercial garage housing multiple bays for automotive testing. Engineers, scientists, social scientists and students develop sustainable technology and business solutions for the auto industry. The site houses an Electric Vehicle R & D Centre; Centre for Mechatronics and Hybrid Technologies; Canadian Excellence Research Chair in Hybrid Powertrain Program; McMaster Materials Research Institute and the Bachelor of Technology Program; and
- The CanmetMaterials Laboratory is a research centre dedicated to structural metals and alloys, materials design, pilot-scale processing and performance evaluation. Scientific and technical staff research and development provide materials solutions for the energy, transportation and metals manufacturing sectors.

While support for the manufacturing sector is important, it will be necessary to ensure that policies and programmes do not emphasise this at the expense of providing support to those outside of manufacturing. This is an important consideration with respect to gender equity. Women will be as affected as men with respect to displacement, yet in less visible fields. If some programmes are targeted, such as to manufacturing, where men make up the majority of workers, broader support will be required to ensure other groups do not get left behind.

Box 4.9. Shifting the manufacturing sector into higher value added production: Lessons from the Basque Country in Spain

In 2019, the United Nations Industrial Development Organisation (UNIDO) selected the Basque Country's "Industry 4.0" industrial strategy as a best practice. UNIDO defines "Industry 4.0" as a process in which "the physical world of industrial production merges with the digital world of information technology – in other words, the creation of a digitized and interconnected industrial production, also known as cyber-physical systems". Created as part of the Basque Government's 2017-2020 industrial policy, the strategy is meant to create positive conditions for the Basque industrial ecosystem with the objective of maintaining industry as a central part of the Basque Country's economic and social model.

In practice, the strategy involves programs such as BIND 4.0, a public-private start-up incubator that links entrepreneurs with Basque firms. The plan will also assist SMEs in technological training in new manufacturing methods. The strategy came at a time when industrial employment seemed at risk, as the economic crisis had a particularly noted impact on industrial jobs. The Basque Government aims to restore industry's share in the region's economy to 25%, and sees industrial development as a means to reduce unemployment, consolidate recovery, raise social cohesion and lift the region's GDP per capita to 125% of the EU average

Source: OECD (Forthcoming), *OECD Reviews on Local Job Creation: Preparing the Basque Country of Spain for the Future of Work.*

4.4.5. Providing more training opportunities for low-skill workers to stay relevant in the labour market

The Ontario employment and training system has recently experimented innovative and evidence-based initiatives going in the direction of preparing people for the future of work. For example, the SkillsAdvance Ontario pilot projects aims to support workforce development in identified sectors. It funds partnerships to connect employers with the employment and training services needed to recruit workers with the right skills, and it also supports jobseekers to get into jobs by providing them with sector-specific employment and training services and connecting them to the right employers (Ontario Ministry of Colleges and Universities, 2019). As part of the SkillsAdvance programme, a course was developed specifically aiming to provide low-skill unemployed people with relevant training to get them into jobs. The course, eight weeks in duration, takes cohorts of fifteen at a time and engages them in trainings at Mohawk College to achieve a certification as a production technician for the manufacturing industry. The programme is employer-driven and most graduates of the program find employment easily right after the course ends.

Box 4.10. SkillsAdvance Ontario Pilot

The SkillsAdvance Ontario pilot project is intended to support workforce development in identified growth sectors. It funds partnerships that connect employers with the employment and training services required to recruit and advance workers with the right essential, technical, and employability skills. It also supports jobseekers to obtain employment by providing them with sector-specific employment and training services, and connecting them to the right employers. SkillsAdvance Ontario embodies a sector-focused strategy that takes into consideration the dynamic nature of regional economies and labour markets, as well as the evolving requirements of different industrial sectors. SkillsAdvance Ontario projects provide the ministry the opportunity to test the effectiveness and efficiencies of sector-focused, partnership-based programming.

Source: Ontario Ministry of Colleges and Universities (2019), SkillsAdvance Ontario Pilot, http://www.tcu.gov.on.ca/eng/eopg/programs/sao.html (accessed on 13 January 2020).

The SkillsAdvance programme has been successful in getting low-skill unemployed people to work, but it graduates only 50 persons a year at the local level, meeting only a small portion of the demand for these services. Programmes aimed at supporting unemployed and low-skill people to access basic skills exist in Ontario. For example, Ontario Works runs a programme specifically aimed at the long-term unemployed. However, the programme only admits 15 clients per class, which may not be enough to handle growing caseloads. A programme re-organisation is underway, but it is unclear whether this will result in greater capacity. Ontario has also targeted the need to enhance basic literacy, including basic skills literacy and digital literacy.

Community Literacy of Ontario and Learning Networks of Ontario are examples of how literacy programmes are funded and co-ordinated across Ontario. Community Literacy of Ontario, a non-governmental organisation, is a provincial literacy network of 100 community literacy agencies across Ontario, founded in 1994. It provides many services to Ontario's literacy community such as creating and sharing information via e-bulletins, newsletters, resource guides, website, and via online and face-to-face training events. In addition, the Learning Networks of Ontario is a coalition of 16 regional literacy networks (also called learning networks) located throughout Ontario. They support literacy and essential skills programming in addition to local service planning and co-ordination. The Learning Networks are playing an increasingly important role in system planning, co-ordination and integration. This role is extended beyond the literacy field to include other agencies such as Employment Ontario, responsible for employment services, apprenticeship, etc. (Community Literacy of Ontario, 2017), (Learning Networks of Ontario, 2020).

The Ontario government has also recently tested the feasibility of the Career Pathways approach in Ontario, through a pilot project. The project focused on building the academic and workplace skills that learners need for entry-level employment towards in-demand sectors, while also providing a bridge to more advance college credentials and employment opportunities (Ontario Centre for Workforce Innovation). Despite plans to upgrade the provincial employment services, Ontario's employment and training system currently lacks some elements that could make it more future-looking. The foundation of the system is the Employment Service, providing general career advice, job search assistance and referrals to training programmes. However, responsive and demand-informed training is not a prominent feature of the Ontario system (Myers, Pasolli, & Harding, 2019). A major challenge is that many workers might find it hard to access these services. This is a significant challenge as it exposes a gap in the current system. When it comes to expanding access to such services, several dimensions need to be considered. First there is lack of awareness about many programmes, which could be addressed through digital and online dissemination. Second, people might lack the basic skills to get into the programme they need. Third, some workers have health issues limiting their access to skill development.

Ontario could also draw inspiration from programmes that exist at the local level in the United States, aiming to provide under-qualified workers with the right skills and get them into jobs. For example, in Colorado, a non-profit organisation has recently developed skills programme and employment practices in collaboration with public and private stakeholders to target people without university or college degrees (see Box 4.11).

Box 4.11. Helping low-skill individuals acquire digital skills: Lessons from Colorado, United States

Skillful is a non-profit initiative of the Markle Foundation, developing skills-based training and employment practices in partnership with Microsoft among others, and in co-operation with state governments, employers, educators and workforce development organisations. The intervention targets the nearly 70% of Americans without college degrees, helping them get quality jobs based on the skills they already have or they can acquire, creating new opportunities for success in the digital era. By focusing on a person's skills, rather than their background, Skillful helps businesses find the talent they need to grow, workers find rewarding work in growing fields, and communities better adapt to economic change. Skillful's main initiatives include:

- Outreach and training for employers. Working with local partners, Skillful offers step-by-step guidance on adopting skills-based practices through online resources, training and workshops.
- Support for career coaches. Skillful's coaching initiative provides skill building to career coaches through the Skillful Governor's Coaching Corps, made of participants coming from different backgrounds, including public workforce centres, community colleges, schools and non-profit organisations. The Skillful Coaching Community of Practice, an online community for career coaches that uses the collaboration tool Microsoft Teams to extend its reach, complements the SGCC.
- Access to digital tools and resources. Skillful has invested in digital solutions to provide support at scale, such as the Skillful Job Posting Generator, making it easier for hiring managers to create skills-based job postings. Tech partnerships, such as with BrightHive, SkillsEngine, PAIRIN, Emsi, and Burning Glass Technologies, help Skillful create tools to provide better insights into skills data and solutions supporting the implementation of skills-based practices.

Skillful partners with more than 100 organisations in Colorado, including local workforce agencies, employer associations, state and local government agencies, community-based non-profit organisations, community colleges, K-12 educators, and other local training providers.

Source: Parilla, J. and S. Liu (2019), Talent-driven Economic Development: A new vision and agenda for regional and state economies, https://www.brookings.edu/wp-content/uploads/2019/10/2019.10.15_Brookings-Metro_Talent-driven-economic-development_Parilla-Liu.pdf (accessed on 22 January 2020); SKILLFUL (Skillful website), Skillful website, https://www.skillful.com/ (accessed on 22 January 2020).

4.4.6. Leveraging the potential of micro-credentials in a new world of work

Micro-credentials are mini qualifications often gained by participating in short, free or low-cost online courses. They are also known as digital badges, nano degrees, micro-certifications, web badges, mini degrees and open badges. Compared to a degree, diploma, certificate or other lengthy accredited training, micro-credentials focus on smaller elements of learning. These smaller blocks of learning can formalise soft and hard skills attained at work, such as teamwork, critical thinking and problem solving, and can help fill skills gaps, such as working with big data.

As regular up-skilling becomes more and more important in order to prepare for a changing world of work, micro-credentialing becomes an increasingly popular and accessible option for lifelong learning. Micro-credentials offer students a pathway to higher education and help employees develop specific skills. Because the technology can capture and communicate what skills and knowledge a student has attained, micro-credentials are also a valuable tool for people to demonstrate both what they can do today and their future potential. Employees may consider them more advantageous than unaccredited and in-house training which, while popular with employers, fail to offer formal recognition of learning that can enhance an individual's career development. As they become more prevalent, micro-credentials also have the potential to be an efficient, cost-effective and flexible means for employers to use to certify learning outcomes. Therefore, micro-credentials are likely to improve labour mobility to the benefit of the economy and the individual (VOCEDplus, 2018). Ontario could look to examples from Australia, where research and discussions are at an advanced stage concerning the possibility of integrating micro-credentials within the Qualification Framework (see Box 4.12).

Some challenges still hamper the effectiveness of micro-credentials. Surveys show that employers do not yet seem to view alternative credentials as substitutes for formal higher education qualifications; rather, they appear to see them as complements to formal qualifications. Confusing signalling of alternative credentials can also be another factor limiting their economic impact. Certificates, digital badges and micro-credentials often lack solid standards on delivery modes, duration, assessment processes, areas of focus, and their capacity to be embedded within or cumulate into other credentials (Kato, Galán-Muros, & Weko, 2020).

Some governments across the OECD have taken steps to establish quality assurance of micro-credentials, and subsidised this provision. As offer expands, governments have started seeking ways to standardise, assure the quality of, recognise, and fund alternative credentials. New Zealand is taking a lead in addressing alternative credentials in their policies. The New Zealand Qualifications Authority (NZQA), a government agency responsible for assessment and qualifications, established specific criteria for training schemes and micro-credentials in 2018. The NZQA individually reviews these credentials, which are provided by New Zealand HEIs, and approves and recognises those satisfying their quality standards. The NZQA also evaluates the content of these credentials offered by higher education institutions (HEIs) outside of New Zealand and New Zealand organisations that are not HEIs, and issues statements presenting the credit value and level of such learning activities against the NZQF (Kato, Galán-Muros, & Weko, 2020).

Box 4.12. Responding to the future of work through the use of micro-credentialing in Australia

Micro-credentials are forming part of recent discussions in Australia on the future of work, lifelong learning and tertiary education. Through stakeholder consultation, the Business Council of Australia finds that micro-credentials are being more and more used in vocational education and training and higher education in the country. As an example, the University of Melbourne has partnered with Learning Machine, a US-based company associated with the Massachusetts Institute of Technology Media Lab, to pilot a block chain-based micro-credentialing system. A pilot was launched to create a university-wide credentials program that allows students to create their own portfolio of micro-credentials to complement their qualification. Several of the credentials have been co-created with industry (Business Council of Australia, 2018).

However, the full-cost recovery basis of non-traditional pathways has been identified as a potential barrier to the groups that would benefit the most from micro-credentialing. As freestanding micro-credentials are mostly unregulated in Australia, this might represent a challenge to government funding. Additionally, the fact of being largely unregulated at the moment, poses a further challenge for employers and students, as the quality of courses might be difficult to verify. To assist in the response to the COVID-19 crisis, a new short form higher education qualification type has been added to the Australian Qualifications Framework (AQF), the Undergraduate Certificate, which draws upon units from existing AQF qualifications. If micro-credentials consist of one or more existing components of recognised qualifications, this could contribute to instilling trust and validity to these courses (2018). Micro-credentials have also been identified as recent developments to be taken into consideration in the Australian Qualifications Framework review.

Source: Business Council of Australia (2018), Future-proof: Australia's Future Post-Secondary Education and Skills System, http://www.bca.com.au (accessed on 14 January 2020); Australian Technology Network of Universities (ATN) and PricewaterhouseCoopers Australia (PwC) (2018), Lifelong Skills: Equipping Australians for the future of work, https://www.atn.edu.au/siteassets/publications/lifelong-skills.pdf.

4.5. Supporting firms in a changing world of work

4.5.1. There has been a strong focus within Canada on providing incentives for employer-led training

Policy has a role to play in providing the right incentives for employers to participate in the vocational education and training system (OECD/ILO, 2017). Incentives can be even more beneficial in the context of SMEs that often lack the financial resources or opportunities to conduct workforce trainings, as compared to larger firms. The Government of Canada has introduced the Canada Job Grant Program, providing opportunities for employers, individually or in groups, to invest in their workforce, with support from the government. The Canada-Ontario Job Grant (COJG) is funded by the Government of Canada and delivered by the Government of Ontario. A review of the Canada Job Grant undertaken in the second year of existence of the programme (2016) had found that the programme was generally meeting the needs of employers across the country, but results could be improved in terms of increasing labour market attachment and the overall employment situation of participants (Goss Gilroy Inc., 2016). The Canada-Ontario Job Grant provides direct financial support to individual employers or employer consortia who wish to purchase training for their employees. It is available to small, medium and large businesses with a plan to deliver short-term training to existing and new employees. It should also be noted that:

- Employers can get up to CAD 10 000 in government support per person for training costs;

- The training has to be delivered by an eligible, third-party trainer;
- Employers with 100 or more employees need to contribute 50% of the training costs. Small employers with less than 100 employees need to contribute 1/6 of training costs.

For employer groups who want to apply for training supports the government offers a COJG Consortium Stream. The Consortium Stream allows a group of employers (two or more employers) to pool their resources to support common training objectives and goals. To apply as a consortium, the intermediary organization needs to ensure all the participating employers and trainees meet COJG requirements, and are able to make their required contribution towards the training cost. Most organisations acting as an intermediary are eligible for administrative funding equal to 15% of the government contribution (Ontario Ministry of Colleges and Universities).

4.5.2. While programmes are being offered to encourage firm investments in skills, more could be done to measure employer demand

Both large firms and SMEs often face challenges in accessing the skills needed for the job. The Manpower Talent Shortage Survey shows that nearly a third of employers say the main reason they cannot fill roles is a lack of applicants, while 27% say candidates lack the necessary hard or soft skills (ManpowerGroup, 2018). In a changing world of work, it becomes even more crucial for policy makers to gather data and evidence on employers' skills needs and training initiatives, to develop evidence-based policies aiming to foster skills development and employer-led training.

Initiatives in Ontario have been undertaken throughout the years to measure and collect data on employers' skills needs. As an example, the Conference Board of Canada, a Canadian not-for-profit think tank, conducted the Ontario Employer Skills Survey in 2013 to get a clear picture of employers' skills needs. More than 1 500 Ontario employers, representing over 760 000 employees (13.5% of the workforce) from across the provincial economy, responded to the survey. Survey results showed that employers most need post-secondary graduates in science, engineering, and technology; and business and finance. The most widespread needs are for employees with two- or three-year college diplomas (57%); four-year degrees (44%); and trades (41%) (The Conference Board of Canada, 2013).

However, employer surveys are not conducted regularly in Canada. Stepping up efforts to collect data and information on skills needs of employers in Canada could be a powerful tool to foster evidence-based policy making and bridge companies' skills gaps in Ontario. Both Canada and the Province of Ontario could look to the United Kingdom, where Employers Skills Survey have become a regular tool to inform policy making in the fields of employment and skills. They are conducted every year, reaching out to a broad audience of SMEs and large firms, supporting the development of evidence-based policy making (see Box 4.13).

Box 4.13. Understanding the evolving needs of firms through regular surveys about skills: The example of the United Kingdom (UK)'s Employer Skills Survey

The Employer Skills Survey (ESS) aims to collect comprehensive intelligence on the skills challenges that UK employers report both within their existing workforces and when recruiting; the levels and nature of investment in training and development; and the relationship between skills challenges, training activity and business strategy. The survey has been conducted bi-annually since 2011, and it is conducted by the United Kingdom's Department for Education, that partners with market research companies such as IFF Research, Ipsos MORI and BMG Research to conduct the field work.

The 2017 survey (2019 survey results are not available yet) collected data from over 87 000 employers across the UK, enabling an assessment of how skills deficiencies are affecting business and organisational performance at both UK and a more local level. The survey was carried out in two parts: a core survey of UK establishments and a follow-up survey looking at the investment employers had made in providing training to employees in the previous 12 months (the "Investment in Training Survey"). Both surveys were conducted by telephone. The ESS provides a substantial body of evidence available to a wide range of organisations and audiences. The findings from the survey also informed policy-makers and industry to decide how to invest in national and local skills systems.

Source: Department for Education (2019), Information for participants of the 2019 Employer Skills Survey (ESS19); Department for Education (Employer skills survey 2017, 2018), Employer skills survey 2017.

4.5.3. Promoting the creation of employer-led networks for skills

Digitalisation and new technologies are opening up new opportunities for young firms and SMEs to innovate and grow, including through digital business platforms, big data and financial technology. For example, OECD work shows that between 2016 and 2017, online alternative financing saw double and triple digit growth in many countries, representing a turning point in the diversification of SMEE financing sources and instruments (OECD, 2019). Canada has a vibrant small business sector and healthy attitudes towards entrepreneurship, although it faces challenges in scaling up small businesses, increasing the rate of business dynamism and high-growth firms and fostering productivity and exporting in established small firms (OECD, 2017). Data from Statistics Canada show that there were 1.18 million employer businesses in Canada as of December 2017, of which 1.15 million (97.9%) were small businesses, 21 926 (1.9%) were medium-sized businesses and 2 939 (0.2%) were large businesses. Ontario emerges as the main location of SMEs across Canada, accounting for 417 742 small employer businesses (more than 40% of the total) (Government of Canada, 2019).

Digitalisation and the changing nature of work also have the potential to ease SMEs access to skills through better job recruitment sites, outsourcing and online task hiring. However, SMEs often struggle more than larger companies in accessing the right skills and developing their workforce talent. This can be related among others to lack of financial resources and technical expertise to engage in effective talent development. As SMEs represent the backbone of the economy and account for substantial shares of employment both in Ontario as well as across many OECD countries and regions, it is crucial to develop targeted strategies to ensure SMEs invest in preparing their workforce for future changes in the labour market.

The creation of networks of businesses within the same sector or partnerships between SMEs can play a crucial role in helping SMEs navigate labour market changes and get easier access to skills development information and opportunities. Ontario could look to examples from the United States. The Excellence in Manufacturing Consortium (EMC) is a prime example of knowledge exchange among SMEs within the manufacturing industry (see Box 4.14). In principle, EMC is dedicated to all manufacturers but the bulk of its resources are devoted SMEs. SMEs are less likely to invest in skills because it has fewer resources to spend and also because its scale is not large enough for efficient delivery of skills. SMEs are therefore ideally suited for the type of collaboration offered by EMC. Ontario could also look to Skillnet in Ireland, which has been particularly successful in creating networks (especially among SMEs) for businesses within the same sector of operation or geographical region, to come together and develop targeted skills development solutions (see Box 4.15).

Box 4.14. Excellence in Manufacturing Consortium

EMC founded in the mid-1980s, provides "primary expertise to manufacturers". EMC's unique consortium infrastructure provides need-driven (and real-time) solutions to manufacturing organisations. Services help EMC members "become more globally competitive and produce a variety of high precision products & services marketed throughout the world." EMC collaborates with other organisations based on project need.

EMC's basic model is to use the collective knowledge and other resources of its member companies to educate, increase awareness of best practices and find solutions. This is achieved by creating clusters of knowledge around specific sectors or problem areas. Some illustrative examples include the food & beverage group, which provides manufacturing training, advanced Web networks, and labour-pool building initiatives for food sector manufacturers. Other groups form around issues such as safety (including health and safety prevention into regular duties), energy (expertise to find better energy supply, achieve better energy conservation, cost savings, and environmental safety), purchasing (find suppliers at reduced costs, buy larger volumes, and share container purchases), and learning (sourcing of training, provide training and certification programmes in lean manufacturing, human capital, health and safety, etc.).

EMC provides a forum for members to collaborate and share information to learn about each other's experiences and find better solutions for policies. These procedures can be accessed online and the questions are anonymously grouped together by subject. Peer-to-Peer networking includes field services where members have opportunities to network between members, government, and other organisations. The Strategic Interest Groups meet in monthly/bi-monthly networking sessions where members have a chance to discuss their problems, solutions and new developments in manufacturing at large. EMC members have access to an advertising programme, a bookstore, and classified ads. EMC began in Ontario but has since expanded to three other maritime provinces: New Brunswick, Nova Scotia and Prince Edward Island.

As of 2019, EMC lists more than 110 organisations as members. It operates more than 60 consortia across Canada providing programs for learning, innovation and exchange of knowledge.

Source: EMC Canada (EMC Canada website),, https://www.emccanada.org/ (accessed on 17 January 2020).

Box 4.15. Promoting SME networks and enterprise-led learning: The example of Skillnet, Ireland

Skillnet is a national agency dedicated to the promotion and facilitation of workforce learning in Ireland

Skillnet supports over 16 500 companies nationwide, 56% of which are micro-enterprises, 26% are small enterprises and 13% are medium enterprises and 5% are large companies. Skillnet Ireland provides a wide range of valuable learning experiences to over 50 000 trainees. Skillnet encourages firms to lead the process for training to ensure that programmes delivered are highly relevant to industry needs. Training and up-skilling significantly enhances the career mobility of the workforce. Training is open to management and employees of companies who become members of a Skillnet Network. Skillnet allocates funding to Learning Networks, which are groups of companies within the same industry sector (Single Sector Networks) or region (Multi Sector Networks) with similar training needs, so they can receive subsidised training. With 70 distinct Networks nationwide, businesses can find a Network that has experience in a particular area of interest and understands specific business needs. Networks offer a flexible approach to suit specific business needs: they work with businesses to source and part-fund training partners to provide relevant up-skilling.

Source: OECD (2019), SME and Entrepreneurship Policy in Ireland, OECD Studies on SMEs and Entrepreneurship, OECD Publishing, Paris, https://doi.org/10.1787/e726f46d-en; Skillnet Ireland (About Us - Workplace Learning | Skillnet Ireland), About Us - Workplace Learning | Skillnet Ireland, https://www.skillnetireland.ie/about/ (accessed on 17 January 2020).

4.5.4. Fostering business-education partnerships will be fundamental for local resilience

Ontario is also taking steps to favour the emergence of partnerships between businesses and education institutions, to create innovative and entrepreneurial pathways helping students develop skills needed in the labour market. Six public colleges in Ontario (Cambrian, Canadore, Lambton, Northern, Saint Clair and Saint Lawrence) currently have private partnership agreements for the delivery of programmes leading to an Ontario college credential in Canada (Government of Ontario, 2019). In Hamilton, Ontario, Mohawk College has been a leader in engaging local firms to support skills development opportunities linked to local industry demand (see Box 4.16). Several examples of business-education co-operation exist from around the world that could inspire more action in Ontario. Looking for European examples, the City of Twente, Netherlands has promoted the emergence of business-education co-operation while integrating school-based learning with work-based practices (see Box 4.17). Incentive programmes can also play an important role in facilitating co-operation between businesses and local institutions. As an example, created in 2008, Michigan's New Jobs Training Program in the United States represents an employer-specific customised job training incentive that leverages the state's 21 community colleges (see Box 4.18).

Box 4.16. Building closer connections with industry in Hamilton, Ontario: A good example from Mohawk College

Mohawk College has developed multiple connections with the region's labour market on both the demand- and the supply-side of skills. There are several initiatives and programmes with direct linkages to local demand for skills that contribute directly to regional economic development. The College offers training of skilled labour by developing and delivering appropriate programming to match existing and future demand in the regional labour market. Through its Marshall School of Skilled Trades & Apprenticeship, the college offers programmes to suit different needs: full-time, part-time, or a Certificate of Apprenticeship. They also offer a programme for women in trades. Further, some Continuing Education are offered for already qualified individuals. Through its Centre for Experiential Learning, the College has created a number of programs that facilitate a mutual exchange relationship between education and industry as also between education and the community. Many of these programmes help students acquire applied and practical skills even as they benefit business and community organizations.

Source: Mohawk College (Mohawk College website),, https://www.mohawkcollege.ca/ (accessed on 14 January 2020).

Box 4.17. Techwise Twente in the Netherlands

The overall aim of the project is 'to facilitate the cooperation between education providers and business organisations to organise (higher) VET-training which respond to the needs of the manufacturing industry. The cooperation is mainly focussed on updating curricula, connecting supply and demand through new and currently qualified workers, raising the profile of VET through education in innovative technologies, and mobility of VET students in the region. Because Techwise has a wide scope of member organisations, the cooperation takes place on regional, firm and sectoral levels. A success factor of the initiative is that Techwise is able to efficiently play the role of broker between a company, a student and a VET institute due to low overhead costs, as Techwise officials are employees of VET institutes and companies in the region. This also facilitates the close ties and knowledge sharing between the organisations within the co-operation

Source: (European Commission, 2017), Business cooperating with vocational education and training providers for quality skills and attractive futures, DG Employment, Social affairs and Inclusion, http://dx.doi.org/10.2767/231864.

Box 4.18. Michigan's New Jobs Training Program in the United States

The Michigan New Jobs Training Program is designed as an economic development tool, allowing community colleges to provide free training for employers creating new jobs in Michigan. The training for the newly hired workers is paid by bonding against and then capturing the future state income tax associated with the new employee's wages. The programme operates as an economic development tool to attract new businesses and incentivise existing ones to expand. Employers cannot use the programme to train incumbent workers, as the programme aims to increase the aggregate levels of employment in the state. The programme applied to businesses creating new jobs, which must result in a net increase in Michigan for the employer and the wage paid for the job must be at least 175% of the state minimum wage. Employers then communicate their training needs to one of the 21 participating community colleges, which work with businesses to design, develop and deliver training programmes. Colleges report to the Michigan Department of Treasury on all existing agreements. The Department of Treasury is involved in the administration and oversight of individual income tax withholding some aspects of the programme.

To finance the programme, the state government created a USD 50 million cap on the amount of outstanding training agreements at any one time, which was quickly reached after the creation of the program. As of September 2018, the program has served 194 employers and supported 21 855 new jobs over the past decade.

Source: (Parilla & Liu, 2019) Talent-driven Economic Development: A new vision and agenda for regional and state economies, https://www.brookings.edu/wp-content/uploads/2019/10/2019.10.15_Brookings-Metro_Talent-driven-economic-development_Parilla-Liu.pdf (accessed on 22 January 2020).

References

Acemoglu, D., & Restrepo, P. (2019). *The Wrong Kind of AI? Artificial Intelligence and the Future of Labor Demand.* Retrieved 01 13, 2020

Australian Technology Network of Universities (ATN), & PricewaterhouseCoopers Australia (PwC). (2018). *Lifelong Skills: Equipping Australians for the future of work.* Retrieved 01 14, 2020, from https://www.atn.edu.au/siteassets/publications/lifelong-skills.pdf

Banerjee, A., & Duflo, E. (2019). *Good Economics for Hard Times.* Retrieved 05 14, 2020

Bughin, J. (2018). *Why AI Isn't the Death of Jobs.* Retrieved 01 13, 2020, from https://sloanreview.mit.edu/article/why-ai-isnt-the-death-of-jobs/

Business Council of Australia. (2018). *Future-proof: Australia's Future Post-Secondary Education and Skills System.* Retrieved 01 14, 2020, from www.bca.com.au

Communitech. (n.d.). *Communitech website.* Retrieved 01 14, 2020, from http://www.communitech.ca/

Community Literacy of Ontario. (2017). *Community Literacy of Ontario.* Retrieved 01 13, 2020, from http://www.communityliteracyofontario.ca/

Department for Education. (2018). *Employer skills survey 2017.* Retrieved 02 03, 2020

Department for Education. (2019). *Information for participants of the 2019 Employer Skills Survey (ESS19).* Retrieved 02 03, 2020

Department of Finance. (2019). *Investing in the Middle Class: Budget 2019.* Retrieved 05 14, 2020, from https://www.budget.gc.ca/2019/docs/plan/budget-2019-en.pdf

EMC Canada. (n.d.). *EMC Canada website.* Retrieved 01 17, 2020, from https://www.emccanada.org/

European Commission. (2017). *Business cooperating with vocational education and training providers for quality skills and attractive futures.* DG Employment, Social affairs and Inclusion. doi:10.2767/231864

Future Skills Centre. (2020). *Innovation Projects.* Obtenido de https://fsc-ccf.ca/innovation-projects/

Goss Gilroy Inc. (2016). *Canada Job Grant Year 2 Review: Pan-Canadian Report-Final Draft.* Retrieved 01 17, 2020

Government of Canada. (2019). *Key Small Business Statistics - January 2019.* Retrieved 01 17, 2020, from https://www.ic.gc.ca/eic/site/061.nsf/eng/h_03090.html

Government of Canada. (2020). *Benefits, credits and financial support: CRA and COVID-19* . Retrieved 05 14, 2020, from https://www.canada.ca/en/revenue-agency/campaigns/covid-19-update/covid-19-benefits-credits-support-payments.html

Government of Canada. (2020). *Canada's COVID-19 Economic Response Plan* . Retrieved 05 14, 2020, from https://www.canada.ca/en/department-finance/economic-response-plan.html#businesses

Government of Ontario. (2019). *Newsroom : Ontario Supports Innovative College Partnerships.* Retrieved 01 17, 2020, from https://news.ontario.ca/maesd/en/2019/11/ontario-supports-innovative-college-partnerships.html

Government of Ontario. (2020). *Ontario's Initiatives to Support Jobs and Businesses Impacted by COVID-19.* Retrieved 05 14, 2020, from https://news.ontario.ca/opo/en/2020/05/ontarios-initiatives-to-support-jobs-and-businesses-impacted-by-covid-19.html

He, D., & Guo, V. (2018). *4 ways AI will impact the financial job market.* Retrieved 01 13, 2020, from https://www.weforum.org/agenda/2018/09/4-ways-ai-artificial-intelligence-impact-financial-job-market/

Higher Education Quality Control of Ontario. (2018). *On Test: Skills, Summary of Findings from HEQCO's Skills Assessment Pilot Studies.* Retrieved 05 15, 2020, from http://www.heqco.ca/en-ca/Research/ResPub/Pages/On-Test-Skills-Summary-of-Findings-from-HEQCO%E2%80%99s-

Skills-Assessment-Pilot-Studies.aspx

Higher Education Quality Council of Ontario. (n.d.). *About us.* Retrieved 05 15, 2020, from http://www.heqco.ca/en-ca/About%20Us/Pages/Home.aspx

Hosanagar, K. (2019). *A human's guide to machine intelligence : how algorithms are shaping our lives and how we can stay in control.* Retrieved 01 13, 2020

International Labour Organization. (2018). *The future of work in a changing natural environment: Climate change, degradation and sustainability.* Retrieved 05 15, 2020, from https://www.ilo.org/wcmsp5/groups/public/---dgreports/---cabinet/documents/publication/wcms_644145.pdf

Kato, S., Galán-Muros, V., & Weko, T. (2020). *The Emergence of Alternative Credentials.* Retrieved 05 14, 2020, from http://www.oecd.org/officialdocuments/publicdisplaydocumentpdf/?cote=EDU/WKP(2020)4&docLanguage=En

Lamb, C., Vu, V., & Huynh, A. (2019). *Lost and Found: Pathways from disruption to employment.* Retrieved 01 23, 2020, from https://brookfieldinstitute.ca/wp-content/uploads/Lost-and-Found-ONLINE-2.pdf

Learning Networks of Ontario. (2020). *Learning Networks of Ontario.* Retrieved 01 13, 2020, from https://learningnetworks.ca/

Local Employment Planning Council. (2020). *Local Employment Planning Council website.* Retrieved 01 14, 2020, from http://www.localemploymentplanning.ca/

London Local Employment Planning Council. (2020). *About Us.* Obtenido de http://www.localemploymentplanning.ca/about

ManpowerGroup. (2018). *Solving the Talent Shortage: Build, Buy, Borrow and Bridge.* Retrieved 02 03, 2020

Ministry of Training, Colleges and Universities. (2020). *Chapter 3, Section 3.02 - Employment Ontario: Standing Committee on Public Accounts Follow-Up on Section 3.04, 2016 Annual Report.* Retrieved 05 15, 2020, from www.auditor.on.ca/en/content/

Mohawk College. (n.d.). *Mohawk College website.* Retrieved 01 14, 2020, from https://www.mohawkcollege.ca/

Myers, K., Pasolli, K., & Harding, S. (2019). *Skills-Training Reform in Ontario: Creating a Demand-Driven Training Ecosystem.* Retrieved 01 14, 2020, from https://on360.ca/policy-papers/skills-training-reform-in-ontario-creating-a-demand-driven-training-ecosystem/

OECD. (2014). Employment and Skills Strategies in Canada. In *OECD Reviews on Local Job Creation.* OECD Publishing, Paris. doi:https://dx.doi.org/10.1787/9789264209374-en

OECD. (2014). Employment and Skills Strategies in the United States. In *OECD Reviews on Local Job Creation.* OECD Publishing, Paris. doi:https://dx.doi.org/10.1787/9789264209398-en

OECD. (2017). SME and Entrepreneurship Policy in Canada. In *OECD Studies on SMEs and Entrepreneurship.* OECD Publishing, Paris. doi:https://dx.doi.org/10.1787/9789264273467-en

OECD. (2018). Economic Outlook for Southeast Asia, China and India 2019: Towards Smart Urban Transportation. *2019/1.* doi:https://dx.doi.org/10.1787/saeo-2019-en

OECD. (2018). Indigenous Employment and Skills Strategies in Canada. In *OECD Reviews on Local Job Creation.* OECD Publishing, Paris. doi:https://dx.doi.org/10.1787/9789264300477-en

OECD. (2018). Job Creation and Local Economic Development 2018: Preparing for the Future of Work. doi:https://dx.doi.org/10.1787/9789264305342-en

OECD. (2019). Getting Skills Right: Future-Ready Adult Learning Systems. In *Getting Skills Right.* OECD Publishing, Paris. doi:https://dx.doi.org/10.1787/9789264311756-en

OECD. (2019). Indigenous Employment and Skills Strategies in Australia. In *OECD Reviews on Local Job Creation.* OECD Publishing, Paris. doi:https://dx.doi.org/10.1787/dd1029ea-en

OECD. (2019). *Individual Learning Accounts : Panacea or Pandora's Box?* OECD Publishing, Paris. doi:https://dx.doi.org/10.1787/203b21a8-en

OECD. (2019). OECD Employment Outlook 2019: The Future of Work. doi:https://dx.doi.org/10.1787/9ee00155-en

OECD. (2019). *OECD Skills Outlook 2019 : Thriving in a Digital World.* OECD Publishing, Paris. doi:https://dx.doi.org/10.1787/df80bc12-en

OECD. (2019). *OECD SME and Entrepreneurship Outlook 2019.* OECD Publishing, Paris. doi:https://dx.doi.org/10.1787/34907e9c-en

OECD. (2019). SME and Entrepreneurship Policy in Ireland. In *OECD Studies on SMEs and Entrepreneurship.* OECD Publishing, Paris. doi:https://dx.doi.org/10.1787/e726f46d-en

OECD. (2020). Better using skills in the workplace in the Leeds City Region, United Kingdom. In *OECD Local Economic and Employment Development (LEED) Papers* (Vol. 2020/1). OECD Publishing, Paris. doi:https://dx.doi.org/10.1787/a0e899a0-en

OECD. (2020). *From pandemic to recovery: Local employment and economic development .* Retrieved 05 12, 2020, from https://read.oecd-ilibrary.org/view/?ref=130_130810-m60ml0s4wf&title=From-pandemic-to-recovery-Local-employment-and-economic-development

OECD. (Forthcoming). *OECD Reviews on Local Job Creation: Preparing the Basque Country of Spain for the Future of Work.*

OECD/ILO. (2017). *Engaging Employers in Apprenticeship Opportunities: Making It Happen Locally.* OECD Publishing, Paris. doi:https://dx.doi.org/10.1787/9789264266681-en

Ontario Centre for Workforce Innovation. (n.d.). *Career Pathways: Exploring promising avenues and evaluating impact .* Retrieved 01 14, 2020, from https://ocwi-coie.ca/project/career-pathways-exploring-promising-avenues-and-evaluating-impact/

Ontario Government. (2020). *Ontario Moving Ahead with the Reform of Employment Services.* Recuperado el 2020, de https://news.ontario.ca/mol/en/2020/02/ontario-moving-ahead-with-the-reform-of-employment-services.html

Ontario Ministry of Colleges and Universities. (2019). *SkillsAdvance Ontario Pilot.* Retrieved 01 13, 2020, from http://www.tcu.gov.on.ca/eng/eopg/programs/sao.html

Ontario Ministry of Colleges and Universities. (n.d.). *Canada-Ontario Job Grant.* Retrieved 01 17, 2020, from http://www.tcu.gov.on.ca/eng/eopg/cojg/

Oxford Workforce Development Partnership. (2018). *Local Employment Planning Council (LEPC): London Economic Region (LER).* Retrieved 01 14, 2020

Parilla, J., & Liu, S. (2019). *Talent-driven Economic Development: A new vision and agenda for regional and state economies.* Retrieved 01 22, 2020, from https://www.brookings.edu/wp-content/uploads/2019/10/2019.10.15_Brookings-Metro_Talent-driven-economic-development_Parilla-Liu.pdf

SKILLFUL. (n.d.). *Skillful website.* Retrieved 01 22, 2020, from https://www.skillful.com/

Skillnet Ireland. (n.d.). *About Us - Workplace Learning | Skillnet Ireland.* Retrieved 01 17, 2020, from https://www.skillnetireland.ie/about/

SkillsFuture. (2019). *SkillsFuture: 2018 Year In Review.* Retrieved 01 14, 2020, from https://www.skillsfuture.sg/NewsAndUpdates/DetailPage/a35eccac-55a5-4f37-bd2f-0e082c6caf70

Southampton City Council. (2019). *Executive response to the Future of Work in Southampton Inquiry.* Retrieved 03 13, 2020, from http://www.southampton.gov.uk/moderngov/documents/s42135/Enc.%201%20for%20Executive%20response%20to%20the%20Future%20of%20Work%20in%20Southampton%20Inquiry.pdf

Southampton City Council. (2019). *Getting Southampton ready for the AI revolution.* Retrieved 02 03, 2020, from https://www.southampton.gov.uk/news/article.aspx?id=tcm:63-418034

Statistics Canada. (2020). *Labour Force Survey, April 2020.* Retrieved 05 12, 2020, from https://www150.statcan.gc.ca/n1/daily-quotidien/200508/dq200508a-eng.htm

Statistics Canada. (2020). *Labour Force Survey, May 2020.* Retrieved 06 09, 2020, from https://www150.statcan.gc.ca/n1/daily-quotidien/200605/dq200605a-eng.htm?HPA=1

The Conference Board of Canada. (2013). *Skills Shortages Cost Ontario Economy Billions of Dollars Annually.* Retrieved 02 03, 2020, from https://www.conferenceboard.ca/press/newsrelease/13-06-21/Skills_Shortages_Cost_Ontario_Economy_Billions_of_Dollars_Annually.aspx?AspxAutoDetectCookieSupport=1

Tibando, A., & Do, A. (2018). *Breaking into Tech.* Retrieved 01 14, 2020

VOCEDplus. (2018). *Focus on Micro-credentials.* Retrieved 01 14, 2020, from https://www.voced.edu.au/focus-micro-credentials

www.ingramcontent.com/pod-product-compliance
Ingram Content Group UK Ltd.
Pitfield, Milton Keynes, MK11 3LW, UK
UKHW051504290926
15471UKWH00008B/1412

9 789264 946798